Growing Child Intellect

The Manifesto for Engaged Learning in the Early Years

Edited by

Judy Harris Helm & Karrie A. Snider

TEACHERS COLLEGE PRESS
TEACHERS COLLEGE | COLUMBIA UNIVERSITY
NEW YORK AND LONDON

Supplemental material (see pages 100, 109) is available for free download and printing from tcpress.com/growingchildintellect

Published by Teachers College Press, 1234 Amsterdam Avenue, New York, NY 10027

Copyright © 2020 by Teachers College, Columbia University

All rights reserved. No part of this publication may be reproduced or transmitted in any form or by any means, electronic or mechanical, including photocopy, or any information storage and retrieval system, without permission from the publisher.

Cover photos courtesy of Judy Harris Helm.

Text design by Lynne Frost

Library of Congress Cataloging-in-Publication Data

Names: Helm, Judy Harris, editor. | Snider, Karrie A., editor.
Title: Growing child intellect : the manifesto for engaged learning in the early years / edited by Judy Harris Helm & Karrie A. Snider.
Description: New York : Teachers College Press, 2020. | Includes bibliographical references and index.
Identifiers: LCCN 2019040142 (print) | LCCN 2019040143 (ebook) | ISBN 9780807761601 (paperback) | ISBN 9780807763162 (hardback) | ISBN 9780807778135 (ebook)
Subjects: LCSH: Early childhood education—Activity programs. | Project method in teaching. | Activity programs in education. | Cognition in children.
Classification: LCC LB1139.35.A37 G76 2020 (print) | LCC LB1139.35.A37 (ebook) | DDC 372.21—dc23
LC record available at https://lccn.loc.gov/2019040142
LC ebook record available at https://lccn.loc.gov/2019040143

ISBN 978-0-8077-6160-1 (paper)
ISBN 978-0-8077-6316-2 (hardcover)
ISBN 978-0-8077-7813-5 (ebook)

Printed on acid-free paper
Manufactured in the United States of America

To our loving families, who supported and encouraged us to press on; to the many educators and stakeholders across programs, classrooms, and communities who made this work possible through thinking, teaching, and learning together; to our colleagues, whom we treasure as bearers of the torch; and to you, the reader, who—like other passionate educators—has longed for deepened, exhilarating, and authentic teaching and learning, and for whom we now share our Manifesto for Engaged Learning.

Contents

PART I
Why Engaged Learning? Why Now?

1 Bringing Intellectual Deserts to Life   3
Judy Harris Helm & Karrie A. Snider, with Sue Vartuli

The Classroom as an Intellectual Desert   4

Growing and Sustaining Classrooms Where Thinking Happens   8

Overview of This Book   9

References   9

VOICES FROM THE FIELD: The Path Project   10
Rebecca Teall, Prekindergarten Teacher

2 Curriculum That Supports Intellectual Development   14
Judy Harris Helm, Maggie Holley, & Sue Vartuli

Insights from Mind Brain Education Science   14
Judy Harris Helm

A Reexamination of Common Curriculum Approaches   20
Maggie Holley & Sue Vartuli

Conclusion   23

References   24

VOICES FROM THE FIELD: The Power Lines Project   25
Nick Pettit, First-Grade Teacher

3 Curriculum Research on the Project Approach:
Illuminating the "What" and the "How" of Teaching and Learning   29
Karrie A. Snider & Sue Vartuli

Why We Don't Know More:
Challenges to Project Approach Curriculum Research   29

What We Do Know! The Current Research Base on Project Work   31

Conclusion   36

References   36

VOICES FROM THE FIELD: Engaging Teacher Candidates in Project Work   39
Karrie A. Snider & Natalie Tye, Teacher Educators

PART II
Making Engaged Learning Happen: Navigating the Diverse Nature of Teaching, Thinking, and Learning

4 Creating 21st Century Learners: Integrating Projects and Standards — 45
Rebecca A. Wilson, Pam Scranton, & Tricia DeGraff

Developing 21st Century Learners — 45
Rebecca A. Wilson

Standards Come to Preschool — 48
Pam Scranton

Projects—A Woven Tapestry of Learning Standards and Integrated Concepts — 52
Tricia DeGraff

Summary: Putting It All Together in Our Programs — 57

References — 57

VOICES FROM THE FIELD: The Construction Project — 58
Pam Scranton, Center Director

5 Project Work: A Path to Engaged Learning for All Children — 64
Karrie A. Snider, Rebecca A. Wilson, Pegi Stamps, & Carol Bolz

Integrating Research-Based Strategies and the Project Approach to Support Dual Language Learners — 65
Rebecca A. Wilson

Implementing Projects in Special Education Classrooms — 70
Pegi Stamps & Carol Bolz

Understanding the Potential of Children's Capacity to Learn — 74
Karrie A. Snider

The Potential of the Project Approach for Today's Youth — 78

References — 79

VOICES FROM THE FIELD: The Reptile Project — 80
Crystal Woodin, Kindergarten Teacher

6 Professional Development Models to Support Teaching with the Project Approach — 83
Carol Bolz, Catherine Wilson, Erika Gray, Pam Scranton, Lisa Roti, Pegi Stamps, & Liz Smith

Characteristics of Successful Programs — 83
Catherine Wilson & Carol Bolz

Kohl Children's Museum Early Childhood Connections Program — 83
Erika Gray

Becoming Young Thinkers Summer Institute — 85
Pam Scranton

Nature Connections: The Power of Collaboration — 87
Lisa Roti

Coaching with the Project Approach and CLASS *Carol Bolz, Pegi Stamps, Liz Smith, & Catherine Wilson*	90
Conclusion	94
References	94
VOICES FROM THE FIELD: Bringing Project Work to an Elementary School *Tricia DeGraff, Executive Director*	95

PART III
The Manifesto on Active, Engaged Learning Through the Project Approach

7 Moving Forward with the Project Approach *Karrie A. Snider, Sue Vartuli, & Judy Harris Helm*	99
The Manifesto Delphi Study	99
The Manifesto for Engaged Learning	103
Call to Action: How We Move Forward	106
References	106
8 Manifesto Call to Action: **Growing Child Intellect Through the Project Approach** *Karrie A. Snider, Sue Vartuli, & Judy Harris Helm*	107
Calling Teachers to Action	107
Calling Administrators to Action	110
Calling Other Stakeholders to Action	110
Implications for the Future	112
Our Beliefs: The Manifesto Creed	112
Index	113
About the Editors and Contributors	119

PART I

Why Engaged Learning? Why Now?

CHAPTER 1

Bringing Intellectual Deserts to Life

Judy Harris Helm & Karrie A. Snider, with Sue Vartuli

IT WAS a beautiful October day and the classroom of active 3- and 4-year-olds at the Roosevelt Prekindergarten were seated in their child-sized chairs at tables filled with art materials. There were five tables with four children at each table. In front of each child was a brown paper lunch bag, a cup of orange paint, and a paintbrush. The teacher reminded the children to keep their hands quiet and listen for directions, which was a difficult task for these very small children. The children would be making paper bag pumpkins to create a "pumpkin patch" in their room. The teacher then instructed them to open the paper bag and set it by their chair.

Next, the teacher told the children to take the sheet of newspaper that the assistant teacher brought to them and crush it into a ball, then to stick the ball into the paper bag. However, some children's balls were too large to fit in the paper bag. The teacher was reminded again of how young children's hands work differently than a grown-up's hands. One child's ball was way too big for the bag, and the child could not get it into the open end of the bag. Coming to the child's aid, the teacher unfolded the newspaper, made a new ball, and stuck it in the paper bag for the child. Everyone waited until all had accomplished this step.

Then the two adults moved around the room twisting the top of each paper bag to make a point. When the teachers had finished twisting the bags, the children could then pick up their paintbrushes and paint the paper bags orange. They were cautioned to be very careful and not paint the twisted top of the bag, which they would later paint green to make a stem for their pumpkin. At the appropriate time, the teachers replaced the orange cups with cups of bright green paint and new brushes so the children could paint the twisted tops of their paper bags.

Jeremiah, who was 4, pointed to a real pumpkin sitting on a shelf, proclaiming loudly that the stem of that pumpkin was not green at all but a muddy brown. Alicia, 3 years old, left her seat to look at the pumpkin. She agreed with Jeremiah, pointing out that there was not just brown but also a little bit of yellow on the stem. The teacher fetched Alicia and led her back to her chair. Jeremiah asked for brown paint, to which the teacher replied, "In our pumpkin patch the stems are all green."

After the children had carefully lined up their pumpkins along the wall, the teacher brought out green ribbon and explained that this would be a vine. She wound the ribbon through and over the pumpkins and pronounced that now they had a pumpkin patch in their room. She closed the learning experience by making a big sign that read "Our Paper Bag Pumpkin Patch," saying the names of each letter as she wrote the word and having the children "read" the sign (see Figure 1.1).

Children created their pumpkin patch by following the teachers' directions. Although time-consuming, this was an enjoyable activity. The students practiced small-motor coordination, followed directions, talked about letters, identified colors, and conversed about their painting. The teacher probably had listed these as "goals" in her lesson plans and had mentally checked them off as "covered." The

FIGURE 1.1 • The product of the Pumpkin Patch hands-on learning experience

children seemed to enjoy this hands-on sensory learning experience.

The same month, in another classroom of 4-year-olds, the children gathered around a teacher and were deeply involved in a very lively discussion about what materials would be best for constructing a path for toddlers to be able to access their new mud kitchen. There were lots of ideas as children remembered what they had learned about the characteristics of different materials used for making paths. The teacher asked if they wanted to record their ideas. They said *yes,* and she took out a large piece of paper and listened to the children talking. "What do we need to write?" she asked. "We need to talk about what would be the best kind of path." "Yeah, we need to have a path that will be wide enough for toddlers to walk on side by side." The teacher wrote, *Must be wide.* "It has to be smooth so they won't trip and fall." "Babies fall a lot," said another. *Smooth,* wrote the teacher. "Have you thought about what shape the path should be?" asked the teacher. This created a long discussion about the shapes of paths and square corners versus curves. The children finally told the teacher to write down, *Curved Path.*

Now the children moved on to a discussion about which materials they could use to build this path. The ideas flowed quickly from child to child, from children to teacher, and from verbal words to written plans. The children became more and more excited. The children seemed to be unable to stay seated on the floor. As the ideas came, they moved closer to the teacher and the chart paper on which she wrote.

"Maybe," said the teacher, "we should make some plans of what we think this path should be like. Would you like to do that? Would you like to work together with a friend and draw up a plan?" Yes, they did want to do that. "What do you need?" asked the teacher. They wanted paper and pencils, and some wanted markers, and one pair decided to get the LEGOs out. Off they went, happy with their purpose and confident in their abilities to build a path for the toddlers, which they subsequently did (see Figure 1.2).

THE CLASSROOM AS AN INTELLECTUAL DESERT

Both of the learning experiences described here were designed to take advantage of young children's natural sensorimotor approach to learning. Both teachers had in mind early learning and development standards that were a required part of the curriculum shaping their classrooms and the learning experiences within them. In both of these classrooms, children were experiencing hands-on learning. Both teachers focused on a topic they thought would be of interest to preschool children. One could make a

FIGURE 1.2 • Preschoolers begin the process of building a path for toddlers to reach the mud kitchen.

rather extensive list of objectives covered, including eye–hand coordination, color recognition, understanding the purpose of writing, identification of characteristics of materials, sharing materials, and working with others. Both of these experiences were probably enjoyable for the children.

However, if asked to identify the biggest, overarching learning accomplishment for the Pumpkin Patch activity for these 30 minutes of precious preschool learning time, one could probably conclude that the children learned primarily how to follow directions and wait, and that the teacher always knows what to do. The most active people in this classroom were the teachers, who scurried from table to table, hauling out materials, directing children's work, and troubleshooting any failure to follow through on directions. To be fair, the teacher had earlier read aloud a book about pumpkins, and the children did see a drawing in a book about growing pumpkins. The teacher showed the children a real pumpkin, which she then placed on a shelf. Making paper bag pumpkins was certainly not harmful. No child was ever hurt painting a paper bag pumpkin. Or were they? When considering how these children could have been spending that 30 minutes, based on what we now know about how children's intellect develops, we would have to say that the contributions to their development and future school success were minimal.

In contrast, if asked to identify the biggest, overarching learning accomplishment in the Path Project during this same 30 minutes, the list would be very different. These children also experienced eye–hand coordination, understanding the purpose of writing, identification of characteristics of materials, sharing materials, and working with others. Did they learn to follow directions? Yes; however, they also experienced listening to and debating with peers, setting goals, developing plans, weighing alternatives, solving problems, and using language and drawing to communicate their ideas to others. These children were asked to do their own thinking, communicate their own thoughts, and engage others in meaningful dialogue.

In the Path Project, children accomplished what Lilian Katz (2015) described as intellectual goals. These are goals that

> address the life of the mind in its fullest sense (e.g. reasoning, predicting, analyzing, questioning, etc.), including a range of aesthetic and moral sensibilities. The formal definition of the concept of "intellectual" emphasizes reasoning, hypothesizing, posing questions, predicting answers to the questions, predicting the findings produced by investigation, the development and analysis of ideas and the quest for understanding and so forth. (p. 2)

Besides these intellectual goals, Katz, Chard, and Kogan (2014) remind us of the importance of developing dispositions—the ways in which a person's mind wants to think, the habits of their inner intellectual world. These include "the disposition to be experimental, reflective, analytical, and critical when confronted with a range of problems and issues" (p. 69). The types of experiences that children have can strengthen or weaken such dispositions. One would be hard pressed to find evidence of many of these intellectual goals or much support for strengthening intellectual dispositions in the Pumpkin Patch experience.

More recently, neuroscience research has given us a window into the physiological processes that occur with intellectual thought, as discussed in Chapter 2. A critical component is the development of executive function, an interconnection of processes that occurs largely in the prefrontal cortex of the brain (Blair, 2008). It develops rapidly in early childhood and includes the intellectual goals of problem solving, reasoning, and planning. More discussion of executive function can be found in Chapter 5.

What conclusions can we draw from revisiting the contrasting learning experiences and development of intellect? Classrooms and learning experiences can support the life of the mind and growth of child intellect; however, not all do this well. One way to think about supporting growth is to think about gardeners. Plants in gardens tended by good gardeners bloom and grow to their full potential. In contrast, plants in deserts struggle. When thinking about growing child intellect, we might ask ourselves if our classrooms are more like intellectual gardens where growth is supported or more like intellectual deserts.

Projects—A Potential Solution

One way early childhood teachers move away from the didactic, teacher-scripted lessons of a classroom intellectual desert to using more child-sensitive and intellectually stimulating learning experiences is to integrate project work into their classrooms. As teachers learn how to organize and integrate required curriculum goals and standards into project work, they create intellectually stimulating learning opportunities while meeting the demands for accountability. As the reader will see in the rest of this book, the Project Approach provides a structure, methods, and strategies that can scaffold such a change in teaching. The Project Approach is derived from a tradition of hands-on, child-directed, investigative learning. Most scholars who write about project work and its many forms (Edutopia, 2014; Glassman & Whaley, 2000; Helm & Katz, 2016; Katz & Chard, 2000; Markham, Larmer, & Ravitz, 2003) credit John Dewey's work at his experimental laboratory school at the University of Chicago, 1896–1904, for articulating the basic concept now known as a project (Dewey, 1902, 1916).

There are many variations of project work because of differences in the developmental ages of students and age-level variations in their skills. When projects occur in preschool with children who are beginning to learn about the world of literacy, they look significantly different from project work in a 5th-grade classroom, where students use literacy as a research tool. The ability to proficiently read and write enables older children to use the Internet for research, read and analyze original written materials, and create written reports (Boss & Krauss, 2007). These differences affect how children investigate, research, and represent their learning. Although there are variations, certain consistent characteristics differentiate projects from other approaches to curriculum, and all of the approaches have the goal of developing students' intellectual skills.

The most common way that projects are introduced into curriculum for young children is called the Project Approach, and the work presented in this book is based on this form of project work. *Project Approach* has a precise meaning. In *Engaging Children's Minds: The Project Approach,* Lilian Katz and Sylvia Chard (1989, 2000) define a project in the following way:

> We use the term *project* to refer to an in-depth study of a particular topic usually undertaken by the whole class working on subtopics in small groups, sometimes by a small group of children within a class, and occasionally by an individual child. The key feature of a project is that it is an investigation—a piece of research that involves children in seeking answers to questions they have formulated themselves or in cooperation with their teacher and that arise as their investigation proceeds. (p. 2)

As an approach to curriculum, the Project Approach has a structure, strategies, and methods. Readers new to the Project Approach should refer to *Young Investigators: The Project Approach in the Early Years* (Helm & Katz, 2016), which provides a detailed guide to project work. For an overview of the basic structure of the Project Approach, see Figure 1.3. The teachers guiding the Path Project followed the structure of the Project Approach, as described in more detail in the Voices from the Field feature at the end of this chapter.

Although the two classrooms that were contrasted at the beginning of this chapter were both prekindergarten classrooms, the Project Approach is just as, if not more, effective for fostering child intellect in the early primary grades. As children develop more and more academic skills, project work provides a vehicle for integration of those skills. Solving problems and investigating topics of great interest becomes a way for children to understand the value of learning academic skills and applying those skills within real-world opportunities. This can be seen in the Power Lines Project conducted in Nick Pettit's 1st-grade classroom, as described in Voices from the Field at the end of Chapter 2.

Rising Frustration of Teachers and Families

Unfortunately, all children do not experience child-initiated and child-directed project work. This is especially true in kindergarten. Fowler (2018) conducted a survey of kindergarten teachers in Massachusetts classrooms. The results are typical of what is seen in other states. Fowler reported that, overall, schools have reduced the time kindergartners have for child-directed learning and the scheduling of child-directed activities. Those children who would most benefit from the intellectual stimulation of active, engaged learning are less likely to get it. In some schools with higher concentrations of children from families with backgrounds of low socioeconomic status, child-directed learning was minimal or nonexistent. Fowler reports that administrators with little or no knowledge of early childhood education have placed increasing restrictions on kindergarten teachers' control over curriculum and instruction. Organizations such as Defending the Early Years have taken strong positions on the importance of child-initiated learning and play. Levin and Van Hoorn (2018) have documented the distress and frustration of teachers and parents regarding the effect of standards and mandated curriculum. "Everything is supposed to be structured for a specific lesson and rigidly timed to fit into a specific, tight, preapproved schedule" (p. 4). According to another kindergarten teacher,

> With this extreme emphasis on what's called "rigorous academics," drills are emphasized. It's much harder for my children to become self-regulated learners. Children have no time to learn to self-regulate by choosing their own activities, participating in on-going projects with their classmates, or playing creatively. They have to sit longer, but their attention spans are shorter (p. 6).

Teachers and families know when children are engaged, when they are learning, and when school is an exciting and meaningful place to be. They are beginning to gather together and to speak out. Given a choice, and understanding the differences, most parents would choose the intellectually stimulating classroom for their children.

Challenges in Creating Classrooms Where Engaged Learning Happens

Equipped with quality experiences, education, skills, and developmentally appropriate teacher beliefs, any teacher in any program can create a classroom where engaged learning happens. We have learned this from our own teaching practices, our own roles as leaders of school programs and as teacher educators, and through conducting our own research in the field. We have also learned this from the wide array of stories, presentations, case studies, and research that has been conducted on the Project Approach and similar project-based teaching and learning methods.

What we observe is that for some teachers and for some programs, implementing project work for the first time or even the first several times can be challenging. Trying new things can be laborious for a variety of reasons. Teachers need adequate time to prepare, implement, and conduct

FIGURE 1.3 • The three phases of the Project Approach

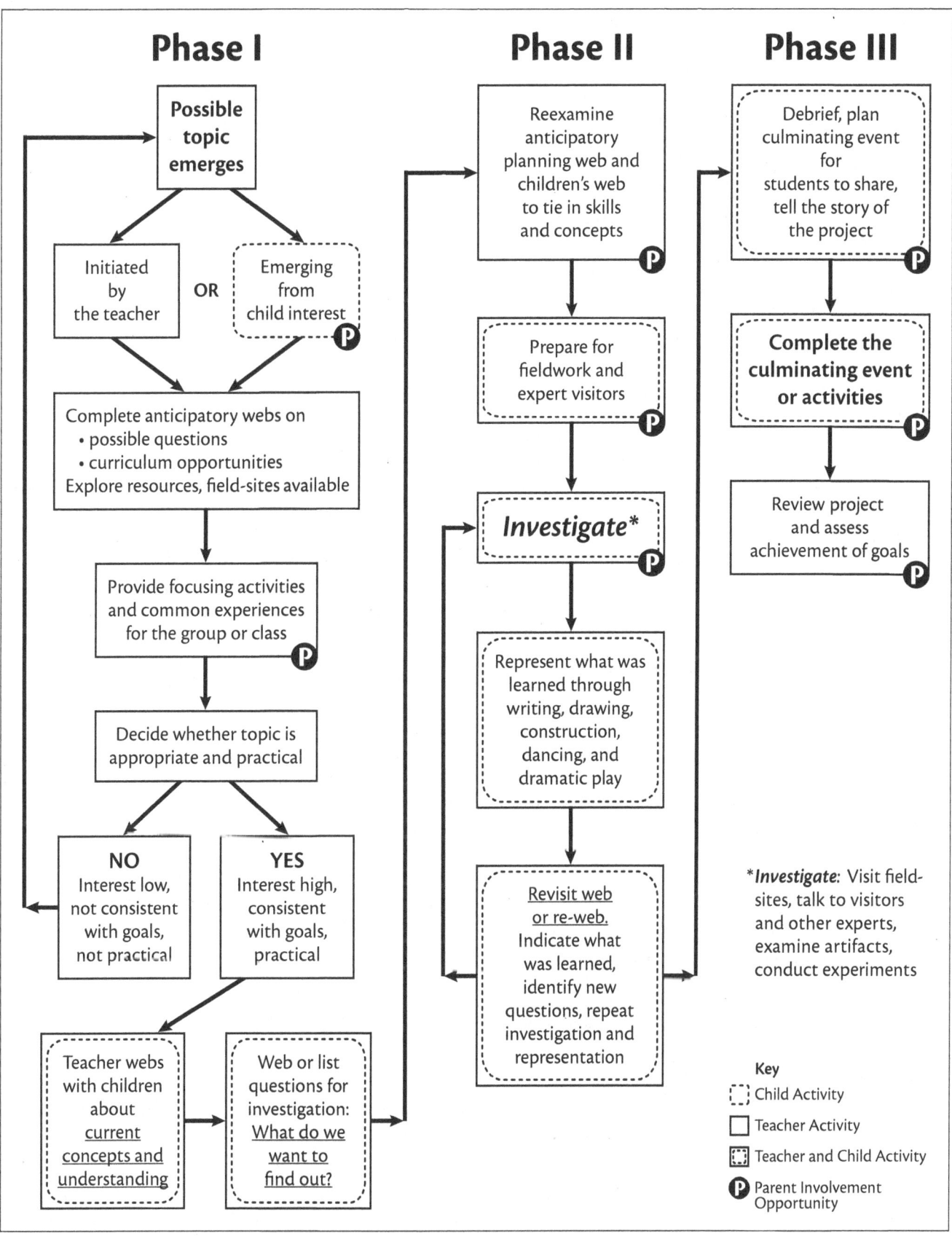

project work with children. Teachers vary in their comfort with the emergent quality of the Project Approach, with numerous activities occurring simultaneously, which requires adjusting classroom management strategies. Teachers have to learn to web, chart, document learning, facilitate small-group work, and differentiate instruction through scaffolding, as children collect information to answer child-posed questions. Knowledge is co-constructed through problem solving, surveys, experimentation, field trips, expert visits, and use of technology. Teachers sustain children's motivation and thought through active investigation of curriculum content.

We believe when it comes to implementing the Project Approach, certain perceived barriers exist when teachers or administrators have limited early childhood knowledge or experience with project work, which may hinder a more widespread adoption of this curriculum approach. Within the current teacher-preparation system, there is minimal constructivist theory-based coursework. Teachers are not always prepared to teach using observing, questioning, and experimenting in a learner-centered environment. Since most of a teacher's own educational experience has been a behavioral-transmission educational experience, a teacher's personal beliefs about how children learn and how teachers teach reflect more systematic instruction and teacher-driven learning.

The complexity of our current educational system makes change very slow and extremely difficult. Katz et al. (2014) have stated that projects can complement and enhance current, more formal curriculum, but the different approaches to teaching and learning, especially between systematic instruction and the Project Approach, make this possibility problematic. When early childhood teachers (pre-K through 2nd grade) try to implement the Project Approach, they often run into roadblocks. These may include time constraints; lack of administrative, familial, and system support; and uncertainty with alternative teaching and learning processes.

GROWING AND SUSTAINING CLASSROOMS WHERE THINKING HAPPENS

From our experiences, we know that the Project Approach is a powerful tool for meeting inclusive, culturally responsive, and standards-based teaching and learning for all children. Project work cultivates a collaborative climate of inquiry, significantly enabling diverse learners to be more engaged with peers, teachers, and tasks, and more connected to curriculum. Children develop stronger academic skills within a meaningful context and are more prepared for the demands of formal schooling. We encounter many individuals who acknowledge their own joy from teaching through projects or through their many observations of student, family, and teacher successes in using this emergent curriculum approach. They say, "Why don't more schools incorporate this approach?" "How can we challenge others to do this kind of teaching?" Indeed, how can we help all stakeholders in the early education field be confident and supported in implementing the Project Approach?

How This Work Came to Be

The purpose of this book, the stories told, and the research shared percolated over time and then emerged during a catalytic event last year when a community of colleagues connected and relaxed over dinner after a regional training event on project work. At the table that evening were administrators, teachers, researchers, teacher educators, and an educational consultant. Conversation focused on what they had seen in the day's training—the child-initiated learning and engagement of not just children but teachers in Project Approach investigations.

As the group relaxed, the conversation turned to sharing thoughts about what the group perceived as a strong push into developmentally inappropriate and intellectually inadequate curriculum approaches due to curriculum and assessment mandates. Instead, they were observing and envisioning project work as a way to respond to the push, as a way to meet standards and requirements yet still maintain that intellectual environment.

"Why don't more schools incorporate this approach?" Emboldened by being with colleagues who were passionate about teaching and learning, the group began with a "someone ought to . . . ," "what needs to be done is . . ." type of discussion. When these kinds of conversations happen, they often serve as a safety valve for frustration and a bonding activity but they seldom lead to real action. This time, however, someone said, "Who is going to do this?" The answer was, "It is up to us, we have to do it." A pen was pulled out, a napkin turned over, and the group began to brainstorm what it would take to spread the word about project work:

- "How can we inspire more teachers, more administrators, and more programs?"
- "What needs to be done and who needs to be told?"
- "How can we help teachers and early education stakeholders advance their own adoption or implementation of this valuable emergent curriculum approach?"

The ideas flew, and then someone asked, "What shall we call this?" Everyone agreed that "Recommendation" was not strong enough. "Position statements" have already been written with uncertain impact of effectiveness. Something stronger was needed, something that matched the value and importance of the issue and the passion of the group. "What about a *manifesto,* a manifesto of engaged learning?" Someone else asked, "What is a manifesto?" "It is a written statement declaring publicly the intentions, motives, or views of a group." It is basically a call to stand up, be counted, and take a position, to speak as one voice together. As Dewey reminds us, ideas . . . beget ideas . . . beget ideas (Dewey, 1910). And just like that, the idea of this Manifesto was born.

The Manifesto Delphi Study

The group agreed that research should be a key component of this Manifesto. From there, the research team determined that we needed a comprehensive literature review of what we already know about project work in the early years (see Chapter 3). We needed the opinions of experts in the Project Approach, who might bring different viewpoints based on their roles and expertise. We also needed a format or systematic way in which these stakeholders could think, respond, communicate, and reflect, while being separated geographically across the world. A Delphi study could be that format, as it consists of assembling a group of experts around a pertinent issue that needs to be addressed or solved. This was the mechanism we needed. And so, the research team conducted a Delphi research study about the Project Approach. This study shaped the contents of this book, and most importantly, the *Manifesto for Engaged Learning.*

For the Delphi study, the research team invited expert educators, administrators, teacher educators, community leaders, and scholars with significant Project Approach experience to participate. Seventeen experts, with diverse roles and experiences in early education, comprised the final Delphi panel. (See Figure 7.1 for biographical sketches of the Delphi panel participants.) Delphi panel experts engaged in a process of creating multiple feedback loops between themselves and researchers to identify characteristics of successful project work implementation and also to identify common challenges. The panel identified the significance of each challenge across different roles, such as teachers, administrators, coaches, researchers, and so forth. Finally, their consensus, which includes prioritized recommendations, key actions, and responsibilities, shaped the *Manifesto Call to Action.* These results, discussed in Part III of this book, provide detailed insights for understanding the challenges described within the research base in Chapter 3 and within the experiences in chapter authors' work with projects.

OVERVIEW OF THIS BOOK

You are invited to join those who saw the vision of this Manifesto on that fall night. In this book the chapter authors have pulled together research, stories, and lessons they have learned from the variety of early childhood settings and the variety of professional positions they have held in the field of early childhood education. In the coming chapters, you will be able to deep dive with them into the world of project work. The other chapters in Part I present the neuroscience foundation of project work and curriculum approaches (Chapter 2) and the research in the field (Chapter 3). In Part II, education stakeholders across prekindergarten through primary grade experiences provide rich examples of how project work addresses critical needs of education today, including how project work meets standards, reflects principles of 21st century thinking skills, supports diverse learners, and enhances executive function development of the brain. Also, in Part II, readers encounter the characteristics of successful professional development and training models. In Part III, the work of the Delphi panel is presented, including identification of the challenges and possible solutions. Lastly, the reader will be invited to join the Call to Action—what each of us can do, no matter our position or program, to again nurture children's development in our early childhood classrooms.

REFERENCES

Blair, C. (2008). Executive functions and school readiness intervention: Impact, moderation, and mediation in the Head Start REDI program. *Developmental Psychopathology, 20*(3), 821–843.

Boss, S., & Krauss, J. (2007). *Reinventing project-based learning: Your field guide to real-world projects in the digital age.* Washington, DC: International Society for Technology in Education.

Dewey, J. (1902). *The child and the curriculum.* Chicago, IL: University of Chicago Press.

Dewey, J. (1910). *How we think.* Boston, MA: Heath.

Dewey, J. (1916). *Democracy and education: An introduction to the philosophy of education.* New York, NY: Macmillan.

Edutopia. (2014). *Project-based learning.* Available at www.edutopia.org/project-based-learning

Fowler, R. C. (2018). *The disappearance of child-directed activities and teachers' autonomy from Massachusetts' kindergartens.* Jamaica Plain, MA: Defending the Early Years.

Glassman, M., & Whaley, K. (2000). Dynamic aims: The use of long-term projects in early childhood classrooms in light of Dewey's educational philosophy. *Early Childhood Research and Practice, 2*(1). Available at ecrp.illinois.edu/v2n1/glassman.html

Helm, J. H., & Katz, L. G. (2016). *Young investigators: The Project Approach in the early years* (3rd ed.). New York, NY: Teachers College Press.

Katz, L. G. (2015). *Lively minds: Distinctions between academic versus intellectual goals for young children.* Jamaica Plain, MA: Defending the Early Years.

Katz, L. G., & Chard, S. C. (1989). *Engaging children's minds: The Project Approach.* Greenwich, CT: Ablex.

Katz, L. G., & Chard, S. C. (2000). *Engaging children's minds: The Project Approach* (2nd ed.). Stamford, CT: Ablex.

Katz, L. G., Chard, S. C., & Kogan, Y. (2014). *Engaging children's minds: The Project Approach* (3rd ed.). Santa Barbara, CA: ABC-CLIO.

Levin, D. E., & Van Hoorn, J. L. (2018). *Teachers speak out: How school reforms are failing low-income young children.* Jamaica Plain, MA: Defending the Early Years. Available at dey.org/wp-content/uploads/2019/03/teachersspeakfinal_rgb.pdf

Markham, T., Larmer, J., & Ravitz, J. (2003). *Project based learning handbook: A guide to standards-focused project based learning for middle and high school teachers.* Novato, CA: Buck Institute for Education.

VOICES FROM THE FIELD

The Path Project

Rebecca Teall, Prekindergarten Teacher

PHASE I: HOW THE PROJECT STARTED

The prekindergarten classrooms at St. George's Episcopal School (New Orleans, Louisiana) don't usually do projects across classrooms, but the Path Project began when children shared the same experience. As the project progressed and sharing of ideas occurred across classes, the children did not want to be separated. All of the pre-K teachers—Jessie Kutcher, Jackie Miller, Katie Steinhardt, and myself—were engaged in the project and were excited to learn from each other and from the children in each other's classrooms.

At the beginning of the year, the pre-K children were amazed by the fact that two classes could go in different directions out of their classrooms and end up at the same place. They never crossed each other's path! We heard the children saying things like, "Wait, how did you guys get out here?" and "Where did you come from?" In the beginning of the year, we have several places that we have to take our classes for special events, and we like to visit them so the children feel comfortable during these events. We decided that we would take a tour of the whole school, which covers two blocks. While walking to the theater, we took different paths so the children could see if they all ended up in the same place. There are three stairwells and an elevator; each of us took a group of children in a different direction, and once again the children were excited and confused. Every time another door would open the children were surprised.

When we discussed what we had observed, we originally thought the classes were interested in a topic of "Doors" because the children wanted to stop and predict what was behind each door. The children didn't even know what was behind all the doors in our own hallway.

In the classrooms, the children drew maps and created paths out of different materials (see Figures 1.4 and 1.5). We attempted to take the children out in small groups with two teachers so one teacher could lead the group while the other recorded what the children were talking about. We were only able to do this a few times because the children wanted to stay together and talk; they didn't want to be separated.

When a small group would return to the classroom, the other children would crowd around them and ask them

---

FIGURE 1.4 • Small groups of children take pictures of the different ways to get to their favorite places on campus.

FIGURE 1.5 • Beau and Raul make tape paths leading out of the main door of our classroom.

where they went: "What door did you go out of? How did you get back? What did you see?" The best moment was when Jackie decided to take her class a different direction out of the gym. She nodded to me to indicate she was going out a different door. She had done that several times during the year before, but this time she was with a substitute teacher who didn't really know her way around the middle school. My class waited and waited for her class so the two classes could cross the street together, but eventually we crossed without them. When Jackie's class finally made it to the playground, Jackie was laughing and her class was really excited. She said they had gotten lost, and the children wanted to tell us everything they saw on the "big kid" side of campus. Of course, my class had to check out that side of campus as soon as we left the playground. The classes walked all over campus many times over the next two weeks. We teachers had a very hard time identifying the focus of the project. We knew that the children were excited about something, but we didn't know *what* it was that they were so excited about.

As we started using the word "path" with the children, it became clear that *that* was what they were the most interested in—how people get from one place to another.

The children started asking if only people use paths or if animals and vehicles also use paths when they move from place to place.

PHASE II: DEVELOPING THE PROJECT

After webbing with the children about what they knew and what they had questions about, we teachers identified two big questions: "Where do you find paths?" and "Who uses paths?" We planned a field trip to the Couturie Forest, a New Orleans City Park, which we knew had several paths that all lead to the top of a small hill. One of our parents shared that her husband's landscape architecture firm had just redesigned the forest by adding and eliminating some of the paths. The children were very excited to talk to someone who designed paths, so we asked him to come to talk to the classes before they went on the field trip. The landscape architect brought aerial views of the forest as well as blueprints. The children used the blueprints to plan various pathways that the classes would use to get to our shared lunch spot. The children were very interested in what the paths in the park were made of and how they were shaped (see Figure 1.6).

FIGURE 1.6 • Students explore paths in a forested park.

When our classes returned from the field trip, we noticed that the children's focus had changed from "who uses paths" to "what paths could be made of." Arrangements were made for a contractor to come and talk about how he chooses different materials for different paths.

This led the children to experiment with different materials for paths. Because the classes had different schedules, they had to do some experiments in their separate classrooms, which made it very important for all of us teachers to be doing the experiments, recording knowledge, and documenting work in a similar way. We realized that the only way this would work would be to reflect on the project daily. The children were convinced that paper would make a great path and that glue could hold anything together. They tested many different path materials under lots of different conditions. They tested how the materials would feel on their bare feet and with shoes on, they tested them in wind and rain, and they tested the materials for durability. Smooth rocks worked well in most of our experiments, but the rocks didn't stay together and the path would lose its shape. One morning during free play we noticed that two children were using blocks to contain their rock path (see Figure 1.7). We quickly took pictures of their work to start a discussion about using multiple materials when building a path.

Several children were convinced that LEGOs would make a great path because they had a lot of them, they are strong, and they stick together. The biggest problem with the LEGO test paths was that the bricks were so appealing to the little children that the minute they put them down the LEGOs would get picked up again.

The children then wanted to know if they could add more paths around campus. We let them take pictures of paths they used around the school. While checking out other paths on campus, the class also noticed that paths were many different shapes; some were curved, and some were straight. One of our children asked, "Why are paths curvy or straight?" Of course, the children now needed to find the answer to that question! They noticed that the curvy paths were in "pretty" areas and straight paths were usually in areas where people were "just walking by." The children also timed themselves using straight and curvy paths: "You can run so much faster on a straight path." "Where else would we need a path?" "Should it be straight or curvy?" "What materials should we use to build the path?" After spending time in the Butterfly Garden and observing the preschoolers, our pre-K children decided that the toddlers needed a path that would lead the little ones to their mud kitchen. This became a goal of the project.

PHASE III: CONCLUDING THE PROJECT

Planning construction of the pathway took several weeks. The pre-K students wanted to make sure the toddlers would use a new path. They decided to put down a temporary path and observe whether it was used or not. We observed that the younger children loved the path—they used it every day for a week (see Figure 1.8). During the week observing the toddlers, we noticed other things that helped us decide how wide the path should be and that the path should be smooth because "babies fall a lot." The children also had to decide on the shape of the path. The class ultimately decided to use bricks to build a curved path. They measured and remeasured a lot! They also wanted to make sure they had the right supplies and the right number of bricks.

Many parents volunteered to donate materials and help build the path with the children. We planned for the path building to take about a week, but we were slowed by several weather events (it actually snowed in early December!). Also, the pre-K children couldn't build a path while the 1-year-olds were in the yard. We eventually were able to build the path during lunch. The path was built completely by the children. Each child chose a part of the process that they wanted to do, and we broke them into groups for each step of the path building. There was a group that measured and staked off the exact location of the path, a group that dug and leveled the ground, a group

FIGURE 1.7 • Alona and Fern build walls around their rock path to help hold its shape.

FIGURE 1.8 • The pre-K children observe the toddlers using the temporary path.

FIGURE 1.9 • Members of the bricklaying small group work together to place the bricks in a pattern they all agree on.

that placed the bricks (see Figure 1.9), and a group that swept sand into the spaces between the bricks.

The path turned out to be amazingly level, and it is used every day by the younger children. Even the teachers were surprised at how stable and useful the path is without concrete. Everyone was also surprised that prekindergarten children would choose to tackle such a complicated job, would stick to it, and would create something so useful.

CHAPTER 2

Curriculum That Supports Intellectual Development

Judy Harris Helm, Maggie Holley, & Sue Vartuli

READERS WHO have extensive experience as early childhood educators may recognize the Pumpkin Patch learning experience described in Chapter 1. In fact, they may have actually used this lesson in a classroom some time ago. And they may even say, "We used to do that, but now we know better." These educators will find the Pumpkin Patch activity outdated and old-fashioned and may express surprise that young children are still attending schools where sitting and following directions are the primary goals. Other early childhood educators may feel chastened by the description of the activity because it is too close to what happens today in their own classrooms. "This is how we were taught to teach," they might protest. Each of these responses is probably authentic to the coursework and training these individuals received while preparing to be a teacher. More important, their reaction to the learning experiences might be traced to when and where they learned how to teach as well as the teaching expectations in the setting in which they have found themselves. What is taught and how it is taught has changed over the 20th century and continues to change in the 21st century. In this chapter we focus on why that change has occurred and how it has resulted in different approaches to curriculum, and we present a framework for examining different curriculum approaches.

INSIGHTS FROM MIND BRAIN EDUCATION SCIENCE

Judy Harris Helm

Learning About Learning

One of the reasons that teaching has changed (or in some cases needs to change) is that our understanding of learning has changed. Much of that change is the result of new technology. Just as technology has changed our health care, communication, and transportation systems, technology has also changed our understanding of how the brain learns and how we develop intellect. Technology has enabled us to "see" through the skull and observe the brain in action. Until this happened, what occurred in a child's head was theory and speculation based on what children do and say. If a child did not know the name of a letter, then later could tell us the letter name, we concluded that something had happened within the head of that child to create this change. Our conclusions were based on observation and then speculation. It wasn't until near the end of the 20th century—through technology such as scans and sophisticated brain monitoring equipment—that we began to get glimpses of how learning actually occurs. With technology we could capture changes in heart rate, breathing, and even the rate of sucking of babies using a pacifier. In the early 1970s computerized axial tomography (CAT) scans, later also called CT scans, enabled a more accurate viewing of the structures of the brain. In the 1980s magnetic resonance imaging (MRI) provided high-quality two- and three-dimensional images of the brain. In the 1990s functional magnetic resonance imaging (fMRI) captured blood flow in the brain, and we were at last able to see what neural activity looked like.

Brain 101

The brain is very complex, and our understanding of the process of learning changes daily. However, one does not need to be a neuroscientist to use what we are learning to improve our teaching. At the risk of oversimplifying a very complex process, here is an overview (Brain 101) of how thinking and learning occur. There are four main ideas that all teachers should know and understand. These are (1) the connected nature of a neuronal network, (2) how neurons communicate with one another, (3) the location of processes within the brain, and (4) pruning.

Connected Learning. The brain is part of the nervous system. Communication happens throughout this system through the use of cells called neurons. Each human brain has billions of neurons, and each neuron has many, many dendrites and axon terminals that connect with the dendrites or terminals of other neurons, forming networks that enable thinking. When a stimulus occurs, such as touching a rabbit's fur, or a question pops into our head, the brain responds by creating connections to other experiences by a neuron literally reaching out and connecting with another neuron created from previous experiences with a similar event or a similar thought.

The brain connects over and over again, creating neuronal networks that are complex and rich. For example, when a child experiences something new, such as the feel of rabbit fur, the child's brain connects that experience with a neuron from a relevant experience, creating a chain of neurons, or more accurately, a web of neurons. Unless this web links all the information and input from that past experience to this new experience, the new experience has no meaning (such as learning vocabulary words out of context). In that case, the neuronal network supporting storage of this new experience is very short lived (short-term memory), and the neuronal network related to the experience will gradually disappear. But if the experience has meaning—that is, the child attaches the new experience to other prior experiences—then the child will be able to recall what was learned in the future. This in turn creates more neuronal networks that can be built upon, constructing a neuronal foundation for learning. Academic learning relies on connections to prior experiences and on the development of meaning.

Synaptic Junctions. Technology has enabled researchers to watch how these neuronal connections actually occur. In photos and videos of neurons connecting to other neurons, the dendrites and terminals of one neuron reach out to other neurons to make these connections. It appears that each connection is made by the grasping of the dendrite or axon terminal with those of another neuron. Now that more advanced technology has enabled an even closer look at this connecting, it is clear that rather than physically grasping the next neuron, the neuron lines up with the other neuron, not actually touching it but creating a gap. Into that gap between the two neurons, chemicals (neurotransmitters) are released and taken up by the other neuron. Which neurotransmitters are released into the gap makes a big difference in whether or not the connection becomes strong, building a foundation for more connections, or whether it fades away. The strength of the connection, hence the strength of the memory, is determined by these neurotransmitters. Which neurotransmitters are released can be influenced by emotions. When emotions are positive, such as curiosity, excitement, or joy, the neurotransmitters released can increase the likelihood that information will be remembered and that skills will be learned. Engagement and curiosity have a direct impact on the chemistry of the neuron connection. Likewise, if a child is not interested or is under stress, then other neurotransmitters fill the gaps and the connections are weakened, and learning is impacted. Likewise, if a child is unengaged in a learning experience—finds it to be boring or repetitive—the child is less likely to connect it to other experiences and to build a network to support future learning related to that experience. In the Path Project described at the end of Chapter 1 and the Power Lines Project described at the end of this chapter, children were deeply engaged, creating powerful chemical readiness for learning.

Brain Structures. Educators and other adults have a sophisticated way of thinking about how various curriculum content areas should be organized. They separate subjects and create hierarchies of concepts and skills. It is easy to forget that organizing knowledge and skills in this manner is not always the same way that children organize knowledge and skills. For example, children will often learn letters in the order they encounter them in words that are important to them, such as in their name or in "Daddy." Adults understand that all letters must be learned, so they may think that going letter by letter through the alphabet is the logical way to teach letters.

Many adults also mistakenly think that the brain is subdivided into areas that match our content divisions, such as a math area and a reading area. It is true that there are specific areas of the brain that are connected to other areas, and specific structures that think in one way, as well as some specific neuronal networks that are, predictably, the same from one person to another. However, the brain is complex. Different areas of the brain function in different ways and relate to other areas of the brain. Neuronal networks that involve many different areas of the brain create pathways related to specific ways of thinking that are located in specific areas of the brain. Other ways of thinking about the same subject will activate different areas of the brain. Consider the case of a musician, for example. Performing music by reading the notes from a prewritten sheet of music will involve neuronal pathways that are located in particular areas of the brain. However, when a musician improvises (as he or she might when playing jazz), different areas of the brain are activated. Even though similar-sounding music may emerge from the two approaches, the music is the result of activation of different neuronal networks within the musician's brain (Limb & Braun, 2008).

When experiences repeatedly use a specific area of the brain, these experiences can make physical changes in the brain. Brain scans of London taxi drivers who must pass tests on the location of streets and addresses revealed that areas of the brain used in this geographic processing were larger than those of people who did not drive taxis (Maguire et al., 2003). The more a neuronal network is used, the more effectively that area functions in the future. The more a musician improvises music, the better he gets at doing it. This is true for taxi drivers and for musicians and for any number of other kinds of experts.

Some of the development of the brain is based on heredity, but more often it is experiences that build mind–brain capacity by creating neuronal connections and pathways. It is true that we shape our own brain, and it matters which kinds of connections we use and where they are located in the brain, because it is these connections that determine our ability to think in certain ways in the future.

Pruning. Many adults still have the image of the brain as a computer. In this image the brain has limited memory and learns only what is programmed into it. With such an analogy, the way to teach would be to simply program or put into children's heads what we want them to know. From this point of view, teaching is the process of identifying what is to be learned, organizing it as we think it makes sense to us in our adult brains, then "getting it into" children's heads. A more appropriate image, however, is that of the brain as part of a living thing. It functions through biological processes, and like all living things needs nutrition, rest, and exercise to develop.

One of the most important biological processes for educators to understand is the process of pruning. This process shapes the brain. Pruning naturally occurs early in life when there is an overgrowth of neurons. It is as if the brain is prepared for all possible learning; however, only those connections that are made and used survive, creating the foundation for other connections. Similar to the way a gardener might prune a lilac bush to fit in a designated space in the yard, the brain prunes itself to function most efficiently in its environment. Those connections that are not used are pruned away. In this way the brain grows, changes, and adapts. The adage of "use it or lose it" applies to young children as well as it does to senior citizens. It is important to remember that opportunities for thinking in the early years will determine what neuronal structures are there to support different ways of thinking in the future.

Moving Beyond Neuromyths

In our search to understand the brain, it is possible that we simplified too much of the knowledge that was emerging about learning. As neuroimaging became more and more sophisticated, those who studied the process of learning eagerly jumped on findings from neuroscience, applying them directly to teaching. Unfortunately, some of these applications turned out to be "bridges too far" and in the end were found not to be scientifically sound (Tokuhama-Espinosa, 2018). Some of the misunderstandings included that people are either "left-brained" or "right brained"; it's all over by age 3; or the brain is like a computer with limited memory storage (Dekker, Lee, Howard-Jones, & Jolles, 2012; Tokuhama-Espinosa, 2018). The hoopla that followed left educators wary. Drawing valid implications for classroom practice from the work of neuroscientists was difficult for educators. It was also difficult for neuroscientists and researchers. There is, however, enormous potential in using the research and drawing truly valid implications for educational practice, and the first glimmers of educational neuroscientific research are promising. Since 2000, there has been a growing movement to recreate those bridges, to conceptualize a scientifically substantiated art of teaching, perhaps a biologically based revolution (Fischer & Immordino-Yang, 2008). If we are talking about supporting the development of child intellect, we need to start with what we now know about how children learn.

To effectively bridge the gaps between the sciences, the International Mind, Brain, and Education Society was formed in 2004 (Dawson & Fischer, 1994; Fischer, 2009; Fischer et al., 2007). The goals of the organization were to develop resources for scientists, practitioners, public policymakers, and the public; and to create and identify useful information, research directions, and promising educational practices. To define standards for this new collaborative science of Mind Brain Education and to separate myths from the facts, Tokuhama-Espinosa (2008, 2010) facilitated a group decision-making process. This process supported interaction and joint reflection by bringing together experts in these fields to address and reach a consensus regarding the applicability of neuroscience research to teaching and learning. Utilizing grounded-theory development, the study determined the parameters of the Mind Brain Education field with a meta-analysis of over 2,200 documents from the past 30 years. This was followed by a Delphi survey (a survey process by which a group can reach agreement) of 20 international experts from six different countries that further refined the science content over several months of reflection. As a result, there are now standards for the emerging new field of Mind Brain Education Science (also called MBE Science). This meta-analysis of the literature and the Delphi response (Tokuhama-Espinosa, 2008) culminated with the development of a model of learning. This model includes tenets that address individual learning, principles of learning that are true for all learners, and 10 instructional guidelines.

In 2016, a new Delphi panel that was formed as a 10-year follow-up on the original MBE Delphi study confirmed the principles of learning and the instructional guidelines of the first Delphi. This study also documented that, unfortunately, there is still extensive perpetuation of the neuromyths in curriculum approaches, classrooms, and mainstream teacher education programs (Tokuhama-Espinosa, 2017).

At this point, you may be wondering exactly how a classroom might look where Mind Brain Education guidelines are being utilized. The answer is that it would look a lot like the classrooms where deep investigations of topics of interest to children are occurring, that is, classrooms where projects are a mainstay of the curriculum. Deep investigations of topics that children care about are not only compatible with what we now know about learning but also may be one of our best hopes for supporting the development of intellect in children in the 21st century. At the preschool level, an MBE Science classroom would be like the classroom where the Path Project occurred. In the primary grades, the classroom would look like the classroom where the Power Lines Project occurred (which is described at the end of this chapter). Classrooms where students are doing projects meet most of the 10 practical guidelines identified in the Delphi study. Figure 2.1 lists

FIGURE 2.1 • MBE Science instructional guidelines and the Project Approach

Instructional Guidelines	Implications for Instruction	How the Instructional Guidelines Occur in Project Work
Instructional Guideline 1: Learning Environments	"Good learning environments are made, not found." Teachers model and require respectful intellectual exchanges. Learning experiences begin with "assessment of what students already know." Teachers have "a clear vision of what students need to know to learn." "Learning activities that are student-centered and dynamic." (p. 115)	Small-group, large-group, and teacher/child conversations occur regularly as a topic is selected; children discuss what they know about the topic and then generate questions for investigation. Teachers plan integration of required curriculum and standards by anticipating child needs in the investigation and opportunities for children to learn and practice academic skills. Children plan how to represent what they learn through drawing, writing, painting, presentations, and building models and play environments.
Instructional Guideline 2: Sense and Meaning	Teachers "link what is taught in class with applications to the students' lives." Teachers know students' needs. "Facts and skills are embedded in authentic experiences (natural contexts)." Teachers appreciate students' "culturally based neural network (knowledge)." (p. 116)	Project topics are chosen based on relevance to children's lives and child interest. During anticipatory planning the teacher identifies where learning knowledge and skills *naturally occur* in the topic. For example, in a project on shoes the teacher anticipates that numeral recognition will naturally occur as children study shoe sizes and prices. The teacher uses the children's interest and involvement in shoes to assess numeral knowledge and teach numerals.

Instructional Guideline 3: Memory	Teachers "understand the vital link between memory and learning."
	
	 "Modes of instruction take advantage of different sensory pathways in the brain."
	
	 Teachers "teach to auditory, visual, and kinesthetic pathways . . . to improve the chances of recall."
	
	 Experiences utilize the three forms of long-term memory:
	 • Associative memory—"links past knowledge with new information"
	 • "Emotionally important or value-laden memory"—"what the student gives importance to"
	 • Survival-value memory—"students learn things that help them survive"
	
	 Recall experiences help students "develop a 'habit of mind' about how to store and retrieve important information." (p. 117)
		The project process maximizes memory. As children investigate, they
		
		 • make notes, take photographs, draw pictures, create models, design and use play environments, give presentations, organize materials, and so on
		 • interview experts in large and small groups, read books, view videos and photos, discuss findings, theories, and ideas for representation of what they learned
		 • utilize all three forms of long-term memory by
		   · beginning the project by remembering and sharing what they know about the topic
		   · investigating topics that are relevant and of high emotional interest
		   · learning and using academic skills because they need them to do their work (e.g., tallying because they need to know how many windows they need in their construction; learning how to ask questions because they need to get answers from experts)
		 • discuss their findings, reviewing each day the status of the process and their goals

(continued on the next two pages)

FIGURE 2.1 • Continued

Instructional Guidelines	Implications for Instruction	How the Instructional Guidelines Occur in Project Work
Instructional Guideline 4: Attention Spans	Attention spans "vary by individual, subject, and activity." Teachers should - "minimize passive activities" - engage learners and maximize opportunities to gain new knowledge - vary experiences with persons (teacher to student, for example), place (a change of seat), or topic at least every 20 minutes Students reflect and summarize new information to maximize memory consolidation. Teachers use primacy-recency principle. Children will "remember best what occurs first, second best what occurs last, and least what occurs in the middle." (pp. 118–119)	Project work is active learning. The project process requires experiences that children find engaging such as visiting field sites, interacting with adults who are experts on the topic, and investigating authentic artifacts. Children review and share their findings with the group on a regular basis, often daily when project work is going on. Teachers document what children are doing with photographs and notes that are shared with children for reflection. Children also take photographs and discuss what they have observed.
Instructional Guideline 5: The Social Nature of Learning	"Learning often occurs in social contexts" and "can often be enhanced through social interaction, as in student group work or discussions." Teaching activities should "encourage active exchanges of perceptions and information." Encouraging debate enables students "to think critically and to interact with each other" and "prepares them to deal with counter opinions." Small-group work "requires a few students to interact collaboratively." Orchestrate activities "in such a way as to encourage maximum participation and thus allow students to construct their own learning." (pp. 119–120)	Project work in the early years of schooling is done in groups of children. Groups of children may focus on a specific aspect of a project such as the wheels of a truck. The teacher and children create webs and lists of what they know and what they have learned, which children review when deciding on next steps in the process. Children create plans for representing what they have learned. They may create models or play environments, plays, or presentations. Children discuss what to do and how to do it. Theories and plans are shared, recorded, and revisited by the group.
Instructional Guideline 6: Mind–Body Connection	Teachers teach children about nutrition, sleep, and exercise. Teachers recognize that "students' brains learn best when the needs of the body are met." (p. 120)	Project work often provides opportunities for teachers to integrate knowledge about the needs of their bodies (e.g., topics on health-related facilities such as the dentist's office, food providers such as restaurants, or sports and hobbies). Because project work is centered on topics of great interest to children, knowledge and skills developed during the investigation are easily learned and remembered. Project work in classrooms more often occurs during flexible work times, enabling response to children's individual attention and activity levels.
Instructional Guideline 7: Orchestrated Immersion	Teachers create interactions that integrate the strengths and weaknesses of the learners to maximize experiences of all, "similar to an orchestra director who immerses students in complex experiences that support learning by calling on individuals one by one to bring out their voices and then weaving them into a single class experience." "Teachers integrate different gifts and help each player perform to their best abilities for the good of the group." "This means picking up on all of the cues students provide in class." (p. 121)	Project work involves many different kinds of activities so each child has many opportunities to contribute to the project and also to focus on aspects of the topic of the most interest. All children have a place in the project. The role of the teacher is to enable the complex process of project work to occur through classroom management and access to resources and experts. The teacher documents and assesses throughout the project process so that children are learning knowledge and skills appropriate for each child's developmental needs and skill level. The teacher uses anticipatory planning that maps the concepts and skills which can authentically be encountered in the project so opportunities are not missed. Anticipatory planning includes special needs and abilities of all children in the classroom.

FIGURE 2.1 • *Continued*

Instructional Guidelines	Implications for Instruction	How the Instructional Guidelines Occur in Project Work
Instructional Guideline 8: Active Processes	Teachers must integrate active learning and reflective activities to enhance learning potential. Active learning classrooms include • more than passive listening • opportunities to use higher-order thinking skills • less emphasis on knowledge transmission and greater emphasis on developing skills • encouragement to explore attitudes and values • immediate feedback from teachers (Bonwell & Eison, 1991) Teachers should "design significant learning experiences that require students to act on their own knowledge. This means teachers not only help students acquire knowledge; they also show them how to put that knowledge into action in order to develop skills." (p. 122)	Project work is active learning, even when the children are involved in listening to experts or having reading materials related to the topic read to them. Because they are investigating with specific knowledge goals about the topic, they are involved in actively listening and looking for specific information. Higher-order thinking skills are developed as children generate questions for investigation, analyze data and findings, and hypothesize about what experts might tell them or how a process might work. Children think about what they have learned, talk about it, and plan as a group how to create representations related to what they have learned about the topic. Projects usually involve a significant amount of problem solving. Some of this occurs when children are trying to figure out a process. For young children, a significant amount of the problem solving in project work occurs when children paint, build, draw, and construct representations.
Instructional Guideline 9: Metacognition	Activities stimulate metacognition and provide time for students to reflect and to "think about thinking." Students are given time to reflect and "consider new information . . . to maximize memory consolidation." Teachers "allow time for metacognition during class and to assign homework that requires metacognitive skills." End-of-day or end-of-class reflections or questions about content develop "habits of mind that encourage reflection." (p. 122)	The project process requires children to think about what they know about a topic and what they want to learn. The webbing process done by children and teacher together at the beginning of the project records their initial knowledge about the topic. Revisiting the web throughout the process focuses children on what they have learned in their investigation and what more they might want to learn. Recreating a web at the end of the project enables them to reflect on what and how much they have learned. Reviewing progress on the project in discussions in both large and small groups enables ongoing reflection.
Instructional Guideline 10: Learning Throughout the Lifespan	Skills are taught "at an appropriate time based on the characteristics of the learner." "Developmentally appropriate age-related activities should be milestones and benchmarks, not roadblocks." Students who don't meet the standard developmental milestones are not labeled. "Be sure the student understands that he can improve, but only with effort; the student's willingness to do better is crucial to improvement." (pp. 123–124)	In project work children can contribute at their current skill level but are continually challenged to reach beyond typical expectations by the open-ended nature of investigation and representation. A 3-year-old is often seen creating signs for constructions, a process which motivates them to write and learn about letters. Children role play adult work in the project process (e.g., a waiter taking orders for pizza or a real estate agent interviewing a customer wanting to buy a house). Children learn to write large numbers because they want to record them. In project work, children often attempt difficult tasks, such as designing a play car that they can get in and pretend to drive. A common experience is for first attempts to fail, and children have to figure out what went wrong and another way to do a task.

Note: Content from *The New Science of Teaching and Learning: Using the Best of Mind, Brain, and Education Science in the Classroom*, by T. Tokuhama-Espinosa, 2010, pp. 114–124.

each instructional guideline, the implications of the guideline for instruction, and how it occurs in project work.

With this foundational understanding of how learning occurs from MBE Science, let us reexamine curriculum approaches most common in early childhood classrooms.

A REEXAMINATION OF COMMON CURRICULUM APPROACHES

Maggie Holley & Sue Vartuli

As described earlier, children learn and develop through active interactions with adults, peers, and the environment, which are understood more fully through MBE Science. When children make choices and are given real tasks and responsibilities in their classrooms, they begin to see themselves as competent, capable learners. Children gain a sense of agency when they help teachers, other adults, and peers make meaningful decisions. Teachers support children to develop decision-making skills as their ability to make and reflect on choices grows. When the amount of involvement in curriculum participation, engagement, experimentation, and investigation increases, the child's sense of agency grows. The development of the child's sense of agency has been associated with persistence, intentional action, self-regulation, leadership skills, self-esteem, desire to learn, and other developmental outcomes (Bandura, 2006; Correia, Camilo, Aguiar, & Amaro, 2019). In this section, we examine early childhood curriculum approaches and children's roles within each approach. Then we examine how children can develop a sense of agency as they are involved in curriculum component decisions.

Children's Roles in Learning in Curriculum Approaches

Early childhood curriculum approaches vary as to who makes and informs curricular decisions. Two main developmental learning theories have guided teachers' approaches to implementing early childhood curriculum: *behaviorism* and *constructivism.* John Watson's (1924) pioneering contributions to the field of behavioral psychology influenced the development of the Behavioral-Transmission Model, which is a teacher-centered curriculum approach suggesting that knowledge and behavior are learned in response to environmental stimuli. The child's primary role in learning is to replicate what the teacher demonstrates and to appear engaged, not to initiate learning.

In this model, the children are passive and they lack agency, because they are asked only to describe or report what they notice, copy the teacher, or practice a learned skill. Relying almost only on what is termed "convergent thinking," a child is not asked to discover any new ideas or hypothesize reasons or new methods. Teachers using a behaviorist approach believe that teaching is conveying a set body of knowledge to the learner in a preset way. Teachers use props, such as alphabet flash cards and step-by-step strategies, and the children's tasks should be completed in one correct way. In a teacher-directed classroom, the child will not have opportunities to experience feelings of efficacy or control over the school day, leading to a failed sense of agency for the child (Bandura, 1997). For a harried teacher, lecturing and directly instructing children to do a specified task can be more efficient, but comes at the cost of limiting or diminishing the children's input and creativity, engagement, and increased learning. The Behavioral-Transmission Model is what is mostly seen in public school classrooms today. The Pumpkin Patch learning experience described in Chapter 1 is a good example of a classroom where children lack agency.

Constructivism, on the other hand, is a concept that goes back to Socrates in classical antiquity and is often attributed to Jean Piaget, John Dewey, and Lev Vygotsky, among others. Piaget (1924) was one of the first to believe that a child's mode of thinking is different from that of adults, Dewey (1902) believed education should be grounded in real life, and Vygotsky (1934) extended this to include the social and cultural influences on learning. The constructivist model is one in which a teacher co-constructs knowledge and learning with children. Constructivist teachers believe that children are very capable thinkers and learners, including those with diverse cultural, intellectual, and linguistic backgrounds. Constructivist teachers believe even preschool children are not too young to be able to select curriculum topics of interest, formulate questions, research answers, work independently, think for themselves, or succeed in small groups without direct supervision. These learning-process skills are seen as part of the curriculum. Constructivist teachers ask children what they want to know, and how they might go about finding answers to their questions. Children have agency—the freedom to initiate learning and share in real dialogue with peers, teachers, and other adults.

The Path Project described at the end of Chapter 1, in which children made the decision to design and build a brick sidewalk for toddlers, is an example of a classroom supportive of agency. In this active teaching and learning curriculum model, children have the opportunity to create, analyze, evaluate, and problem solve. As they think divergently, and work with peers and teachers, children learn to construct knowledge through interactions with adults, peers, materials, and their own ideas. Teachers can organize small groups, games, provocations, problems to

FIGURE 2.2 • Agency spectrum for teacher–child curricular decisions

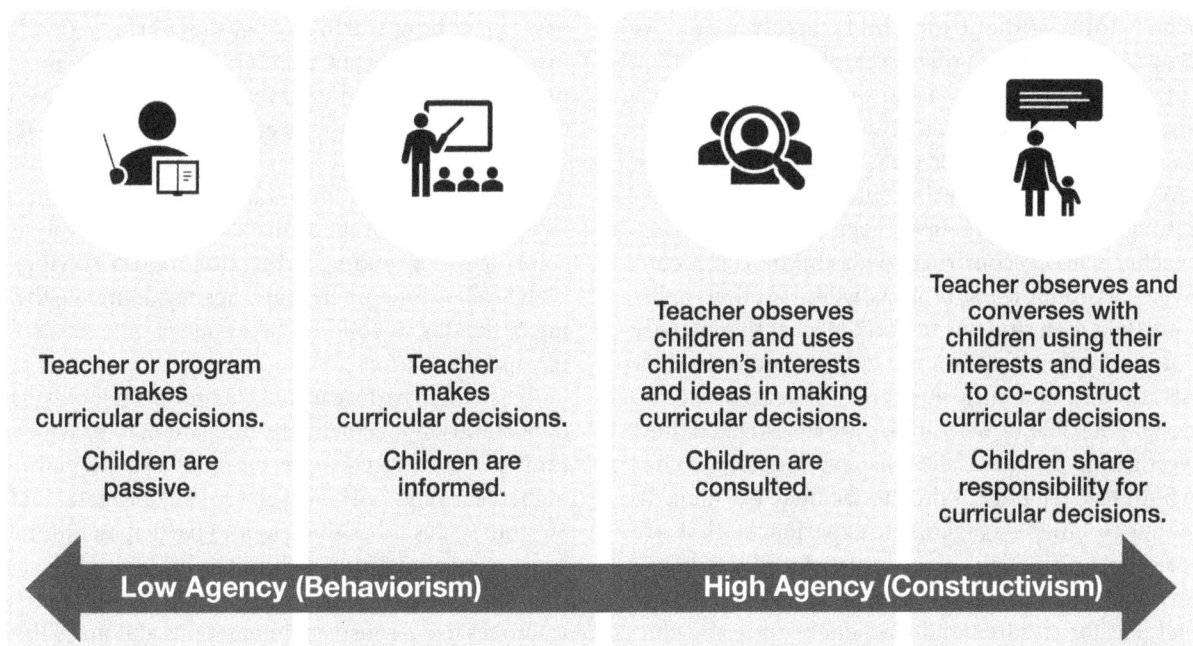

solve, role-plays, and investigations through projects as the mainstays of the classroom. As children make connections between parts of their lives, and relate new information to their prior experiences, they begin to see the "big picture" and consequently learn more and retain their new information longer.

Of course, teachers rarely use all behaviorist practices or all constructivist interactions, but instead enact a range of techniques every day that influences how children learn. The type of curriculum in an early childhood classroom is actually more a range of choices than a dichotomous pair. Teachers select certain curricular components in which children can have input and control. For example, some teachers encourage children to make choices during center time, but still direct large-group settings. Other teachers support genuine dialogue, problem solving, and planning together in large-group activities, and guide children in how to conduct research during center or project time.

In reality, teacher–child curriculum decisions occur across an agency spectrum: from teacher-controlled decisions to teacher–child co-constructing and sharing responsibility for curricular decisions (see Figure 2.2). All parts of this curriculum range have a valid place in the classroom. For example, if the teacher is supporting the children in learning how to say "please" and "thank you," then direct teaching and modeling is appropriate, because a child cannot intuit conventional language. But for most cognitive work in the classroom, teacher–child co-planning is more effective. For example, a child in the block area will discover more about inclines and balance by experimentation rather than by teacher presentation (Kamii, 1982).

All teachers hold beliefs about their teaching, students, subject matter, roles, and responsibilities (Pajares, 1992), and these beliefs affect, to varying degrees, teacher performance in the classroom (Hamre et al., 2012; Vartuli, 2005). Teachers vary in beliefs due to higher education, exchanging points of view, making implicit beliefs explicit through dialogue and discussion, observing exemplary models of master teachers, and the extent and quality of professional development (Vartuli, 2005). When teacher beliefs shift from behaviorist to constructivist practices there is a paradigm shift: from teacher as instructor to teacher as facilitator; from teacher as knower to teacher as coordinator; and from teacher as director to teacher as partner (DeVries & Zan, 2012).

Curriculum Components in Various Approaches

Curriculum includes both content and instruction, and consists of components such as planning, interactions and relationships, environments and materials, and documentation and assessment. In this section, these four curriculum components are addressed.

Planning. Teachers organize curriculum content by using single lessons, units, themes, and projects. Units are mainly teacher-driven and children are passive, perhaps consulted and informed. In the behaviorist classroom, teachers will use direct instruction from textbooks and/or prescribed units, without the child's involvement. As teachers gradually begin to share control of planning, they begin by integrating subject matter in their teaching, then introducing observed children's interests using a theme. Classes will "study" pizza, or cars, their favorite things. Teachers gradually begin placing "provocations" or interesting things to explore and investigate out on the table.

A teacher who co-constructs with children in a constructivist classroom using projects will first observe, listen to, and talk with students to find out what they already know, stories of their families and culture, and what their interests, desires, and curiosities are. The teacher will be intentionally flexible in what topics are investigated, how the investigation proceeds, and what experiences are chosen by both teacher and children to facilitate learning. To help enhance child engagement, experiences that are direct, authentic, firsthand, child-initiated, and interactive are most important for young children. These experiences are emergent for children and teachers because the children chose the topic and the methods of investigation.

In a constructivist classroom, teachers are faced with a dilemma of how to include child agency without giving away all of the decision making. One solution to how to begin with child planning is through genuine conversation, with contributions from both teachers and children. Many teachers use "I wonder . . ." statements in planning. This is a gift that enables children to "follow their interests, listen to each other, and negotiate suggested ideas to solve turn taking issues . . . in a co-constructed exchange" (Houen, Danby, Farrell, & Thorpe, 2016, p. 272).

Sometimes, children's inflated sense of omnipotence leads them to not fully comprehend and even to underestimate task demands, but this leads them, if they have agency, to be excited about planning and learning, and not be daunted by the size of the task. This empowerment of children, and the value their teachers place on their authentic participation, leads to greatly increased engagement on the part of the children, because they are genuinely interested in topics they chose. This interest and engagement has a physiological effect on the brain, with an increase in those positive neurotransmitters that enable development of new neuronal networks and long-term memory. This is important not just for increased daily engagement and fewer behavioral issues, but also for increased agency and self-efficacy (Bandura, 1997).

Interactions and Relationships. When teachers view themselves as being in charge, and view children as passive learners in a behaviorist-transmission classroom, then the teacher often addresses whole groups of children at the same time, answering their questions as needed. As teachers begin to shift their beliefs toward the idea that children have something worth saying, they include small-group instruction and begin to interact more individually and personally with children, eventually including free choice time and class discussions engaging children. As teachers fully engage children's ideas, they seek a balance between child-initiated and adult-supported learning in a constructivist classroom. Many engaged and lively discussions, question asking, authentic problem solving, and a high level of child interest and agency dominate the learning of the day, as children take control of their own learning and the teacher watchfully guides.

Teachers in early learning classrooms not only have the opportunity, but actually the obligation, to provide opportunities for children to be set on a positive path toward higher learning. Correia et al. (2019), in a meta-analysis of 36 studies, describes the "right to participate" in the classroom, conceptualizing children as having rights, as agents in their own social worlds, and as "competent to use resources to co-construct interactions and make their own choices" (p. 80).

Environments and Materials. On the agency spectrum for teaching environments, behaviorist teachers in control select all materials and completely decide room arrangement, according to the curriculum guide. As teachers include accommodations for some individual child needs, they see that perhaps other individual children have some specific needs and interests as well. Soon, as their beliefs shift, they begin setting up learning centers based on researched children's interests. In a co-constructed constructivist classroom, the children's agency, thinking, learning, and work are evident throughout the room. Together teachers and children select and gather concrete, authentic materials. Real objects, photos, and books are accessible to children, many contributed by children and family members. According to Loris Malaguzzi, founder of the well-known early childhood schools of Reggio Emilia, Italy, the third "teacher" is a flexible environment, responsive to the need for teachers and children to create learning together (Edwards, Gandini, & Forman, 1998).

A change in environment changes the way the child becomes engaged and responds to materials. If all educational materials in the classroom have only one use, such as battery-operated toys or coloring sheets, then no creativity can happen. If, on the other hand, most materials are open ended, allowing the child to decide how to use them—such as blocks and related accessories, open-ended art materials, and scientific experimentation items—then discovery is possible and more learning occurs. When a child makes the choice, the child is able to activate neuronal networks already established, tapping into an existing knowledge base or existing skills. For example, a child might have a dog at home and have had many experiences with the dog. This has created neuronal networks related to dogs (vocabulary words, physical characteristics such as fur texture, or the feel of muscles under the fur). This child might choose to use clay to create a model of a dog for a play veterinarian's office the class is creating.

Documentation and Assessment. Documentation also distinguishes a co-constructed constructivist classroom from a behaviorist one in which the only assessment is a teacher- or text-constructed test. The constructivist room is filled with child representations, charts, lists, graphic organizers, artwork, child theories and stories, and portfolios. Both teachers and children co-assess. Teachers capitalize on making keen observations of children in multiple settings: stepping back and really watching, listening, and wondering about children's behaviors and engagement. Then, teachers use observations to drive further learning experiences to support children's progress in learning and furthering their autonomy. Children use their agency to make sense of their own learning and use the artifacts to document learning and to plan next steps in an investigation. But in a behaviorist classroom, all assessment is skills-based, with text-constructed tests, benchmarks, and fill-in-the-blank worksheets.

Learning is cyclical. When documentation and assessment are effective in a constructivist classroom, teachers and learners are both looking for the next experience to engage and challenge. New ideas are connected to prior experience, questions are asked, hypotheses are formed and tested, and children's representation demonstrates their new understanding. Children can easily see their work, compare it to previous work, and judge growth and learning, setting them on a path to be capable of evaluating future learning.

Teachers' Learning Processes

Through trainings, reading, and team collaboration, a teacher can learn the steps of any curriculum or approach to teaching. For behaviorist classrooms, training can help a teacher know when and how they can use rewards and how to reinforce or extinguish behavior. Teachers can be supported in using a curriculum that is clear and direct, with suggestions for activities every day, along with questions to ask children.

Teachers seeking to engage in more constructivist approaches in the classroom can benefit from workshops and classes that demonstrate how to create anticipatory webs; how to journal and reflect; how to help children learn to ask questions, dialogue and work cooperatively, and investigate the answers to their questions; and how to document children's understanding and their own teaching journey. Teachers can learn how to keep learning active and authentic, providing down time for the children to consolidate their memories. Training can demonstrate to the teacher how to "think out loud," summarize learning, and reflect on what is being observed to model practices that the children can do as well, and how to "transform the material . . . to develop it within the range and scope of the child's life" (Dewey, 1902, p. 30).

More challenging to learn from others is a commitment to experimentation (Edwards, Gandini, & Forman, 1998), a belief that children have agency and that it can be fostered through a more communal teaching experience. Harder to develop from workshops are the ability to share the control of learning in the classroom with children; the encouragement of child agency; the dispositions of flexibility, sense of humor, and risk-taking; the excitement for learning new things; and the willingness to put in extra time to read up on a topic, create anticipatory webs, and reach out to experts in the community. The teacher who holds these beliefs and dispositions will be able to make real differences with children's learning in the classroom. The rewards of increased child engagement and learning are worth it.

Constructivist teachers do not believe that children are empty vessels. Children come with rich funds of knowledge and prior experiences already on the first day of class. They are *ready to learn*. Their brains are rich with neuronal networks that they have been building since early infancy. They have prior knowledge of many things in their environment, both active and passive vocabulary in their home language, a sense of relationships between people, and a varying amount of content knowledge. They are capable of developing a sense of agency, inquiry, new ideas, and reflective thought. Teachers have the opportunity and responsibility to collaborate with children, as both teacher and child learn even more new things together. The tools for increased children's agency, engagement, and investment in their own learning are the co-planning, interactions, materials and environment provisions, and co-assessment, as a part of curriculum in the early childhood classroom.

CONCLUSION

This chapter began with insights from Mind Brain Education Science into the process of learning and the role of experience and emotions in building neuronal networks. These networks form the foundation of all learning in the future. Different curriculum approaches were then examined regarding the degree of child agency and emotional involvement in learning. In contrasting four curriculum components from behaviorist and constructivist approaches, the strengths of the constructivist classroom were introduced. Finally, the learning processes teachers can undertake to engage more fully in constructivist approaches were discussed. The Voices from the Field section that follows illustrates how constructivist principles can be applied in a primary grade classroom.

REFERENCES

Bandura, A. (1997). *Self-efficacy: The exercise of control.* New York, NY: Freeman.

Bandura, A. (2006). Toward a psychology of human agency. *Perspectives on Psychological Science, 1*(2), 164–180.

Bonwell, C. C., & Eison, J. A. (1991). *Active learning: Creating excitement in the classroom.* ASHE-ERIC Higher Education Report No. 1. Washington, DC: The George Washington University, School of Education and Human Development.

Correia, N., Camilo, C., Aguiar, C., & Amaro, F. (2019). Children's right to participate in early childhood education settings: A systematic review. *Children and Youth Services Review, 100,* 76–88.

Dawson, G., & Fischer, K. W. (1994). *Human behavior and the developing brain.* New York, NY: Guilford Press.

Dekker, S., Lee, N. C., Howard-Jones, P., & Jolles, J. (2012, October 18). Neuromyths in education: Prevalence and predictors of misconceptions among teachers. *Frontiers in Psychology.* Available at doi.org/10.3389/fpsyg.2012.00429

DeVries, R., & Zan, B. (2012). *Moral classrooms, moral children: Creating a constructivist atmosphere in early education* (2nd ed.). New York, NY: Teachers College Press.

Dewey, J. (1902). *The child and the curriculum.* Chicago, IL: University of Chicago Press.

Edwards, C., Gandini, L., & Forman, G. (Eds.). (1998). *The hundred languages of children: The Reggio Emilia approach to early childhood education* (2nd ed.). Norwood, NJ: Ablex.

Fischer, K. W. (2009). Mind, Brain, and Education: Building a scientific groundwork for learning and teaching. *Mind, Brain, and Education, 3*(1), 3–16.

Fischer, K. W., Daniel, D. B., Immordino-Yang, M. H., Stern, E., Battro, A., & Klizumi, H. (Eds.). (2007). Why Mind, Brain, and Education? Why now? *Mind, Brain, and Education, 1*(1), 1–2.

Fischer, K. W., & Immordino-Yang, M. (2008). Introduction: The fundamental importance of the brain and learning. In J.-B. E. Team (Ed.), *The Jossey-Bass reader on the brain and learning* (pp. 183–198). San Francisco, CA: Jossey-Bass.

Hamre, B. K., Pianta, R. C., Burchinal, M., Field, S., LoCasale-Crouch, J., Downer, J. T., et al. (2012). A course on effective teacher–child interactions: Effects on teacher beliefs, knowledge and observed practice. *American Educational Research Journal, 49*(1), 88–123.

Houen, S., Danby, S., Farrell, A., & Thorpe, K. (2016). Creating spaces for children's agency: "I wonder . . ." formulations in teacher–child interactions. *International Journal of Early Childhood, 48*(3), 259–276.

Kamii, C. (1982). *Number in preschool and kindergarten: Educational implications of Piaget's theory.* Washington, DC: National Association for the Education of Young Children.

Limb, C. J., & Braun, A. R. (2008). Neural substrates of spontaneous musical performance: An fMRI study of jazz improvisation. *PLoS ONE, 3*(2): e1679. Available at doi.org/10.1371/journal.pone.0001679

Maguire, E. A., Spiers, H. J., Good, C. D., Hartley, T., Frackowiak, R. S. J., & Burgess, N. (2003). Navigation expertise and the human hippocampus: A structural brain imaging analysis. *Hippocampus, 13,* 208–217.

Pajares, M. F. (1992). Teachers' beliefs and educational research: Cleaning up a messy construct. *American Educational Research Association, 62*(3), 307–332.

Piaget, J. (1924). *Judgment and reasoning in the child.* London, UK: Routledge & Kegan Paul.

Tokuhama-Espinosa, T. (2008). The scientifically substantiated art of teaching: A study in the development of standards in the new academic field of neuroeducation (Mind, Brain, and Education Science) (Doctoral dissertation, Capella University, 2008). *PQDT Open,* 3310716.

Tokuhama-Espinosa, T. (2010). *The new science of teaching and learning: Using the best of Mind, Brain, and Education Science in the classroom.* New York, NY: Teachers College Press.

Tokuhama-Espinosa, T. (2017). The science in the art of teaching: Using Mind, Brain, and Education to dispel neuromyths and improve education. *Conference Abstract: 2nd International Conference on Educational Neuroscience.* doi: 10.3389/conf.fnhum.2017.222.00001

Tokuhama-Espinosa, T. (2018). *Neuromyths: Debunking false ideas about the brain.* New York, NY: Norton.

Vartuli, S. (2005). Beliefs: The heart of teaching. *Young Children, 60*(5), 76–86.

Vygotsky, L. S. (1934). *Mind in society.* Cambridge, MA: Harvard University.

Watson, J. B. (1924). *Behaviorism.* New York, NY: People's Institute.

VOICES FROM THE FIELD

The Power Lines Project

Nick Pettit, First-Grade Teacher

My 1st-grade classroom of 7- and 8-year-old children is a very supportive and caring place. It's common for the children to be interested in one another's backgrounds and experiences. This interest is exemplified by one afternoon during the Power Lines Project, which was related to Sudan, the home country of one of my students. On the easel is a concept web depicting the students' understandings of all things related to power lines (see Figure 2.3).

Next to the easel is a poster that has a list of different words written by students, such as *cables, utility, and insulation.* Under the list of words are various sketches of different electrical grids, power generators, and physical structures labeled *cross and diagonal brace.* At one table, students are building physical structures with loose materials and analyzing different types of string. The students are discussing what type of string best represents their new learnings about aluminum and carbon fiber. At another table, students are using technology to look up pictures of Sudanese villages, while their peers are using these pictures to paint and make collages for the backgrounds of the physical structures. All through the classroom are artifacts on tables that have been used for inquiry: copper wires from the city's power and light company, blueprints of electrical grids donated by a parent, and safety equipment borrowed from the school's custodial crew.

While students are focused on their work at the tables, a small group of students is circled around a classmate who is explaining what life is like in villages in Sudan. As this "student expert" is answering questions, a student who identifies herself as the "researcher" takes notes in a notebook that she will later use to add to the class question, prediction, and answer chart (see Figure 2.4). To this student, the information her peers are sharing is important and vital to the project because the reason the class began studying about power lines and villages in Sudan was because they were trying to solve a problem for a friend.

PHASE I: BEGINNING THE PROJECT

A few weeks before the Power Lines Project developed, the students in my 1st-grade classroom at Crestview Elementary School in the North Kansas City Public School District (Kansas City, Missouri) sat down for their daily community meeting. During this brief time, students would share concerns or ideas for future learning. One particular day the students were discussing wildlife conservation, and a student who had recently arrived in Kansas City from Sudan, in Africa, spoke up and described a problem in her home village. She explained that wildlife and pets were getting hurt or electrocuted by what she described as electricity lines. Immediately the students fired away with questions:

- How were the animals getting caught in the power lines?
- Why are the power lines so low?
- What kind of wildlife is in Sudan?
- Is a village like a city?

FIGURE 2.3 • Using a concept web to organize thinking, I recorded 1st-grade students' knowledge and growing vocabulary during the Power Lines Project.

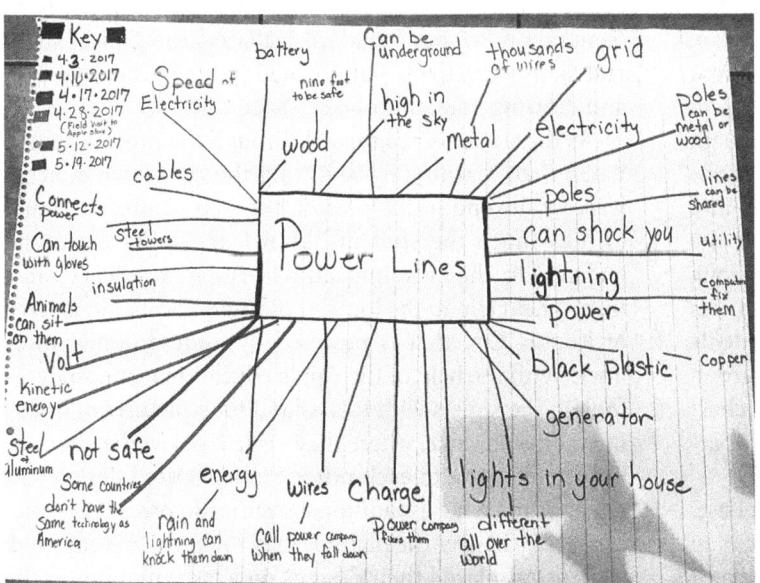

FIGURE 2.4 • Throughout the Power Lines Project as 1st-grade students co-constructed knowledge, I recorded their thinking (questions, predictions, and research) on a graphic organizer.

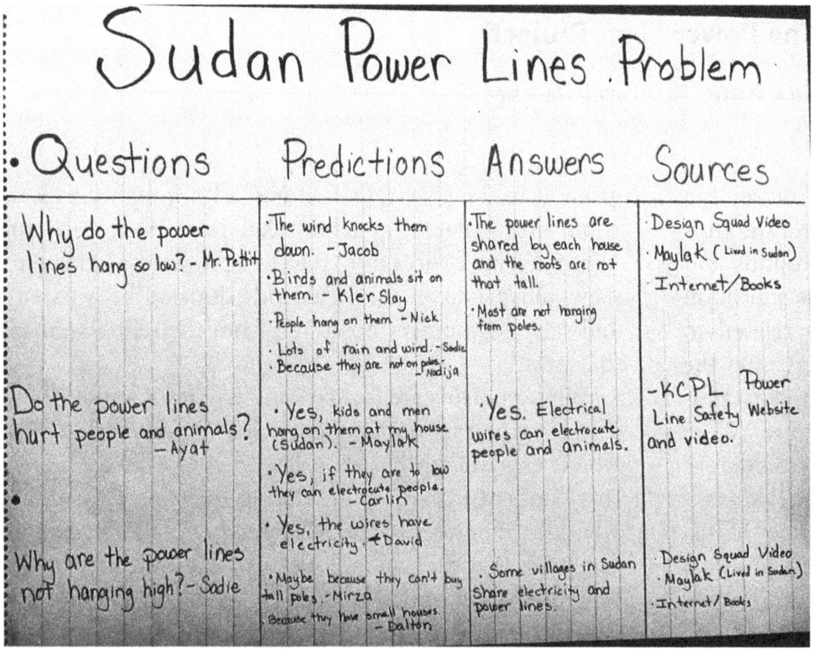

Questions	Predictions	Answers	Sources
Why do the power lines hang so low? – Mr. Pettit	• The wind knocks them down. – Jacob • Birds and animals sit on them. – Kler Slay • People hang on them – Nick • Lots of rain and wind. – Sadie • Because they are not on poles. – Nadija	• The power lines are shared by each house and the roofs are not that tall. • Most are not hanging from poles.	• Design Squad Video • Maylak (Lived in Sudan) • Internet/Books
Do the power lines hurt people and animals? – Ayat	• Yes, kids and men hang on them at my house (Sudan). – Maylak • Yes, if they are to low they can electrocute people. – Carlin • Yes, the wires have electricity. – David	• Yes. Electrical wires can electrocute people and animals.	– KCPL Power Line Safety Website and video.
Why are the power lines not hanging high? – Sadie	• Maybe because they can't buy tall poles. – Mirza Because they have small houses. – Dalton	• Some villages in Sudan share electricity and power lines.	• Design Squad Video • Maylak (Lived in Sudan) • Internet/Books

For the next few days, the daily classroom meetings consisted of asking this student about her experiences. Seeing the interest of all of the students, I casually started to chart the questions that arose during these community meetings. After a few days, I began to gather students' specific questions and documented what the class wanted to learn about power lines. This led to students breaking off into committees and discussing their thoughts in greater detail.

The 1st-graders began using their iPads to look up digital books on the topics of electricity, the country of Sudan, and villages. Students were also beginning to sketch designs in their notebooks using rulers and other forms of measurement that were being taught at the time in math workshop. As the children worked in collaboration, I conferred with students and jotted down their ideas and thinking. I used these notes to bring in artifacts for the class to explore. From the beginning, there was a strong desire to learn about electricity. I brought in different types of wires, batteries, circuits, and controllers for the students to investigate. As students began to wind down their group discussions, I added another column to the question chart for recording the predictions students made about the particular questions they were interested in.

A week before the project moved to the second phase, I met the students on the carpet and shared my conferring notes. I explained that by meeting with all the groups, I had discovered a strong desire to learn about electricity safety and villages in Sudan. I also asked a student to share some learning that he had received from his parents one night. This student began to explain to his classmates that some villages in the world do not have the same electrical systems as we do. While confirming this information with our student from Sudan, this student explained that some electricity in some villages is supplied by generators and that some power lines hang low, even on top of roofs. The student from Sudan raised her hand and stretched out her body with a smile on her face. She yelled, "Yeah that's the problem!" The rest of the class began to chatter with excitement and refer back to their original questions. Trying to contain my own excitement, I brought the students back and calmly asked the class, "Should we work together to try to solve this problem?" The students collectively clapped their hands and shouted "Yes!" A student hugged their friend from Sudan.

PHASE II: INVESTIGATION

For the next month, my 1st-grade class focused on learning more about power lines and power grids. Students were able to meet with electrical linesmen from the power and light company who were able to provide the class with artifacts, knowledge, and the technical terminology needed to deeply study how power lines supply power to communities. Project activities integrated current Next Generation Science Standards (NGSS Lead States, 2013) and skills as students participated in modeling, building, and drawing diagrams of electric circuits.

As the students progressed through the project, I facilitated their learning by revisiting the classroom concept web. By the end of the project, the web painted a picture of how much the students' knowledge about electricity had grown. The most impactful learning experience came from a field trip to the local Apple Store located in an area of Kansas City that is powered by underground power lines. With the help of the Apple education team, students took to the streets with tablets and took pictures of buildings and sidewalks, where they visualized overhead power lines connecting to each other. Students used design studio apps to create a traditional overhead power line structure and grid over the pictures they took. Once completed, students displayed their designs on a large monitor in the store and presented their ideas to their peers and eventually to shoppers who were curious about what the children were doing.

During this long-term investigation, the students were also very interested in learning about their classmate's village in Sudan. The students relied on information from their peer to answer their questions and get her perspective on their thinking. The students in the classroom organically and silently appointed the student the "leader" of the project. This was beneficial to the student, as she was relatively new to the classroom and was shy and reserved. During her first few months in the classroom she had private conversations with me about missing her home country and friends she had made at her former school. Entering a new country and school in the middle of the year was a challenge. As the year progressed, the students were very interested in supporting their peer's transition to America. Students were quick to explain American customs and help their friend with the English language. They were also very curious about her background and experiences. But the student from Sudan was not ready to share.

Structures for classroom meetings were used to create a safe place for all students to express concerns and ideas, but in particular this environment allowed the student from Sudan to find her voice in a new country and new classroom. Once she had shared her experiences and problems in Sudan, she opened herself up to collaboration with peers. As the Power Lines Project progressed, I observed her becoming more animated and passionate when speaking to peers. She also began to demonstrate self-confidence in the classroom. One day when the classroom was talking via Skype with an ambassador from Sudan, the student stood up from the carpet and begin to prompt the guest speaker to give the class information about her homeland that she felt they would find interesting. This new self-confidence poured into the rest of her school day. She began to play more with peers and engage them in nonacademic conversations within the classroom. Her parents also expressed seeing a difference in her at home and a new desire to come to school.

PHASE III: CONCLUDING THE PROJECT

As the class concluded the project, they decided that they wanted to share their learning by designing various structures that could safely distribute power lines to the village in Sudan. One day, while struggling to get a three-dimensional wood structure to stay connected, one of the students in the classroom began to explain that they could still display their structures in two dimensions by using a background to connect to. As the students begin to explore their peer's idea, they also began discussing the idea of collage work, which they were currently learning in their art class. Immediately, some students began to research images of Sudanese villages while others began to cut and

FIGURE 2.5 • First-graders present their Power Lines Project at a school district community outreach event.

tear strips out of classroom magazines. They took these strips and sorted them by shades of color. Once students found an image they wanted to represent, they began to construct a village background by using a collage of colors. When this step was completed, they attached their two-dimensional structures and power lines using a variety of materials.

As student representations were completed, the class held two project culminations. One culmination included the students exhibiting their project at the annual North Kansas City Educational Foundation Breakfast. This is an event held by the school district in conjunction with community stakeholders. Getting up as early as 5:30 a.m. to set up for the breakfast, students showcased the project to members of the North Kansas City School District and community members who had contributed to the district's educational foundation. As students discussed their journey and processed their project, they emphasized the need for developed power grids in Sudan. Many community members made their way over to the group of proud parents that were watching to give praise for the awareness and passion the students showed in their discussion of the project (see Figure 2.5).

The second culmination was a classroom celebration where students displayed their representations, thinking, and artifacts used in the project. In a last-minute decision, some students decided that they would like to be experts on parts of the project and be available to explain in more detail the project web, questions and answers chart, and artifact table. The students opened the classroom up to their 1st-grade peers, school staff, and parents. During the classroom celebration, students were seen explaining the origin of the project and their desire to solve a problem for a peer. Students would find their friend from Sudan and bring her over to meet their parents. In a humorous moment, two students grabbed the hand of their friend from Sudan at the same time, pulling her in both directions! Once realized, all three students begin to laugh and hug each other in the middle of the celebration. At that moment I began to realize that the real work accomplished during this project wasn't the math and science skills embedded throughout the project or the numerous creative and communication skills that were developed through collaboration and inquiry. Rather the most important accomplishment was helping a student feel comfortable joining our classroom community. And that made sense to me because caring and supporting were what my class loved to do the most.

REFERENCE

NGSS Lead States. (2013). *Next Generation Science Standards: For states, by states.* Washington, DC: The National Academies Press.

CHAPTER 3

Curriculum Research on the Project Approach

Illuminating the "What" and the "How" of Teaching and Learning

Karrie A. Snider & Sue Vartuli

AS PRESENTED in the previous chapters, teaching and learning need to be enriched with provocative experiences to engage children in active exploration of their immediate world and connect them to culturally relevant curricula. Active, engaged *learning* and active, engaged *teaching*, as in the Project Approach, promote opportunities for children and teachers to think together, which enhances the intellectual development and learning outcomes of both children and teachers. This is particularly important for ensuring that all learners, especially children from diverse backgrounds, build strong dispositions for learning, which in turn builds active citizens for our future world. How does research on the Project Approach help us understand what impact this active, engaged curriculum has on such outcomes?

Curriculum involves both content and instruction. To determine curriculum effectiveness, researchers must examine curriculum fidelity, which is "adherence to curriculum practices, teacher–child interactions, and environmental conditions being met" (Vartuli & Rohs, 2009, p. 511). In other words, to be valid, research on any curriculum must include assessment of curriculum fidelity—that is, how closely a teacher implements the content, environmental materials, and instructional practices of the curriculum as it was intended. By examining fidelity to processes and outcomes, researchers can understand, interpret, and accurately report the degree to which an intervention (i.e., curriculum model or approach) was implemented (Vartuli & Rohs, 2009). Because content and instruction selection is predominantly individual, curriculum research also assists *teachers* in making the best curriculum choices for young children and informs individual teachers' decisions about what and how to teach in their own classrooms (Steiner, 2017).

Focusing specifically on the Project Approach as a curriculum model, we have found the research base to be sparse (Beneke & Ostrosky, 2009). Researching project work is challenging because of the complex, authentic nature of this teaching and learning approach. On one hand, we know from many descriptive accounts that the Project Approach, as a guide for active, engaged learning, is incredibly beneficial for developing the intellectual capacities of both adults and children. On the other hand, project work has been challenging for teachers to implement *and* for researchers to study and examine the benefits of this type of approach to learning.

In this chapter we first discuss the reasons why there are challenges in researching the Project Approach. Then, we present an extensive review of the existing research. Finally, we conclude by examining the issues related to the current research base on project work.

WHY WE DON'T KNOW MORE: CHALLENGES TO PROJECT APPROACH CURRICULUM RESEARCH

One reason why there isn't a lot of research on the Project Approach is that there are relatively few Project Approach classroom examples available for *researchers* to observe and study. Far more prevalent are classroom examples reflecting the prevailing philosophy of education in the contemporary pre-K through 20 education system—the Behavioral-Transmission Model of teaching. As explained in Chapter 2, the teacher's role in the Behavioral-Transmission Model focuses on teacher-directed, systematic, and skills-based instruction, with learning depicted as test-driven student outcomes.

In contrast, teachers implementing the Project Approach distinguish between academic and intellectual goals, integrate a focus on dispositions of learning within content-area activities, and promote lifelong learning, not grade-level test scores. Teachers implementing projects assume constructivist teaching roles: *facilitator* rather than instructor, *researcher* rather than director, and *co-investigator* rather than knower (see Chapter 2). The Project Approach encourages deeper understanding of meaningful concepts and emphasizes complex learning activities that often have no right answer or one way to be accomplished, rather than surface learning exercises focused on rote facts. Selection of authentic curriculum topics and materials guides instruction during project work, rather than use of preselected materials about content that may or may not be connected to children's backgrounds or interests. The Project Approach has distinct guidelines (Helm & Katz, 2016; Katz, Chard, & Kogan, 2014), but there are no specific directions, teachers' manuals, or lesson plans (Clark, 2006). These characteristics of the Project Approach make research into curriculum fidelity a complex undertaking.

The Nature of the Project Approach

Positive characteristics inherent in projects, as observed by teachers and families, include

- responsiveness to children's interests,
- promotion of high expectations of children as co-investigators, and
- enhancement of positive learning dispositions.

Yet, such characteristics present obstacles to research into Project Approach teaching and learning outcomes.

First, the child-centered, responsive nature and elasticity of the Project Approach focuses on the child as the center of classroom content, instruction, and assessment. Project topics selected, for the most part, are based on children's interests, and learning is built on children's existing knowledge. Dewey (1916) has stated that experiences are interconnected with children's past and future activities, and education is the reconstruction of experience. Therefore, the knowledge, skills, and dispositions will vary from project to project, within and across classrooms (Beneke & Ostrosky, 2009). This variability increases the challenge of comparing classroom outcomes within a research study.

Second, children involved in project work are co-investigators, and teachers promote exploration of appropriate content knowledge and metacognitive learning process skills. Teaching with the Project Approach becomes a dance between child and teacher (Dewey, 1916). Research on the Project Approach has to capture both the content and the learning process outcomes of children. Teachers encourage process skills by promoting a high level of child learning, so that children can pose and investigate questions, solve problems, make predictions, hypothesize, analyze, and develop theories. Teachers must become learners right along with the children (Glassman & Whaley, 2000). Teachers have to shift from the role of instructor to facilitator of learning, giving up appropriate levels of control of the classroom learning (Clark, 2006). Children represent learnings and understandings so outcomes can be documented in many formats. Capturing what teachers and children do—what they discuss, decompose, and construct through interactions and experiences, and what they reconstruct in documentation—makes selection of research tools difficult. To capture authentic, consistent evidence of the dynamic levels of interaction is complicated.

Finally, the Project Approach nurtures positive learning dispositions for children and teachers and positive teaching dispositions for teachers. When implementing the Project Approach in a classroom, most teachers have to shift their thinking and practices to anticipate the possibilities of learning. New approaches can be perplexing even to veteran teachers. Teachers must move from a teacher-directed approach to a child-centered inquiry approach to learning—from an instructor role to a facilitator role. Teachers must also learn the distinction between skill acquisition and the dispositions to apply skills in everyday life. Beliefs about how children learn and how teachers teach are very resistant to change. Many teachers implementing the Project Approach for the first time lack positive teacher efficacy, so the risk of attempting something new proves to be daunting. Strengthening the dispositions of teachers rather than changing entrenched beliefs (Clark, 2006) has been a recommended approach to this problem. Documenting the changes in children's and teachers' learning and dispositions within a research study is a complex process.

Complex Teaching and Learning Equals Complex Research

Researching multiple systems that impact growth, development, learning, and thinking is formidable. Capturing the influences of every level on thinking and learning (children's and teachers') requires use of an ecological research model (Bronfenbrenner, 1977; Rimm-Kaufman & Pianta, 2000). Variables and factors have to be separated and nested to explore the dynamic nature of learning during the Project Approach. Advanced statistics, such as multilevel modeling in the research design, are needed to explore the many facets of the Project Approach. Measuring standards of curriculum implementation (fidelity) for any curriculum is a complicated hurdle for researchers to capture; yet, fidelity is required so that comparisons can be made across studies. The current descriptions of teaching methods and thinking processes that have been implemented within research studies concerning the Project Approach demonstrate a continuum of practice with various degrees of fidelity to the Project Approach guidelines. Capturing the adherence to the principles and practices of the Project Approach and demonstrating the effects on the learners is intricate and complex.

Lack of Resources for Research

Research tools to capture multiple vantage points from multiple perspectives remains a complication. Logistical issues such as the lack of funding of research projects using the Project Approach, including finding support for teachers to be educated on the Project Approach and coached as they attempt to try new teaching methods, are also reasons why we do not know more about Project Approach outcomes. Keeping these barriers in mind, let's now examine the most recent research that has been conducted and what we have learned about the outcomes of implementing the Project Approach.

WHAT WE DO KNOW! THE CURRENT RESEARCH BASE ON PROJECT WORK

To investigate the current research on project work, we asked the question, "What past and current peer-reviewed research contributes to our understandings about the implementation and effectiveness of the Project Approach on children's learning and development?" We performed electronic searches for publications within the last two decades, using the publication date of Katz and Chard (2000) as rationale for this time frame, and identified 127 articles, which were then further reduced by reviewing abstracts of potential studies fitting our criteria. We conducted ancillary searches to ensure that a broad scope and sample were included (i.e., international contributions, infant/toddler through 3rd-grade examples, Reggio Emilia, etc.). Lastly, we conducted a separate supplementary search regarding pedagogical documentation, which has greatly contributed to the understanding of children's and adults' active engagement within constructivist classrooms. More than 500 articles involving pedagogical documentation were previewed, with 75 abstracts reviewed, and finally 40 full articles identified.

In the following sections we present research on project work in early childhood. First, we describe characteristics of the research examples, including two meta-analyses that confirmed our literature-review results. We then organize the research examples by qualitative and quantitative studies. Within each of these sections, we share the research results as they relate to teacher and child outcomes. We highlight pedagogical documentation examples and program evaluation efforts. We conclude by examining the implications of the current research base on project work.

Research in this review represents experiences of teachers, preservice teachers, families, and children within classrooms and programs all over the world, including Australia, Bhutan, Canada, China, Finland, Germany, New Zealand, Spain, Sweden, Turkey, and the United States. Studies included early childhood age groups: infants, toddlers, preschoolers, kindergartners, and school children in primary grades. Researchers examined teachers' and children's experiences, teachers' and/or parents' perceptions of the Project Approach, and how teachers' beliefs regarding early childhood practices changed as a result of utilizing projects. Research highlighted teaching children with special needs and teaching curriculum content such as science and math concepts. Most research studies noted the challenges of conducting research on the Project Approach and that more research on project work is needed. See Figure 3.1 for focus areas, contexts, and associated child age levels for the current research base.

Our review yielded primarily qualitative research. We found few quantitative studies. The available literature includes samples from across the birth–20 education system. Studies represented the various applications of project work inspired by Dewey (1916) and Kilpatrick (1918). Studies varied in describing fidelity to the Project Approach framework (i.e., three phases that span the processes of investigation, representation, and culmination of learning; refer to Figure 1.3) or other modern conceptions of project work.

Meta-Analyses

Two meta-analyses confirmed the results of our literature review. Holm (2011) isolated 16 U.S. and international studies published between 2005 and 2011 that included varied age levels of student samples (pre-K, primary, upper elementary, and high school grades). Of these studies, three targeted pre-K/K contexts in order to examine teachers' efficacy for implementing projects with children with special needs (Beneke & Ostrosky, 2009) and to examine children's developmental outcomes before and after learning through projects (Aral et al., 2010; Bıçakçı & Gürsoy, 2010). The other meta-analysis by Merritt, Lee, Rillero, & Kinach (2017) focused on how quantitative researchers examined the effectiveness of project work. None of the studies included a sample of children below 4th grade. As such, Merritt et al. (2017) found little investigation of how

FIGURE 3.1 • Current research base on the Project Approach in early childhood education

Research Focus	Study	Country	Age Level
Learning of Teachers Implementing the Project Approach	Kogan & Pin (2009) Brewer (2010)	Mexico Midwestern USA	Toddlers
	Beneke (2000) Brooks & Wangmo (2011) [a]Vartuli, Bolz, & Wilson (2014) Serrano, Alfaya, & García (2015) Beneke & Ostrosky (2015) [a]Metin & Aral (2016)	Midwestern USA Bhutan Midwestern USA Spain Midwestern USA Turkey	Preschool
	Wilson (2001) Pui-Wah (2006) Yuen (2009) [a]Bıçakçı & Gürsoy (2010) [a]Aral, Kandir, Ayhan, & Yaşar (2010) Çabuk & Haktanır (2010) Mawson (2010) Chun, Hertzog, Gaffney, & Dymond (2012) Cohrssen, Quadros-Wander, Page, & Klarin (2017) Chen, Li, & Wang (2017)	Midwestern USA China China Turkey Turkey Turkey New Zealand Midwestern USA Australia China	Kindergarten
	Hertzog (2007) Dresden & Lee (2007) Mitchell, Foulger, Wetzel, & Rathkey (2009)	Midwestern USA Southern USA USA	1st grade
	Souto-Manning & Lee (2005)	South USA	2nd grade
Preservice Teachers and University Students	Donegan, Hong, Trepanier-Street, & Finkelstein (2005)	Upper Midwestern USA	Special-needs pre-K to kindergarten
	Hooks & Duarte (2005) Owen (2007) Moran (2007)	Eastern USA Midwestern USA New England, USA	Pre-K
	Çabuk & Haktanır (2010) Wastin & Han (2014)	Turkey Southern USA	Kindergarten
Art	Griebling (2011)	Midwestern USA	3–6-year-olds
Art Media	Swann (2008)	Midwestern USA	3–4-year-olds
Creative Thinking	[a]Gencer & Gonen (2015)	Turkey	Preschool
Infants and Toddlers	McGaha, Cummings, Lippard, & Dallas (2011)	Eastern USA	6-week- to 3-year-olds
Math Concepts	Linder, Powers-Costello, & Stegelin (2011)	South	Pre-K to primary
Sciences	Inan, Trundle, & Kantor (2010)	Midwestern USA	Preschool
Social Studies	Maple (2005)	Midwestern USA	K–1st grade
Teacher Beliefs	Li, Wang, & Wong (2011)	China	Preschool
Early Childhood Special Education	[b]Harte (2010)	Northern Kentucky, USA	Early childhood
	Guven & Duman (2007)	Istanbul, Turkey	6–7-year-olds

Note: [a]Quantitative study. [b]Report or descriptive narrative.

effective project-based learning is for young children in early childhood classrooms.

Results from both meta-analyses included examples of project work as described by Dewey (1916). Yet, we noticed that some included studies lacked distinct characteristics of project work, such as phases and active investigation of children's questions over a period of time. In addition, some studies appeared to focus on thematic approaches rather than the use of projects to guide children's learning.

Qualitative Studies

Similar to Holm's (2011) findings, the greatest abundance of literature we reviewed constituted *case studies*. Researchers select case studies to examine "information-rich" cases and describe features of particular phenomena (Creswell, 2014; Patton, 2014). Researchers use case-study approaches when working with day-to-day realities within real contexts, especially because classroom contexts are already complex. Similar to the case-study approach, *narrative inquiry* is used to think about, study, and describe an experience using narrative. In case studies, as in other qualitative approaches, researchers use original, uniquely constructed content analysis and other methods to review and analyze data (interviews, surveys, documents, classroom observations, conversations and communications, children's work, teachers' reflections and lesson plans, etc.). Study-specific codes assist the analysis process in order to aid researchers in drawing conclusions and making connections to theoretical underpinnings (Creswell, 2014). For these reasons, case studies are advantageous for researching project work but are limited because outcomes cannot be generalized to other populations that do not match the case study.

Teacher Learning and Development.
Case studies and other qualitative research methods yielded variations in how teachers implemented project work and how teaching through projects impacted teachers' perceptions. Studies revealed that teachers felt more comfortable and more excited about shifting their role from instructor to guide (teacher-centered to more child-centered) by the time they had completed project implementation (Çabuk & Haktanır, 2010; Chen et al., 2017; Nariman & Chrispeels, 2016). Teachers developed a sense of efficacy for teaching children with special needs through teaching using the Project Approach (Beneke & Ostrosky, 2009, 2013, 2015). Teachers' increases in confidence were often attributed to professional development experiences and collaborative support (Hertzog, 2007; Nariman & Chrispeels, 2016; Serrano et al., 2015; Yuen, 2009).

Nariman and Chrispeels (2016) described the perceptions of eighteen 1st- through 5th-grade teachers from one elementary school serving predominantly students of low socioeconomic status and Latino students. After receiving professional development for 2 years to support their implementation of science-focused project work, teachers expressed enthusiasm and shifted from teacher-centered to more child-centered practices. Teachers expressed their awareness of the "tensions between the way standardized testing has pushed them to teach and the value of more actively engaging students" (p. 10). During research interviews, teachers also noted that time and resources were significant challenges.

Other case studies depicted how teachers grappled with implementing the core characteristics of the Project Approach (Chen et al., 2017; Hertzog, 2007; Nariman & Chrispeels, 2016; Pui-Wah, 2006). For example, Hertzog (2007) observed and interviewed two 1st-grade teachers about their use of the Project Approach to teach grade-level content. It was challenging for teachers to "give up control," use small-group instructional formats, and help children develop their own researchable questions (i.e., Chen et al., 2017). Teachers often teeter-tottered back to the traditional transmission style of teaching (i.e., Pui-Wah, 2006). For example, Hertzog (2007) noted that teachers assigned worksheets to children when they misbehaved during project activities because teachers perceived this as helping to manage children's behaviors. This was in contrast to the perspective of the researcher, who commented about how little misbehavior actually occurred during children's active engagement in project work. The observed mix of project and traditional teaching practices contributed to the lower adherence to project guidelines.

Researchers concluded that professional development and support would benefit teachers' implementation of the Project Approach (Beneke & Ostrosky, 2009; Vartuli et al., 2014). Chen et al. (2017) detailed the curriculum fidelity processes of 23 kindergarten teachers implementing the Project Approach within Hong Kong kindergarten classrooms. Results included reflections describing how teachers believed professional support would have helped them implement project work with more adherence to the approach.

Preservice teachers have also been subjects of Project Approach research (Çabuk & Haktanır, 2010; Donegan et al., 2005; Hooks & Duarte, 2005; Moran, 2007; Owen, 2007; Wastin & Han, 2014). Hooks and Duarte (2005) studied preservice teachers' understanding of mathematics teaching after observing the Project Approach within their clinical practicum settings. Preservice teachers in this small sample were able to learn the value and type of activities that facilitated teaching of mathematics standards and concepts for young children. "They were amazed at how natural the teaching of math can be if an effective methodology is used, regardless the age of the child" (p. 190). Consequently, teacher education research indicated that preservice teachers benefit from quality settings in which to observe and learn how to conduct project work, as well as mentor teachers who can effectively model and help them develop positive conclusions regarding the nature of project work as constructivist teaching (Owen, 2007; Wastin & Han, 2014).

Children's Learning and Development. Researchers, taking a qualitative approach, illuminated how children benefited from learning through projects by examining child portfolios, conducting direct observations, or completing interviews with teachers and parents. Researchers also analyzed children's representational drawings. These data assisted researchers' development of connections between teachers' use of the Project Approach and improvements in child outcomes.

Serrano et al. (2015), in a study from Spain, described the implementation of the Project Approach across 24 early childhood classrooms, which included a sample of 24 teachers and 485 children. Researchers determined that project work aided children's development of learning dispositions such as autonomy, responsibility, and initiative. Complex themes developed from children's suggestions. Children developed plans, were creative, and used rich vocabulary while asking, answering, and telling about their inquiry-driven learning experiences.

Children's abilities to represent content knowledge through drawings and early writing were strengthened during project work. Yuen (2009) noted children's development of emergent literacy skills (reading signs, booklets, and books) after a project on shoes grew out of a standard curriculum theme ("My Body"). Cohrssen et al. (2017) used formative assessment practices to determine that project work supported children's development of spatial knowledge (exploration of shapes, spatial orientation, and spatial visualization) while further influencing the development of children's mathematical vocabulary.

Project work contributed to building a community of young learners (Brooks & Wangmo, 2011; Harte, 2010; McGaha et al., 2011). Researchers noted that child-centered topics contributed to the success of projects (Çabuk & Haktanır, 2010) and to the promotion of learning as service—as young children impacted their local community through helping others solve real problems (Chun et al., 2012). Child-initiated topics also represented the unique development and nature of the Project Approach (Brooks & Wangmo, 2011). For example:

> A project like the Primary 2 class investigation of the Gangtey Hotel could not have been done by children living in Sakten, a nomadic community, because it has no hotels. Nor could a similar study have been done even in Bhutan's capital, Thimpu, because while it has many hotels, none are converted palaces. Similarly, while children might study any school campus as the Primary 1 class did, each school and each set of children involved will be unique, and the available resources and the activities involved in collecting and representing data will be different in each context. (p. 33)

Perceptions about children's capabilities changed during implementation of the Project Approach. For instance, some teachers believed young children lacked the capabilities and knowledge to participate in and conduct project learning, but these teachers learned firsthand how children became independent leaders in learning (Hertzog, 2007; Pui-Wah, 2006; Serrano et al., 2015; Yuen, 2009); even the youngest of learners (Brewer, 2010; Kogan & Pin, 2009). At first, families believed project work was only for gifted children (Serrano et al., 2015). Families reported an increase in children's conversations at home about school and what they were learning when in project work (Çabuk & Haktanır, 2010; Serrano et al., 2015; Yuen, 2009). Parents valued the Project Approach for developing children's sense of autonomy in learning (Yuen, 2009).

Pedagogical Documentation. Pedagogical documentation captures teaching and learning experiences within constructivist classrooms. As the name implies, pedagogical documentation involves systematic gathering of pedagogical evidence where adults and children collect a wide array of data about teaching and learning. The result combines two facets—the content of the documentation (what data are examined) and the processes of the documentation (the conversations, selections, and decisions made to create the documentation and what occurs as a result of sharing the documentation). Content of the documentation may consist of audio and video recordings, photographs, and representations such as sketches, drawings, writings, constructions, and so forth. Documentation processes may consist of conversations, graphs, comments by teachers with interpretations, notes from children, parents, or teachers, and so forth. Documentation may also include transcriptions of the teacher–child and peer-to-peer interactions revealing what children said, did, or thought within the learning environment. Pedagogical documentation is then shared with others (children, teachers, and parents) through visual representations in order to provoke conversation, reflection, and deeper understandings (Buldu, 2010; Caldwell,

1997). In contrast to other forms of early childhood observation assessment methods, which take a more traditional stance of observing to identify children's capabilities according to developmental norms, pedagogical documentation depicts not only what is being learned but how children are learning.

The challenges associated with conducting pedagogical documentation reflect challenges similar to conducting project work. Teachers have difficulty finding resources, finding time to document, and having time to collaborate with others, such as peers and parents. Because of the authentic nature of pedagogical documentation, it is challenging to compare outcomes across classrooms and programs. Consistent tools for measuring learning outcomes derived within and from pedagogical documentation activities are needed.

Pedagogical documentation research (see Figure 3.2), conducted mainly in Europe, has revealed findings similar to the results from other qualitative studies we reviewed. Pedagogical documentation informed teaching in ways such as the selection of activities or lessons, enabled teachers' reflection on practice, created a professional learning community among teachers and center staff, and increased communication with families (Buldu, 2010; MacDonald, 2007, MacDonald & Hill, 2018; Rintakorpi, 2016). For children, pedagogical documentation scaffolded children's learning experiences and enabled children to think more deeply (Buldu, 2010; MacDonald, 2007). In addition, pedagogical documentation of content and processes increased children's participation, motivation, and interest in learning (Buldu, 2010).

Quantitative Studies

Very few rigorous research studies have explored relationships among teachers' implementation of project work (curriculum), teachers' actual teaching practices (instruction), and children's outcomes (assessment) by applying quantitative approaches. We identified five published research articles and one unpublished study that used quantitative statistical analyses to answer research questions about the Project Approach.

Children's Development. Four quasi-experimental studies compared child outcomes using standardized instruments before and after children experienced learning through projects. Aral et al. (2010) examined the effects of project work on Turkish children's (*N* = 34) conceptual development using the Bracken Basic Concept Scale-Revised. While conceptual development scores increased more over time for the experimental group, the results lacked a statistically significant difference between the groups.

FIGURE 3.2 • Selected research on pedagogical documentation

Study	Country
Buldu (2010)	United Arab Emirates
Katz & Galbraith (2006)	USA
Knauf (2017)	Germany
MacDonald (2007)	Canada
MacDonald & Hill (2018)	Canada
Picchio, Giovannini, Mayer, & Musatti (2012)	Italy
Rintakorpi (2016)	Finland
Rintakorpi & Reunamo (2017)	Finland

Bıçakçı and Gürsoy (2010) determined that Turkish kindergarten children in the experimental preschool group (*N* = 19) scored higher on the Brigance Early Development Inventory II measure, particularly on receptive and expressive language skills. Gencer and Gonen (2015) determined that preschool children's (*N* = 18) creative thinking skills increased after 3 months of project work experiences. Metin and Aral (2016) determined that 5-year-old children's visual perception scores were higher when compared to those of peers who did not participate in learning through projects.

Teachers' Development. Studies frequently focused on the instructional practices that teachers demonstrated when implementing the Project Approach. For example, Vartuli et al. (2014) examined the community of practice between Head Start teachers and instructional coaches implementing the Project Approach across early childhood classrooms in a Midwestern United States metropolitan area. Results indicated that when teachers adhered to Project Approach guidelines (i.e., curriculum fidelity; Vartuli, Bolz, Wilson, & Helm, 2016), they had higher quality instructional interactions with children, based on the Classroom Assessment Scoring System (CLASS; Pianta, LaParo, & Hamre, 2008). Such teacher–child interactions have been identified as necessary for children's academic growth, especially children at risk for school failure.

Vartuli et al. (2014) illuminated that curriculum content does matter. The Communities of Practice Model of ongoing professional development and coaching supported teachers as they learned to conduct project work. A follow-up evaluation study by Snider, Holley, and Usman (2017) replicated the results of Vartuli et al. (2014) and included increases in child outcomes for preschoolers conducting project work. Snider, Marszalek, and Usman

(2019) examined the relationship between project teaching and learning outcomes through a Hierarchical Linear Model. It is evident that more rigorous studies of project work are necessary to move the Project Approach from a research-based to an evidence-based teaching and learning framework.

Program Evaluation. Program evaluation research has many useful purposes, including engaging programs and stakeholders in collaborative, continuous improvement efforts (NAEYC & NAECS/SDE, 2003). Program evaluations focus on program-determined comprehensive goals, which serve as guides to understanding both short-term and long-term impacts of initiatives. Evaluations allow researchers to develop implementation-support tools and research instruments and tailor research questions to the program's interests.

We reviewed the program evaluations of two professional learning communities featured in Chapter 6, the Kohl Children's Museum (Chicago, Illinois) Early Childhood Connections Program (ECC) and the Kansas City Coaching Project Mid-America Regional Council Head Start. Both of these training models have utilized program evaluation research, both for understanding how teachers implemented the Project Approach and for illuminating the impact of teaching with the Project Approach on child and family outcomes.

The Kohl ECC's evaluations contain qualitative and quantitative review of classroom observations, and focus largely on how teachers who completed the Kohl ECC training program independently implemented project work across home-based child care, child care centers, and public school classrooms. The Kansas City project's evaluations incorporated a review of child developmental outcome data, observations of teacher–child interactions, observations of teachers using the Project Approach, and observations of children interacting with peers, teachers, and classroom activities. Overall, each model has multiple-year evaluations that have evolved over time and assisted in the development of trainings and implementation tools (i.e., the Kohl Project Approach Assessment and Coaching Tool; Powell et al., 2013).

Limitations of Current Research

All research has limitations. The current research base on project work is limited for several reasons. The literature contains primarily qualitative research, and these types of studies cannot be generalized to other schools and teachers. Rich qualitative case studies have illuminated the challenges and benefits of project teaching and learning, yet the current research base has focused primarily on novice or first-time Project Approach teachers. Some studies lacked adherence or fidelity to the Project Approach guidelines. Lack of curriculum fidelity evidence diminishes the researchers' ability to suggest that project work is the positive force driving successful study results.

The current quantitative literature lacks the use of authentic, yet standardized and psychometrically sound observation and assessment tools to measure the teaching and learning behaviors enacted within the context of project activities. Examples of behaviors include teachers' instructional strategies, teachers' social and conversational interactions with children, children's level of engagement, and children's growth across early childhood developmental domains. To date, most quantitative research on the Project Approach has occurred in Turkish preschools or kindergartens with small samples of children from low numbers of classrooms using skills-based outcomes. Standardized assessments that focus on discrete skills serve particular purposes but may not necessarily be the best measures of child outcomes within a project. Even with the use of experimental and control groups to compare child outcomes from project and non-project classrooms, these studies lacked research procedures to sufficiently control for impacts of other factors that may be influencing the positive study results (i.e., teacher credentials; children's experiences outside of school; factors related to socioeconomics, culture, gender, and age).

CONCLUSION

The past two decades of research on the Project Approach represents a pioneered trail for researchers and practitioners. We have learned that novice Project Approach teachers need support when implementing projects, especially to overcome barriers of time constraints, lack of systemwide supports, and overreliance on traditional behavioral teaching approaches within contemporary schooling. We have also learned that researchers all over the world have illuminated the extraordinary work of teachers and families who have dedicated teaching and learning to promoting intellectual thinking through the Project Approach. We now understand what is necessary to move project work forward as an evidence-based approach: that is, an accumulation of published mixed-method research that can illuminate "the Project Approach effect" on teaching and learning.

REFERENCES

Aral, N., Kandir, A., Ayhan, A. B., & Yaşar, M. C. (2010). The influence of project-based curricula on six-year-old preschoolers' conceptual development. *Social Behavior and Personality: An International Journal, 38*(8), 1073–1079.

Beneke, S. (2000). Implementing the Project Approach in part-time early childhood education programs. *Early Childhood Research & Practice, 2*(1), 1–22.

Beneke, S., & Ostrosky, M. M. (2009). Teachers' views of the efficacy of incorporating the Project Approach into classroom practice with diverse learners. *Early Childhood Research & Practice, 11*(1), 1–9.

Beneke, S. J., & Ostrosky, M. M. (2013). The potential of the Project Approach to support diverse young learners. *Young Children, 68*(2), 22–28.

Beneke, S., & Ostrosky, M. M. (2015). Effects of the Project Approach on preschoolers with diverse abilities. *Infants & Young Children, 28*(4), 355–369.

Bıçakçı, M. Y., & Gürsoy, F. (2010). A study on the effects of project-based education on the developmental areas of children. *International Journal of Academic Research, 2*(5), 379–388.

Brewer, R. A. (2010). The Canada Goose Project: A first project with children under 3. *Early Childhood Research and Practice, 12*(1), 1–14.

Bronfenbrenner, U. (1977). Toward an experimental ecology of human development. *American Psychologist, 32*(7), 513.

Brooks, M., & Wangmo, T. (2011). Introducing the Project Approach and use of visual representation to early childhood education in Bhutan. *Early Childhood Research & Practice, 13*(1), 1–35.

Buldu, M. (2010). Making learning visible in kindergarten classrooms: Pedagogical documentation as a formative assessment technique. *Teaching and Teacher Education, 26*, 1439–1449.

Çabuk, B., & Haktanır, G. (2010). What should be learned in kindergarten? A Project Approach example. *Procedia—Social and Behavioral Sciences, 2*(2), 2550–2555.

Caldwell, L. B. (1997). *Bringing Reggio Emilia home. An innovative approach to early childhood education.* New York, NY: Teachers College Press.

Chen, J. J., Li, H., & Wang, J.-Y. (2017). Implementing the Project Approach: A case study of hybrid pedagogy in a Hong Kong kindergarten. *Journal of Research in Childhood Education, 31*(3), 324–341.

Chun, E. J., Hertzog, N. B., Gaffney, J. S., & Dymond, S. K. (2012). When service learning meets the Project Approach: Incorporating service learning in an early childhood program. *Journal of Early Childhood Research, 10*(3), 232–245.

Clark, A. M. (2006). Changing classroom practice to include the Project Approach. *Early Childhood Research & Practice, 8*(2), 1–10.

Cohrssen, C., De Quadros-Wander, B., Page, J., & Klarin, S. (2017). Between the big trees: A project-based approach to investigating shape and spatial thinking in a kindergarten program. *Australasian Journal of Early Childhood, 42*(1), 94–104.

Creswell, J. W. (2014). *Research design: Qualitative, quantitative, and mixed methods approaches.* Thousand Oaks, CA: SAGE.

Dewey, J. (1916). *Democracy and education: An introduction to the philosophy of education.* New York, NY: Macmillan.

Donegan, M., Hong, S. B., Trepanier-Street, M., & Finkelstein, C. (2005). Exploring how project work enhances student teachers' understanding of children with special needs. *Journal of Early Childhood Teacher Education, 26*(1), 37–46.

Dresden, J., & Lee, K. (2007). The effects of project work in a first-grade classroom: A little goes a long way. *Early Childhood Research & Practice, 9*(1), 1–16.

Gencer, A. A., & Gonen, M. (2015). Examination of the effects of Reggio Emilia based projects on preschool children's creative thinking skills. *Procedia—Social and Behavioral Sciences, 186*, 456–460.

Glassman, M., & Whaley, K. (2000). Dynamic aims: The use of long-term projects in early childhood classrooms in light of Dewey's educational philosophy. *Early Childhood Research & Practice, 2*(1). Available at ecrp.illinois.edu/v2n1/glassman.html

Griebling, S. (2011, March). Discoveries from a Reggio-inspired classroom: Meeting developmental needs through the visual arts. *Art Education, 64*(2), 6–11.

Guven, Y., & Duman, H. G. (2007). Project based learning for children with mild mental disabilities. *International Journal of Special Education, 22*(1), 77–82.

Harte, H. A. (2010). The Project Approach: A strategy for inclusive classrooms. *Young Exceptional Children, 13*(3), 15–27.

Helm, J. H., & Katz, L. G. (2016). *Young investigators: The Project Approach in the early years* (3rd ed.). New York, NY: Teachers College Press.

Hertzog, N. B. (2007). Transporting pedagogy: Implementing the Project Approach in two first-grade classrooms. *Journal of Advanced Academics, 18*(4), 530–564.

Holm, M. (2011). Project-based instruction: A review of the literature on effectiveness in prekindergarten. *River Academic Journal, 7*(2), 1–13.

Hooks, L., & Duarte, V. (2005). Can 4-year-olds really do math? Using the Project Approach with preservice teachers. *Journal of Early Childhood Teacher Education, 25*(2), 185–192.

Inan, H. Z., Trundle, K. C., & Kantor, R. (2010). Understanding natural sciences education in a Reggio Emilia preschool. *Journal of Research in Science Teaching, 47*(10), 1186–1208.

Katz, L. G., & Chard, S. C. (2000). *Engaging children's minds: The Project Approach* (2nd ed.). Stamford, CT: Ablex.

Katz, L. G., Chard, S. C., & Kogan, Y. (2014). *Engaging children's minds: The Project Approach* (3rd ed.). Santa Barbara, CA: ABC-CLIO.

Katz, L., & Galbraith, J. (2006). Making the social visible within inclusive classrooms. *Journal of Research in Childhood Education, 21*(1), 5–21.

Kilpatrick, W. H. (1918). The project method: The use of the purposeful act in the education process. *Teachers College Record, 19*, 319–335.

Knauf, H. (2017). Documentation as a tool for participation in German early childhood education and care. *European Early Childhood Education Research Journal, 25*(1), 19–35.

Kogan, Y., & Pin, J. (2009). Beginning the journey: The Project Approach with toddlers. *Early Childhood Research & Practice, 11*(1), 1–6.

Li, H., Wang, X. C., & Wong, J. M. S. (2011). Early childhood curriculum reform in China: Perspectives from examining teachers' beliefs and practices in Chinese literacy teaching. *Chinese Education & Society, 44*(6), 5–23.

Linder, S. M., Powers-Costello, B., & Stegelin, D. A. (2011). Mathematics in early childhood: Research-based rationale and practical strategies. *Early Childhood Education Journal, 39*(1), 29–37.

MacDonald, M. (2007). Toward formative assessment: The use of pedagogical documentation in early elementary classrooms. *Early Childhood Research Quarterly, 22*(2), 232–242.

MacDonald, M., & Hill, C. (2018). The intersection of pedagogical documentation and teaching inquiry: A living curriculum. *LEARNing Landscapes, 11*(2), 271–285.

Maple, T. L. (2005). Beyond community helpers: The Project Approach in the early childhood social studies curriculum. *Childhood Education, 81*(3), 133–138.

Mawson, B. (2010). Finding our way: Interpreting Reggio in a New Zealand context. *Early Childhood Folio, 14*(1), 18–22.

McGaha, C. G., Cummings, R., Lippard, B., & Dallas, K. (2011). Relationship building: Infants, toddlers, and 2-year-olds. *Early Childhood Research & Practice, 13*(1), 1–15.

Merritt, J., Lee, M. Y., Rillero, P., & Kinach, B. M. (2017). Problem-based learning in K–8 mathematics and science education: A literature review. *Interdisciplinary Journal of Problem-Based Learning, 11*(2), 1–13.

Metin, S., & Aral, N. (2016). Analysis of the effects of project-based education on the visual perceptions of five-year-old children (60–72 months). *Education and Science, 41*(186), 149–162.

Mitchell, S., Foulger, T. S., Wetzel, K., & Rathkey, C. (2009). The negotiated Project Approach: Project-based learning without leaving standards behind. *Early Childhood Education Journal, 36*(4), 339–346.

Moran, M. J. (2007). Collaborative action research and project work: Promising practices for developing collaborative inquiry among early childhood pre-service teachers. *Teaching and Teacher Education, 23*(4), 418–431.

NAEYC & NAECS/SDE (National Association for the Education of Young Children & National Association of Early Childhood Specialists in State Departments of Education). (2003). *Early childhood curriculum, assessment, and program evaluation: Building an effective, accountable system in programs for children birth through age 8. Position statement.* Washington, DC: NAEYC.

Nariman, N., & Chrispeels, J. (2016). PBL in the era of reform standards: Challenges and benefits perceived by teachers in one elementary school. *Interdisciplinary Journal of Problem-Based Learning, 10*(1), 1–16.

Owen, P. M. (2007). Integrating Katz and Chard's Project Approach with multicultural education in the university classroom. *Journal of Early Childhood Teacher Education, 28*(3), 219–232.

Patton, M. (2014). *Qualitative research and evaluation methods: Integrating theory and practice* (4th ed.). Thousand Oaks, CA: SAGE.

Picchio, M., Giovannini, D., Mayer, S., & Musatti, T. (2012). Documentation and analysis of children's experience: An ongoing collegial activity for early childhood professionals. *Early Years, 32*(2), 159–170.

Pianta, R. C., LaParo, K. M., & Hamre, B. K. (2008). *Classroom Assessment Scoring System (CLASS) manual: Pre-K.* Baltimore, MD: Brookes.

Powell, D., Bynum, S., Gray, E., Helm, J. H., Knable, P., & Trieschmann, M. (2013). *Kohl PAACT: Project Approach assessment and coaching tool.* Glenview, IL: Kohl Children's Museum.

Pui-Wah, D. C. (2006). The translation of Western teaching approaches in the Hong Kong early childhood curriculum: A promise for effective teaching? *Contemporary Issues in Early Childhood, 7*(3), 228–237.

Rimm-Kaufman, S. E., & Pianta, R. C. (2000). An ecological perspective on the transition to kindergarten: A theoretical framework to guide empirical research. *Journal of Applied Developmental Psychology, 21*(5), 491–511.

Rintakorpi, K. (2016). Documenting with early childhood education teachers: Pedagogical documentation as a tool for developing early childhood pedagogy and practices. *Early Years, 36*(4), 399–412.

Rintakorpi, K., & Reunamo, J. (2017). Pedagogical documentation and its relation to everyday activities in early years. *Early Child Development and Care, 187*(11), 1611–1622.

Serrano, R., Alfaya, E., & García, M. A. (2015). RIECU: The early childhood education-centre for teachers-university network. Analysis of children's learning achievements through the Project Approach. *Psychology, Society, & Education, 7*(1), 9–22.

Snider, K., Holley, M., & Usman, A. (2017). *Final report: Project ABC²—Adults building capacities for young children. Commissioned program evaluation report for Project ABC²—Adults building capacities for young children.* Kansas City, MO: Greater Kansas City Community Foundation Grant.

Snider, K., Marszalek, J., & Usman, A. (2019, August). Program evaluation of preschool teachers' implementation of the Project Approach across Mid-America Head Start centers, school districts and family homes. Kansas City, MO: Mid-America Head Start Metropolitan Council on Early Learning.

Souto-Manning, M., & Lee, K. (2005). "In the beginning I thought it was all play": Parents' perceptions of the Project Approach in a second-grade classroom. *School Community Journal, 15*(2), 7–20.

Steiner, D. (2017). *Curriculum research: What we know and where we need to go.* Washington, DC: StandardsWork.

Swann, A. C. (2008). Children, objects, and relations: Constructivist foundation in the Reggio Emilia approach. *Studies in Art Education, 50*(1), 36–50.

Vartuli, S., Bolz, C., & Wilson, C. (2014). A learning combination: Coaching with CLASS and the Project Approach. *Early Childhood Research & Practice, 16*(1), 1–13.

Vartuli, S., Bolz, C., Wilson, C., & Helm, J. (2016). *Early childhood Project Approach fidelity tool.* Unpublished manuscript.

Vartuli, S., & Rohs, J. (2009). Assurance of outcome evaluation: Curriculum fidelity. *Journal of Research in Childhood Education, 23*(4), 502–512.

Wastin, E., & Han, H. (2014). Action research and project approach: Journey of an early childhood pre-service teacher and a teacher educator. *Networks: An Online Journal for Teacher Research, 16*(2), 1–13.

Wilson, R. (2001). The combine project: An experience in a dual-language classroom. *Early Childhood Research & Practice, 3*(1).

Yuen, L. H. F. (2009). From foot to shoes: Kindergartens', families', and teachers' perceptions of the Project Approach. *Early Childhood Education Journal, 37*(1), 23–33.

VOICES FROM THE FIELD

Engaging Teacher Candidates in Project Work

Karrie A. Snider & Natalie Tye, Teacher Educators

One of the challenges we face as teacher educators is to design course- or fieldwork experiences, in the short time that we have, that enable preservice teachers to see the value and possibilities of project work. We have gradually added in ways to engage our preservice teachers in powerful experiences and to connect them with real classrooms where their learning is supported. We believe through a focus on project work during preservice learning, teacher education students more strongly develop the beliefs, dispositions, and skills needed for teaching developmentally appropriate integrated curriculum, instruction, and assessment.

On one particular Tuesday morning in Tiffany Johnson's classroom at Great Beginnings Early Learning Center, Lee's Summit School District (Lee's Summit, Missouri), I (Karrie) observe a buzz in the classroom about all things "fire station." A group of diverse 3- and 4-year-olds are actively engaged in project work after a field visit to a local fire station. Carolyn Jennings, University of Central Missouri (UCM) teacher candidate, engages with two children in "fire truck" play and supports them in creating time-one renderings of a fire truck. During a different day and different semester, I observe Madison Cronley, another UCM teacher candidate, working in Janet Latendresse's classroom with children in the Ice Cream Project. Madison, like her peers, develops initial plans for project work by gathering children's interests, ideas, and questions, and then learns project teaching processes such as Teacher Anticipatory Planning and Tying Standards in a Bow (Helm, 2015, p. 123) (see Figure 3.3).

We find that these planning exercises help our students understand how project work ties topics of great interest to children (left side of bow) with required curriculum standards (right side of bow). Further, our students visualize what the teacher does to create the learning experience (left "tie") and what the children will actively do to explore concepts (right "tie"). Learning to think and plan this way often challenges our students to think differently, as they instinctively want to plan something teacher-directed.

Meanwhile, nearer to our main UCM campus at Ridgeview Elementary, Warrensburg School District, I (Natalie) observe Mackenzie Claas, UCM teacher candidate working in Nikki Richner's classroom. Mackenzie implements an activity based on the Restaurant Project she is developing with two kindergartners. As children explore real restaurant artifacts, they dialogue about their own experiences in visiting restaurants. Around the corner, in Faithia Gillogly's classroom, Abby Frandsen, UCM teacher candidate, brainstorms with children about what dogs need during a project prop box activity. Using new vocabulary and co-constructed ideas, each small group excitedly begins their next steps—one group plans for restaurant play, while the other group determines how they will learn about caring for dogs.

Carolyn, Madison, Mackenzie, and Abby, like other UCM early childhood teacher candidates, spend a semester during their junior year in what we have shaped as our UCM Early Learner Block. Throughout this 8-credit-hour, 16-week practice-based teaching experience, our students develop and implement integrated curriculum through play and project work. We each teach one of the content courses, *Development and Learning through Play* and *Early Childhood Curriculum,* and then together facilitate practicum experiences within partnership schools. During fieldwork, UCM teacher candidates work with two preschool-aged or kindergarten children whom we call *focus children,* so that they may deeply learn about individual differences in children's interests, engagement, and development in learning.

Early in the semester we introduce teacher candidates to the idea of provocations as they gather artifacts and materials while planning a project prop box. They create the prop box (a cardboard box with project-based materials inside) to encourage children's dramatic play and social dialogue around the topic and learning goals from their project work. During the prop box implementation, children experience real tools and materials to further their understanding and allow for exploration and new ideas on the topic.

When observing the prop box and other project activities, we often notice our teacher candidates learning how to ask children guiding questions, how to respond and give their focus children quality feedback, and how to take different teacher roles in children's play. Alongside our students, we also observe that children become very excited

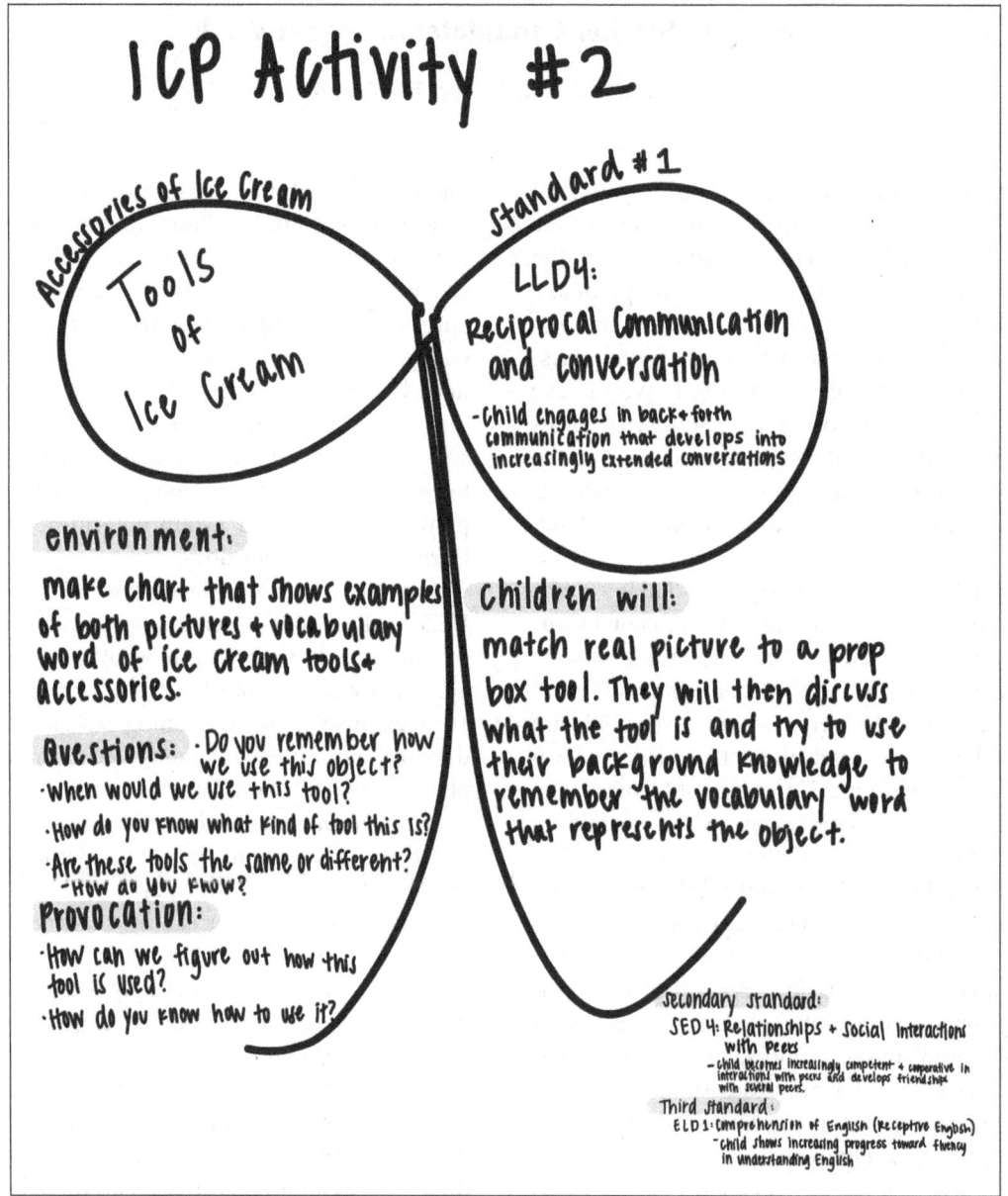

FIGURE 3.3 • UCM teacher candidates learn project planning processes to teach and assess emergent curriculum. Madison Cronley utilized iPad technology to practice tying together standards with teaching and learning experiences.

and really show what they know about the topic. Abby reflected on the dog discussion activity:

> This activity gave me the opportunity to have deeper conversations with my students and showed me they know a lot more about this particular topic than I ever imagined. One of my students used a higher level of vocabulary than I have heard him use before and said "dehydrated" while discussing thirst. As a teacher, in that particular moment, I was reminded just how important it is to never underestimate any single student's knowledge or ability.

Teacher candidates use child observation, instructor and cooperating teacher feedback, and their own reflections to help facilitate their planning of subsequent project-related learning activities. They also make connections to readings throughout the course; these rich publications clearly depict the features and phases of project work so that our students can identify elements of emergent curriculum and then try out project work themselves. For example, Mackenzie reflected:

> When planning and thinking about standards and concepts, I used Judy Harris Helm's [2008] method

FIGURE 3.4 • Integrated Curriculum Plan Summary Grids demonstrate connections between project-related standards and project learning activities.

INTEGRATED CURRICULUM PLAN SUMMARY GRID	
Teacher Candidate: Mackenzie Claas **Project Topic:** Restaurant **Age/Grade Level:** Kindergarten	
Goal 1: There are many jobs and roles in restaurants.	
Standards	**Learning Activities/Lessons**
Language & Literacy • **K.SL.3.A.b.** Speak clearly using conventions of language when presenting individually or with a group by continuing a conversation through multiple exchanges • **K.L.1.B.a.** In written text, print in upper- and lowercase letters • **K.R.1.B.a.** With assistance, develop an understanding of vocabulary by identifying and sorting picture of objects into conceptual categories • **K.R.2.A.d.** With assistance, read, infer, and draw conclusions to recognize different types of texts • **K.W.2.A.a.** With assistance, apply research process to generate a list of open-ended questions about topics of class interest	• Role play restaurant jobs and roles • Write about the restaurant job you want • Ask questions to restaurant employee • Write about a visit to a restaurant • Sort pictures of tools into job categories • Identify the difference between fictional and informational texts about restaurants • Identify research questions about restaurant jobs
Math • **K.DS.A.1.** Classify objects into given categories and count the number in each category • **K.NS.A.4.** Read and write numerals and represent a number of objects from 0 to 20	• Classify restaurant tools by which job needs them • Count and record number of tools sorted into each job • Classify food on menus into food groups • Role play restaurant jobs and roles • Create a restaurant menu

of webbing that I read in "Got Standards? Don't Give Up On Engaged Learning!" When deciding on a topic, I used the "Distance from Self" diagram [Helm, 2015] to be sure my choice was developmentally appropriate for kindergartners.

We guide the learning of the teacher candidates during our college class sessions, as we recognize we are introducing new and challenging tasks. We have found our students gain confidence as we guide them in planning and as we reflect together after observing their actual teaching. We have also found that when students work alongside cooperating teachers who are child-centered, developmentally appropriate teaching beliefs are strengthened.

At the end of the semester, we hold a celebration of learning where students share multimedia presentations and a documentation panel and then submit final written reflections. Final projects include a summary grid of the possible standards and project-related activities they could offer children if they were continuing on with their children (see Figure 3.4).

Madison's end of semester comments provide insights into preservice learning:

Learning how to teach with the Project Approach changed my perspective on what I provide my students with to support their learning. Teaching in a way that is authentic with hands-on activities is something I previously thought was for older grades. My focus children this semester proved my beliefs wrong and showed me how capable preschoolers are of deep level thinking and understanding of a project.

REFERENCES

Helm, J. H. (2008). Got standards? Don't give up on engaged learning! *Young Children, 63*(4), 14–20.

Helm, J. H. (2015). *Becoming young thinkers: Deep project work in the classroom.* New York, NY: Teachers College Press; Washington, DC: National Association for the Education of Young Children.

PART II

Making Engaged Learning Happen

Navigating the Diverse Nature of Teaching, Thinking, and Learning

CHAPTER 4

Creating 21st Century Learners
Integrating Projects and Standards

Rebecca A. Wilson, Pam Scranton, & Tricia DeGraff

ALMOST TWO DECADES into the 21st century, there continues to be a call for the development of 21st century learners. The focus on 21st century learning first began with defining the kinds of learners who will be successful in current and future jobs, and what employers saw as desired skills for future employees. As we become an increasingly global economy, these concerns are ever present. Although 21st century learning and the necessary skills have been defined by different groups of educators in a variety of ways, there is a general consensus that the rapid and pervasive change in society brought on by technology and innovation will require successful adults to possess a set of skills, knowledge, and characteristics that differ in many ways from those required in the past. In response, learning standards and accountability measures for schools have been enacted. What began with an emphasis on preparation for careers and jobs has broadened to recognize that the development of 21st century citizens begins in early childhood. In this chapter, we address how teachers at both the preschool and early primary levels can incorporate learning standards and frameworks into project work in their classrooms.

DEVELOPING 21st CENTURY LEARNERS
Rebecca A. Wilson

Frameworks, Standards, and Project Work

Frameworks and standards are commonly used tools in education to closely examine children's learning and thinking, as well as teacher interactions and child dispositions in classrooms.

The Early Childhood Framework

Recently, the Early Childhood Framework for 21st Century Learning has identified the importance of nurturing children's 4Cs: Creativity, Critical Thinking, Communication, and Collaboration (Partnership for 21st Century Learning, 2019). As demonstrated throughout this book, the Project Approach is a vehicle that can meet all of the 4Cs because of the many common characteristics shared by the Project Approach processes and the Early Childhood Framework's skills and outcomes (Partnership for 21st Century Learning, 2019).

For example, *Creativity* involves skills such as children brainstorming, planning, and evaluating their own creative activities, as well as reflecting on documentation of learning or their work samples. Exercise of these skills is a frequent daily occurrence in project work as children discuss, review, and reflect on project experiences (such as field site visits and expert interviews) through the process of pedagogical documentation.

Critical thinking encompasses all of project work, as that is the main purpose of teaching through projects. Children engage in asking questions, investigating those questions authentically, exploring real-world problems, and making connections to how things function—examining how they fit together or evaluating differences.

The Project Approach relies on extensive *Communication*, which, in the Early Childhood Framework, encompasses both verbal and nonverbal skills. Project work centralizes discussion as a key structural feature for generating, sharing, and critically evaluating ideas. These skills are not only enhanced during project work but also supported in further development, as seen in Chapter 5 where diverse learners are discussed.

Finally, the fourth "C" of the Early Childhood Framework, *Collaboration*, represents another essence of the Project Approach. As seen in the Power Lines Project described at the end of Chapter 2, learning environments that simulate future work environments require a culture of inquiry coupled with caring collaboration to harness mutual understanding, value individual differences, and promote group accomplishment. This means that collaboration grows from the early skills of playing with other peers, planning together to share learning with others, and working together toward a common goal.

Teachers successfully implementing the Project Approach often comment on how project work supports the development of the framework's 4Cs—21st century skills—in young children, as evidenced in their innovations, problem solving, and ability to brainstorm ideas.

A Range of Standards

Educators reading this chapter can probably list the frameworks and standards used within their own programs. In addition to meeting requirements of the Common Core State Standards (see Helm, 2015, appendix C), the Project Approach can also address many other standards of quality in frameworks for both curriculum and teacher interactions. A few of these frameworks might include but are not limited to the Early Childhood Framework for 21st Century Learning (Partnership for 21st Century Learning, 2019); Danielson's Framework for Teaching (Danielson, 2009); the principles of Mind Brain Education (MBE) Science (Tokuhama-Espinosa, 2010); and the Classroom Assessment Scoring System (CLASS; Pianta, LaParo, & Hamre, 2008). In addition, the Project Approach can satisfy standards for individual disciplines, such as the Next Generation Science Standards (NGSS Lead States, 2013) or the C3 Social Studies Standards (National Council for Social Studies, 2013). As educators compare these frameworks more closely, one might notice recurring themes, especially with regard to children's role in inquiry-based learning (see Figure 4.1).

Project work lays a foundation for more in-depth learning and investigation at older age levels. For example, the 3C Social Studies Standards outline a release of responsibility for children to gradually move toward developing and researching compelling questions for inquiry independently in middle school and high school (National Council for Social Studies, 2013). By providing the foundation for children to form questions and seek answers to their own questions at an early age, we are providing children with a chance to master standards in meaningful contexts and are preparing them for higher level inquiry tasks down the road. One such parallel between the early inquiry learning foundation found in the Project Approach and required curriculum standards can be noted in Figure 4.2, as many components in the Next Generation Science Standards align with various components of the Project Approach.

Teachers might be surprised at how many standards for programs can be met through deep project work. However, when they begin project work in Phase I by mapping

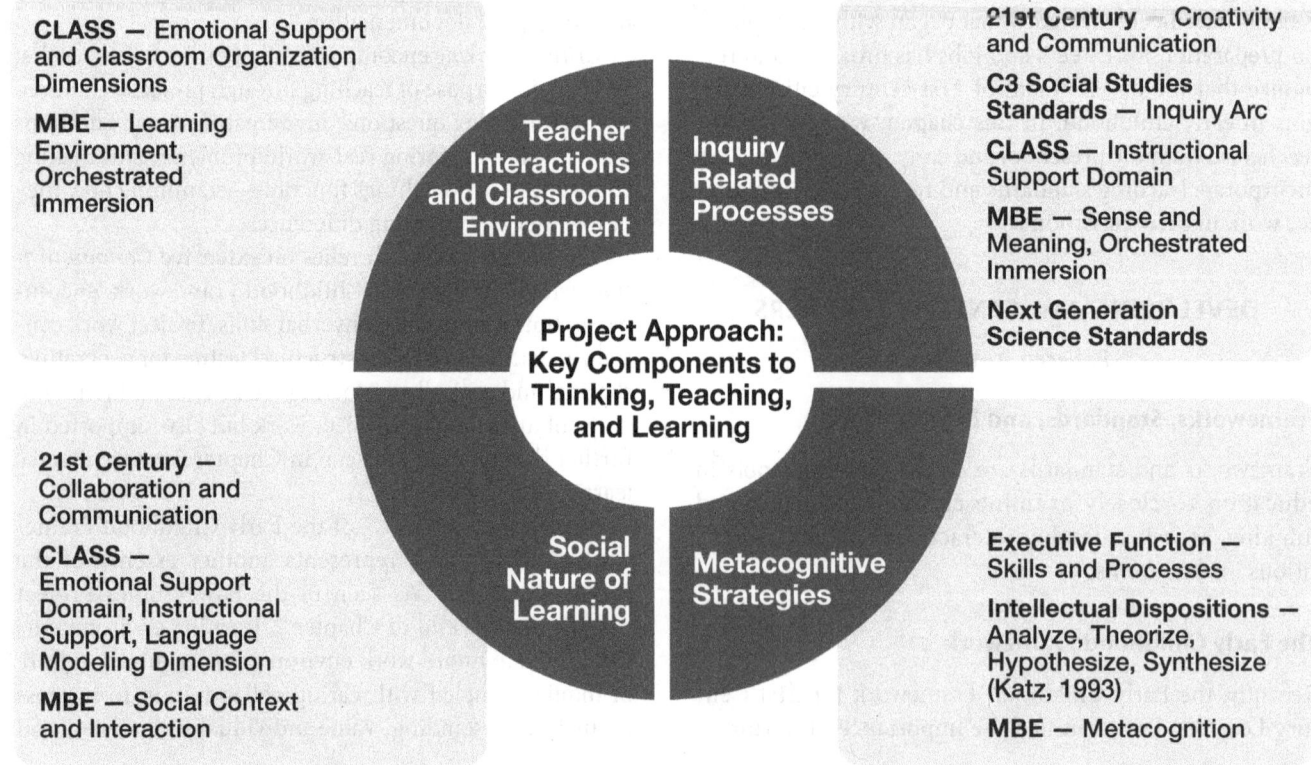

FIGURE 4.1 • The Project Approach and key components of thinking, teaching, and learning related to standards and initiatives

FIGURE 4.2 • Alignment of Next Generation Science Standards (NGSS) and Project Approach components

NGSS 1. Asking questions and defining problems

Phase I Project Approach components:
- Topic is defined
- Teacher collects children's questions and webs current knowledge
- Children develop plans to answer questions
- Teacher and children identify real-world problems to solve

NGSS 2. Developing and using models
NGSS 3. Planning and carrying out investigations
NGSS 4. Analyzing and interpreting data
NGSS 6. Constructing explanations and designing solutions

Phase II Project Approach components:
- Preparation for fieldwork
- Investigation
- Indicate what was learned, identify new questions
- Representation of learning

NGSS 8. Obtaining, evaluating, and communicating information

Phase III Project Approach components:
- Debrief, plan culminating event to share the story of the project
- Review project and assess achievement of goals

out the learning standards and goals through the processes of Teacher Anticipatory Planning and Tying Standards in a Bow (see Helm, 2015), the possibilities become very clear. During training for advanced project work, teachers are often given the exercise of highlighting all of the standards that they felt were met during the project. Many times, teachers are excited to find out the high percentage of learning standards covered over the course of a single project. We can unequivocally say that project work focuses teachers in the right direction for equipping 21st century learners with skills for thinking and success.

Required Curriculum and Accountability

Teachers in state-funded preschool programs are commonly required to complete some type of state literacy assessment, in addition to authentic assessment systems, such as Teaching Strategies GOLD (Heroman & Tabors, 2010) or the Work Sampling System (Dichtelmiller, Jablon, Marsden, & Meisels, 2001), several times a year. Often, they have specific district-required curriculum and professional development goals. Teachers at the primary level struggle to balance required curriculum, progress monitoring, and state assessments with active, engaged learning. At the same time, these teachers feel the pressure to provide updated instructional practices for the children in their classrooms. They want to provide students with developmentally appropriate activities and hands-on learning experiences, and to foster thinking to increase children's metacognition.

Teachers often attend trainings that instruct them to listen to children, problem solve, and teach children to think critically, but then return to classrooms the next day where much of their time with children is predetermined—even down to a particular book that must be read within a certain week.

Often teachers view required curriculum and project work as *required curriculum versus project work*. Teachers ask, "Can we both serve the child's needs and still meet accountability requirements?" "Can we do project work?" "Is it possible to create 21st century learners in our classrooms?" The answer is "Yes." Yes, you can meet both the children's needs and accountability. Yes, you can use a required curriculum and also use the Project Approach. And, yes, you do foster 21st century learning in project-centered classrooms. The key to shifting the mind-set to "*required curriculum and project work*" is to create deep project work and careful documentation of learning standards. As shown in Figure 4.3, documenting the learning that occurs in project work can be the answer to resolving

FIGURE 4.3 • Resolving the dichotomy of demands for developmentally appropriate learning and demands for accountability can be the documentation of achievement of standards in project work (Helm, Beneke, & Steinheimer, 2007).

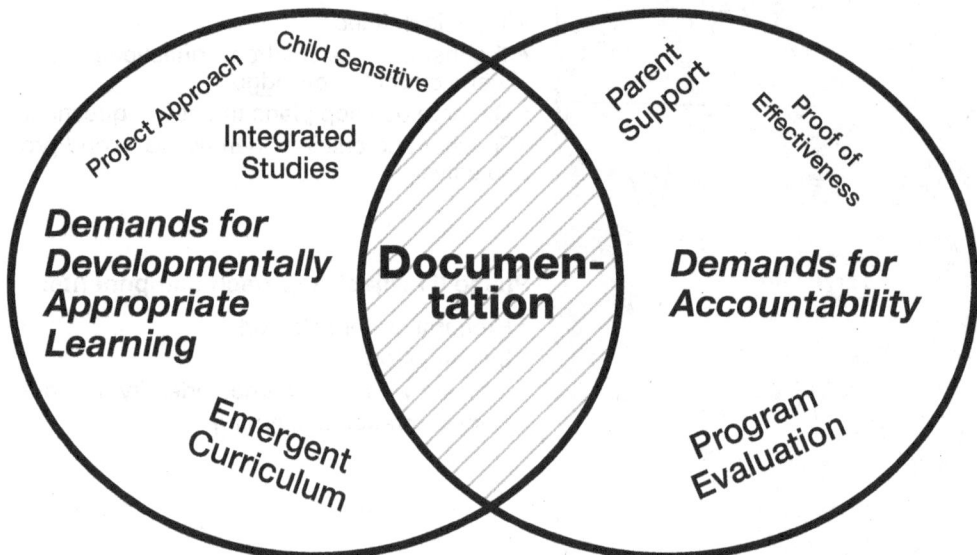

the dichotomy, especially when standards are used as the framework for documentation. This strategy is especially important when communicating to administrators, families, and colleagues how project work accomplishes standards. In the next sections, we show how standards are integrated into the Project Approach at both the preschool and primary levels.

STANDARDS COME TO PRESCHOOL

Pam Scranton

"Will my child learn their letters?" "Will they know how to count?" "Will they learn to write?" These are frequent questions from families with preschoolers as they search for the right preschool for their child. The questions are valid and should be asked. Young children acquire many of these preacademic skills during their preschool years, but *how* they acquire and practice these skills is an equally important question to be answered.

Meaningful and purposeful learning that happens during the context of play is considered the most developmentally appropriate approach to integrating preacademic skills throughout the daily life of the preschool classroom (Copple, Bredekamp, Koralek, & Charner, 2013; Gronlund & Rendon, 2017; Hassinger-Das, Hirsh-Pasek, & Golinkoff, 2017; Heidemann & Hewitt, 2009). The Project Approach fits perfectly within this developmental framework. As children investigate, represent, and document their learning, they have frequent opportunities to practice skills like writing, identifying letters and sounds, counting and graphing, using books as resources, and communicating effectively with their peers. When practiced authentically during a project, these skills have more meaning for children than the alternative of skills being learned in isolation and out of context for the child, as demonstrated by brain research (see Chapter 2).

But how do we as teachers make sure our children are learning and mastering the skills needed to become successful learners? The answer lies in planning for learning, aligning those plans with curriculum goals/state standards, documenting the learning taking place during project work, and using authentic assessment strategies to evaluate children's development.

Let's look at the Duck Project that was conducted in Tracy Raab's preschool class at UPC Discovery, in Peoria, Illinois. The Duck Project began when several Canada geese came to a nearby pond at the same time the children were learning about teeth. Several children wondered if ducks have teeth. After a few days of library research failed to provide the answer, Mrs. Raab found a local farmer willing to be an expert and answer the question. The farmer also brought Green the Duck to the preschool and allowed the children to take care of the duck in their classroom. Mrs. Raab captured children in her class mastering some of the Illinois Early Learning and Development Standards (Illinois State Board of Education, 2013) in the Language Arts and Mathematics domains through participation in the Duck Project. Using photographs and collecting samples of the children's work, she was able to develop documentation that depicted how the children had met such goals (see Figure 4.4). Later in the year, Tracy shared these

FIGURE 4.4 • Documenting learning with the Illinois Early Learning and Development Standards (IELDS)

Language Arts IELDS GOAL 5: Demonstrate increasing awareness of and competence in emergent writing skills and abilities.
  LEARNING STANDARD 5.A. Demonstrate growing interest and abilities in writing.
  LEARNING STANDARD 5.B. Use writing to represent ideas and information.

Liv paints a duck on the easel.

Liv labels the parts of the duck in her painting.

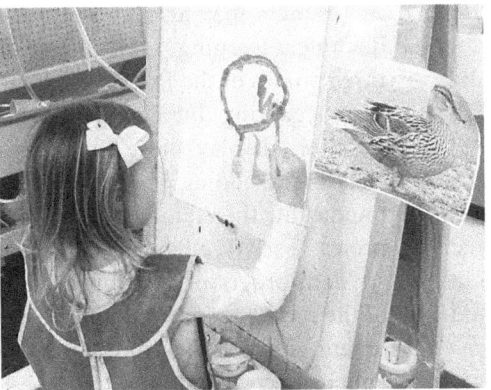

Mathematics IELDS GOAL 10: Begin to make predictions and collect data information.
  LEARNING STANDARD 10.A. Generate questions and processes for answering them.
  LEARNING STANDARD 10.B. Organize and describe data and information.

Children observed Green the Duck eating.

Tucker charts what Green the Duck likes to eat.

Completed chart with data from observations of *What Green Ate*.

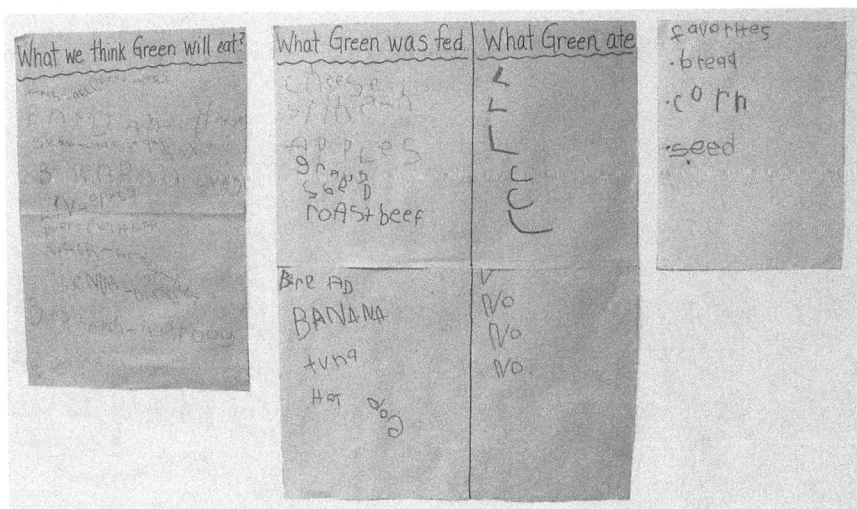

work samples in the children's portfolios with families during conferences.

The very nature of project work—active, engaged learning—dictates the types of assessments used to evaluate the children's development. Authentic assessment measures like the Work Sampling System (Dichtelmiller et al., 2001) and Teaching Strategies GOLD (Heroman & Tabors, 2010) work well for evaluating project work. For example, prior to engaging in project work, 4-year-old Finn was a child who often struggled to engage in positive interactions with his peers, including at times when play deteriorated to shouting and hurt feelings. During the Conductor Project, his preschool teacher at UPC Discovery, Catherine Price, noticed Finn returning to the music stand often to play at conducting a band. He would call children over to be in the band, directing them in their instrument choices and music selections. Mrs. Price documented this new learning disposition using photographs and dictation and organized it in the social/emotional section of Finn's portfolio. She used learning standards to show goals met through the change in Finn's ability to work and collaborate with his friends (see Figure 4.5).

As early childhood teachers learn to implement project work, increasing their understanding of documentation can be a powerful tool to support standards in the classroom, especially when that documentation communicates learning by highlighting the integration of learning standards in the course of the project. Parents, administrators, and colleagues must see that children who do projects are children who are learning in more authentic and engaged ways. Documentation is an effective strategy for communicating that message (see Figure 4.6).

Teachers may also find a project timeline helpful to document learning. The timeline displays the work in the three phases of the Project Approach and describes activities occurring during each phase (refer to Figure 1.3). Teachers display these timelines prominently in their classrooms, adding photos, drawings, dictation, and, most important, the state learning standards met during the project work (see Figures 4.7 and 4.8).

Many programs have found it helpful when the director of the program works alongside the teachers to help document children's learning. The director is a part of the anticipatory planning (where the learning standards are integrated into the project planning), field site visits, and documentation process, often teaching in the classrooms during the second phase of the project to support the teachers and children. Administrative buy-in is key in any program if project work is to succeed. Decision makers at the very top of the educational pyramid must understand that children engaged in project work *are* children who are learning.

FIGURE 4.5 • Documenting a new learning disposition with authentic assessment measures

Work Sampling System Benchmark 1.D: Personal and social development interaction with others
    1.D.3. Participates in the group life of the class (Dichtelmiller et al., 2001)

Teaching Strategies GOLD Social Emotional Development Objective 3: Participates cooperatively and constructively in group situations
    3a. Balances needs and rights of self and others
    3b. Solves social problems (Heroman & Tabors, 2010)

Finn pretends to rehearse an orchestra during the Conductor Project.

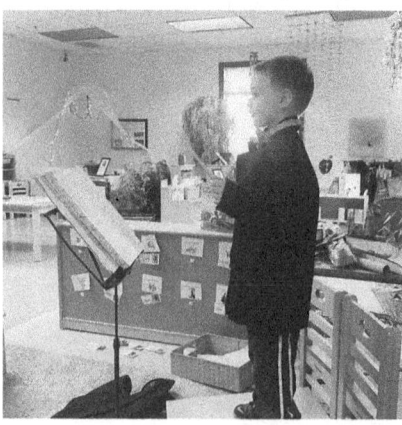

Finn conducts a concert with his classmates playing pretend instruments.

FIGURE 4.6 • Some teachers prepare documentation panels to share with parents and visitors. This panel by preschool teacher Catherine Price describes the value of documentation.

Windows on Learning: How Documentation Supports Project Work

Young children are quite capable of organizing and recording information during project work. This documentation serves to inform and communicate the learning that's happening in the classroom for families, but it also serves to remind the children of the progress they have made during the project.

Children's art and journal work are displayed with pictures and children's explanations. Children have pride in their work and enjoy reviewing the work of others.

Hallway board is used to display the story of St Martin produced and written by the children. It helps parents feel invested in the project and have a deeper understanding of the class achievements.

Children document their individual ideas for making their own lanterns. This information was used to support the child to achieve their goals and displayed to show achievements.

Project timelines with pictures, work samples and anecdotes are displayed in the room for children and parents so they can visualize their learning chronologically.

> It seems to us that high-quality documentation of children's work and ideas contribute to the quality of an early childhood program in at least six ways.
>
> 1. Enhancement of children's learning
> 2. Taking children's ideas and work seriously
> 3. Teacher planning and evaluation with children
> 4. Parent appreciation and participation
> 5. Teacher research and process awareness
> 6. Children's learning made visible
>
> Lillian G. Katz and Sylvia C. Chard
> April 1996

Catherine Price
Preschool Teacher, UPC Discovery

FIGURE 4.7 • Many teachers use a project timeline to document the progress of the project.

During Phase III of a project, where students and teachers *think* about what was learned, teachers will often look at the curriculum goals met during the project work. During the Duck Project, Mrs. Raab reported that her students met over 80% of the benchmarks on the Work Sampling System Developmental Checklist. The children in her classroom not only learned a great deal about ducks that semester, but also met many of their goals for Math, Science, and Literacy instruction while strengthening their dispositions to collaborate and communicate with their peers and other adults. All because of a duck, but that's *real* project work in action! Now, let's take a look at how standards and important skills are accomplished in primary-grade project work.

PROJECTS—A WOVEN TAPESTRY OF LEARNING STANDARDS AND INTEGRATED CONCEPTS

Tricia DeGraff

As demonstrated in Chapter 2, the Project Approach is an effective curriculum approach to create the conditions for a classroom learning environment in which teachers and children are intellectually engaged in learning. Using the Project Approach in primary classrooms allows for teachers to implement state- and district-mandated curriculum in a manner that supports integrated, deeper learning. Instead of limiting the focus to isolated skills and independent single-concept lessons (on the far end of the agency spectrum for curriculum as seen in Figure 2.2), project activities comprise an integration of multiple developmental areas. Teachers intentionally design authentic curriculum maps by weaving district standards into their Teacher Anticipatory Planning Web. Through this cognitive planning process, concepts that are inherent to the topic emerge alongside standards as the content area learning opportunities.

As a child-centered, inquiry-based approach, project work allows children to form their own ideas, questions, and wonderings about project topics, and at the same time motivates young learners to engage deeply in the core con-

FIGURE 4.8 • Parents examine the project timeline for the Pig Project.

tent areas. For example, in order for children to authentically engage in writing related to the project, they must have something compelling and meaningful to write about. Firsthand experiences with content allow children opportunities to learn about and engage a topic deeply. Thus, they gain knowledge and ideas to draw on during the scheduled writing block, and they develop background knowledge to bring deeper questions to the books they are reading during reading workshop. Further, children have the ability to understand the application of math concepts more clearly through strong project experiences related to the integration of mathematical skills and knowledge.

Working Within the Required Curriculum: Overcoming Challenges to Project Work

Elementary teachers have many requirements on their daily schedule to ensure that curriculum concepts at each grade level are taught. In an era of high-stakes testing and accountability, many teachers feel pressured to create daily learning schedules as teaching blocks according to isolated subject areas, rather than relying on the importance of integrated learning experiences. Sometimes, these blocks are planned for them already. Although these challenges are real, they also present opportunities for administrators and teachers to be more strategic and purposeful with planning curriculum and instructional experiences. In the sections that follow, some common challenges—with solutions—are presented in greater detail.

Scheduling

One of the common challenges faced by educators is time management of required curriculum. Using the Project Approach can help to address this issue through the focus on integrated, connected curriculum in which children learn more deeply. The Project Approach presents opportunities for teachers to teach standards across all content areas, thus providing a more strategic use of limited time.

At the Academy for Integrated Arts (AFIA), where I serve as the school's executive director, teachers have addressed scheduling issues by setting a dedicated daily project time in each classroom. During this time, integrated project work is driven by social studies and science standards. Through strategic integration, math, reading, and writing standards are leveraged to allow students to learn content more deeply. Each teacher also schedules time for content-specific workshops—including reading, writing, and math. Additionally, crucial literacy components happen throughout the day, such as interactive read-aloud, word work, and shared writing. Teachers look for natural connections, but they do not force those connections. For example, on some days, the interactive read-aloud book is connected to the project work, but not every day. Teachers often do create text sets, collections of books with different genres, so that children are able to access informational texts that present rich, real photos and expand topic-related vocabulary.

In other instances, teachers capitalize on moments when they observe or notice particular interests of children developing within general curriculum experiences. For example, children in 2nd grade generated many thought-provoking questions about soil after their teacher, Haley Hurst, read them *Sam and Dave Dig a Hole* by Mac Barnett. These questions surprised Ms. Haley, but she saw this as a great opportunity for planning provocations related to soil quality and composition. This interactive read-aloud served as an unintentional jumping off point for a long-term investigation related to soil quality and the life cycle of plants. During this project, the children had the opportunity to work with a community partner, Kansas City Community Gardens (KCCG), to plant garden beds at their school (see Figure 4.9).

The sample schedule presented in Figure 4.10 shows how Ms. Haley integrated project work and addressed the Common Core State Standards (National Governors

FIGURE 4.9 • A student plants seeds in the school garden bed.

Association for Best Practices & Council of Chief State School Officers, 2010) during the Plant Project in her 2nd-grade classroom at AFIA.

During Phase III, students used multiple representations to demonstrate their learning. They produced a display that included artifacts from their project work, such as their child-created concept webs (Figure 4.11). In small groups they choreographed and performed dances that demonstrated the life cycle of a plant. They also harvested vegetables that they had planted and tended, and then served a salad made from their vegetables (Figure 4.12). Families and community members who attended the culminating celebration watched as students performed their dances and were invited to eat the salads the children had prepared.

Gaining Administrative Support

As a school leader, I have noticed that often teachers new to the Project Approach initially use their project time block to mess around with project ideas and topics. This messing around includes creating high-quality provocations and learning activities to promote deeper thinking and provide opportunities for children to ask thought-provoking questions. However, as teachers become more experienced and comfortable with both the Project Approach and grade-level learning standards, project work not only deepens but also is embedded throughout the school day, in addition to the scheduled project time block.

I have learned that it is important for teachers and instructional leaders to give themselves the space and time to improve in Project Approach implementation. Administrators may find it helpful to step back and recognize that even when teachers are beginning their journey with teaching through projects, children are still learning important skills consistent with the Mind Brain Education (MBE) Science instructional guidelines (see Chapter 2 and Helm, 2015) or other frameworks. However, as teachers move along the curriculum continuum from the teaching of single concepts to integrated project work, students benefit even more as MBE guidelines and standards are integrated at a deeper level.

FIGURE 4.10 • A snapshot of how Ms. Haley integrated project work and addressed Common Core State Standards (CCSS) across the school day throughout the Plant Project in a 2nd-grade classroom

Routine or Activity	Activities Integrating Plant Project Work with CCSS Standards
Breakfast/ Morning Meeting	Children began spontaneous discussions about plants (the project topic) as they entered the classroom. They shared artifacts and talked about what they learned from their family members. Ms. Haley's "Morning Meeting" letter to students referenced the Plant Project and invited students to turn and talk about their recent learning, the difference between *tap roots* and *fibrous roots*. **CCSS.ELA-LITERACY.L.2.4: Language Vocabulary Acquisition and Use** *Determine or clarify the meaning of unknown and multiple-meaning words and phrases based on grade 2 reading and content, choosing flexibly from an array of strategies.*
Reader's Workshop	Based on the 2nd-grade scope and sequence, the week's lessons were focused on questions and informational text. The teacher saw a great opportunity to bring in nonfiction text related to the Plant Project and modified the planned lessons to focus on the project topic. In the case of this project, children were given opportunities to read field guides and were introduced to this genre through their interest in the Plant Project. Since the students were interested in field guides, there was a great opportunity to reinforce the following standards: **CCSS.ELA-LITERACY.RI.2.1: Informational Text: Key Ideas and Details** *Ask and answer such questions as who, what, where, when, why, and how to demonstrate understanding of key details in [an informational] text.* **CCSS.ELA-LITERACY.RI.2.7: Informational Text: Integration of Knowledge and Ideas** *Explain how specific images (e.g., a diagram showing how a machine works) contribute to and clarify a text.* The project topic was authentically integrated into the daily mini-lesson. Such mini-lessons taught both the reading standards and concepts related to the project topic.
Word Study	This time of the day was typically an explicit, short, inquiry-based word work lesson. Students were able to apply strategies learned to reading books related to the project topic.

FIGURE 4.10 • *Continued*

Routine or Activity	Activities Integrating Plant Project Work with CCSS Standards
Writer's Workshop	Based on the 2nd-grade scope and sequence, the research unit was scheduled to be taught 2 months after this project. Based on students' interests and questions, Ms. Haley rearranged her scope and sequence and traded the narrative and research units within the year's schedule. The required curriculum lessons for the week were focused on research. Ms. Haley planned writing lessons centered on creating field guides based on research. The writing unit directly connected to both the project *and* the reading unit. **CCSS.ELA-LITERACY.W.2.7: Writing: Research to Build and Present Knowledge** *Participate in shared research and writing projects (e.g., read a number of books on a single topic to produce a report; record science observations).* **CCSS.ELA-LITERACY.W.2.8: Writing: Research to Build and Present Knowledge** *Recall information from experiences or gather information from provided sources to answer a question.*
Interactive Read-Aloud	Ms. Haley compiled a text set of books related to soil and plants. This text set included nonfiction and fiction texts. Books that were appropriate for read-aloud were used during interactive read-aloud. **CCSS.ELA-LITERACY.RI.2.4: Informational Text: Craft and Structure** *Determine the meaning of words and phrases in a text relevant to a grade 2 topic or subject area.* **CCSS.ELA-LITERACY.RI.2.5: Informational Text: Craft and Structure** *Know and use various text features (e.g., captions, bold print, subheadings, glossaries, indexes, electronic menus, icons) to locate key facts or information in a text efficiently.*
Project Time	After learning about soil quality and the life cycle of plants, students engaged in a process to plan out what they would plant in their garden beds and what they need to be ready for planting the garden beds when the field expert visited from Kansas City Community Gardens (KCCG). Throughout this project, students worked with field experts from KCCG multiple times. The field experts helped them determine what to plant, as well as supported students when they planted seeds and harvested vegetables. **CCSS.ELA-LITERACY.W.2.8: Writing: Research to Build and Present Knowledge** *Recall information from experiences or gather information from provided sources to answer a question.*
Enrichment/ Related Arts	Ms. Haley communicated with the enrichment teacher about the Plant Project in her classroom. Sometimes the enrichment teacher was able to integrate project work. For example, during visual art class students engaged in observational drawings of plants.
Math Workshop	Before students planted their garden beds, they planted seeds in cups in the classroom to investigate how different conditions (light vs. no light, amount of water, etc.) impacted the growth of plants. In order to draw conclusions based on this science experiment, students measured these specific plants during math. Drawing on the standards below, Ms. Haley incorporated the project into their math block. **CCSS.MATH.CONTENT.2.MD.A.3: Measurement and Data: Measure and Estimate Lengths in Standard Units** *Estimate lengths using units of inches, feet, centimeters, and meters.* **CCSS.MATH.CONTENT.2.MD.A.4: Measurement and Data: Measure and Estimate Lengths in Standard Units** *Measure to determine how much longer one object is than another, expressing the length difference in terms of a standard length unit.*
Closing Circle	At closing circle, Ms. Haley gave students the opportunity to reflect on their day and make connections across the school day. These conversations often included comments about work related to their project.

FIGURE 4.11 • Students were asked to create a web of what they had learned about plants.

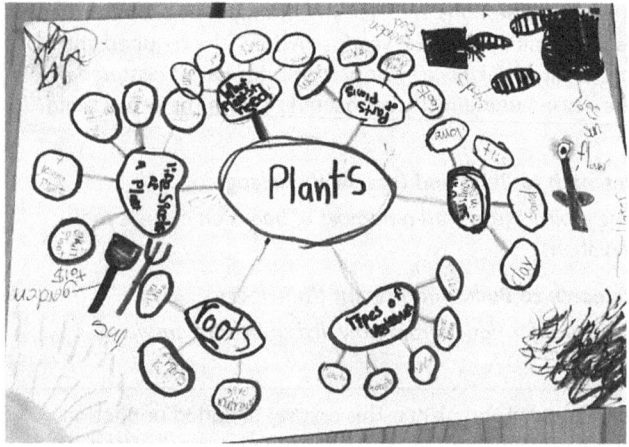

FIGURE 4.12 • To culminate the 2nd-grade Plant Project, students harvested vegetables grown in the school garden and served salads to families and guests.

Creating Access Points for Teaching and Learning Through Projects

It is critical to note that teachers should not force connections across content areas when using the Project Approach. At the primary level, administrators and staff may want to set aside a separate project time each day, as was done at AFIA. This scheduling ensures that projects are being taught daily, and when natural connections exist between and across content areas, teachers are able to integrate project work into reading workshop, writing workshop, or the math block. This practice also ensures that curriculum requirements are addressed and fundamental concepts (i.e., learning how to read) are taught at the appropriate grade levels, creating balanced teaching and learning experiences. Approaching project work in this way gives teachers with various levels of experience with conducting project work a clear access point into this way of teaching.

Addressing the Pressures of Standardized Testing

Another challenge often faced by elementary teachers includes the pressures related to standardized testing. Even though standardized testing does not accurately reflect the full picture of what a child is able to do, including their dispositions for learning or linguistic and cultural background knowledge, we know that it is important that our students show what they know on standardized tests. Since the Project Approach is emergent curriculum, teachers and administrators might feel worried at times that not all standards are covered. This can be addressed through ensuring that teachers follow a scope and sequence during the reading, writing, and math blocks.

However, teachers should follow the scope and sequence flexibly, moving standards around as necessary.

For example, as illustrated in Figure 4.10, 2nd-graders became interested in reading and creating field guides related to their Plant Project. Thus, the teacher moved their research writing unit to occur earlier in the school year, so students could learn about and engage in purposeful, authentic research writing. New teachers may be less likely to do this. However, as teachers grow in their knowledge of their standards, the more likely they are to allow the project work to span across the school day and content areas.

It is important that teachers are given the opportunity to get to know their standards well. It is also crucial that administrators support teachers in learning Project Approach teaching processes such as topic selection, teacher anticipatory webbing, and tying concepts and standards together, so that they become confident in meeting curriculum standards and come to see how projects allow teaching and learning across all developmental and subject areas.

Goal-Oriented Professional Development and Collaboration

Finally, it is critical to discuss the importance of professional learning and collaboration for sustaining powerful teaching in intellectual, thinking classrooms. Teacher educators and building leaders have reported how essential it is that teachers feel confident in their practice. Teaching is incredibly complex work. To do this work well, teachers must not only know their standards well but also develop skills in listening and observing children carefully to understand and learn their strengths, interests, and questions. Powerful curriculum is found at the intersection of formal learning standards and students' backgrounds, interests, and questions. To be able to teach from this intersection is no easy feat, but it is attainable.

Teachers must have opportunities to engage with thought partners to enable them to do this complex work. Specifically, we recommend having teachers engage in intentional, strategic structures for collaboration with colleagues with an eye toward continual improvement. For example, at the beginning of the year, administrators might find it helpful to lead the staff through shared learning related to anticipatory webbing with standards in mind. Then teachers should be given opportunities to dig in and plan with their own students' interests and questions in mind and to engage in discussion with their colleagues. When working in isolation, it is easy to get stuck. However, when given the time and space to process ideas with colleagues, a teacher can be more intentional and strategic in planning. At the beginning of the school year, teachers may find it helpful to collaborate on how they can model and practice key processes of the Project Approach—such as topic selection, class discussions, fieldwork, representation, and investigation—*before* a project topic emerges.

Another area addressed during collaboration time might include documentation. Through an intentional focus on documentation, including mechanisms for teachers to share their documentation with their colleagues, we have found that teachers can learn from one another, while also engaging in authentic self assessment of their own practice. The act of documentation not only solidifies key components of the Project Approach such as following the three phases, webbing, and the planning of provocations, but it also helps teachers make student learning more visible while they learn their standards more deeply. This allows for a recursive process of continual improvement.

SUMMARY: PUTTING IT ALL TOGETHER IN OUR PROGRAMS

Throughout this chapter, we have presented strategies for planning and demonstrating the integration of learning standards within active, engaged learning. For example, the process of linking program initiatives and standards as we did in Figure 4.1 is helpful when planning for professional development or curriculum mapping. Using the Teacher Anticipatory Planning process (Helm, 2008, 2015), especially with colleagues, helps align project work with standards. As mentioned earlier in this chapter, classroom teachers, particularly at the primary level, may also consider moving around standards within the scope and sequence to match the project topic. The daily schedule also helps organize project work and standards across regular routines and activities.

Once teachers ensure that learning standards are being met through deep project work and careful planning, the next step is to share these accomplishments with others. One of the most critical tasks that we can perform as educators is to demonstrate that we are indeed meeting standards through active, engaged learning. We cannot overemphasize the importance of documentation (see Figure 4.3). We must make children's thinking and learning visible to both stakeholders within educational institutions and families alike.

Let's review a few steps educators can take to make this happen in their programs. In this chapter, we mentioned displaying a project timeline and linking children's activities to standards throughout the project. We also recommend displaying learning standards side by side with children's work any time work is displayed. These representations can range from simple bulletin boards to detailed documentation displays. Lastly, we can also link children's individual work to learning standards in portfolios and work samples shared with families.

Classrooms engaged in deep project work are classrooms that create 21st century learners. Teachers know and can see the lines, or connections, to learning standards even when they are not readily apparent to others. It is our job to draw the lines more explicitly to help others see our children's learning and thinking processes. In other words, through documentation, we can make the invisible become visible as children's deep thinking and integration with learning standards are both recognized and valued.

Chapter 5 provides more examples of how teachers integrate learning standards and best practices to engage children's thinking. Specifically, authors examine how project work supports children's learning and thinking within classrooms serving diverse learners.

REFERENCES

Copple, C., Bredekamp, S., Koralek, D., & Charner, C. (Eds.). (2013). *Developmentally appropriate practice: Focus on preschoolers*. Washington, DC: National Association for the Education of Young Children.

Danielson, C. (2009). *Implementing the Framework for Teaching in enhancing professional practice*. Alexandria, VA: ASCD.

Dichtelmiller, M. L., Jablon, J. R., Marsden, D. B., & Meisels, S. J. (2001). *The Work Sampling System: Preschool-4 developmental guidelines* (4th ed.). New York, NY: Pearson.

Gronlund, G., & Rendon, T. (2017). *Saving play: Addressing standards through play-based learning in preschool and kindergarten*. St. Paul, MN: Redleaf Press.

Hassinger-Das, B., Hirsh-Pasek, K., & Golinkoff, R. M. (2017). The case of brain science and guided play: A developing story. *Young Children, 72*(2), 45–50.

Heidemann, S., & Hewitt, D. (2009). *Play: The pathway from theory to practice.* St. Paul, MN: Redleaf Press.

Helm, J. H. (2008). Got standards? Don't give up on engaged learning! *Young Children, 63*(4), 14–20.

Helm, J. H. (2015). *Becoming young thinkers: Deep project work in the classroom.* New York, NY: Teachers College Press; Washington, DC: National Association for the Education of Young Children.

Helm, J. H., Beneke, S., & Steinheimer, K. (2007). *Windows on learning: Documenting young children's work* (2nd ed.). New York, NY: Teachers College Press.

Heroman, C., & Tabors, P. O. (2010). *Teaching Strategies GOLD: Birth through kindergarten assessment.* Washington, DC: Teaching Strategies.

Illinois State Board of Education. (2013). *Illinois Early Learning and Development Standards. For preschool: 3 years old to kindergarten enrollment age.* Springfield, IL: Author. Available at www.isbe.net/Documents/early_learning_standards.pdf

Katz, L. G. (1993). *Dispositions as educational goals. ERIC Digest.* Champaign, IL: ERIC Clearinghouse on Elementary & Early Childhood Education.

National Council for Social Studies. (2013). *The College, Career, and Civic Life (C3) Framework for Social Studies State Standards: Guidance for enhancing the rigor of K–12 civics, economics, geography, and history.* Silver Spring, MD: Author.

National Governors Association for Best Practices & Council of Chief State School Officers. (2010). *Common Core State Standards.* Washington DC: Authors.

NGSS Lead States. (2013). *Next Generation Science Standards: For states, by states.* Washington, DC: The National Academies Press.

Partnership for 21st Century Learning. (2019). *21st century learning for early childhood framework.* Hilliard, OH: Battelle for Kids. Available at static.battelleforkids.org/documents/p21/P21Early ChildhoodFramework.pdf

Pianta, R. C., LaParo, K. M., & Hamre, B. K. (2008). *Classroom Assessment Scoring System (CLASS) manual: Pre-K.* Baltimore, MD: Brookes.

Tokuhama-Espinosa, T. (2010). *The new science of teaching and learning: Using the best of Mind, Brain, and Education Science in the classroom.* New York, NY: Teachers College Press.

VOICES FROM THE FIELD

The Construction Project

Pam Scranton, Center Director

This is the story of a project that began with a catalytic unplanned event at UPC Discovery Early Learning Center (Peoria, Illinois), where I am the director. Usually the projects in the toddler through preschool classrooms are focused on different topics because each project topic is based on children's interests. The projects I now describe, however, all began together. This is how it happened.

PHASE I: HOW THE PROJECT BEGAN

A major road reconstruction project was taking place on the road in front of our school. The children were on our little hill watching construction machines rebuild the road in front of our campus (see Figure 4.13). After watching the machines for about 30 minutes from afar, one class decided they needed a closer look. They walked up the street to observe the machines, hoping to find someone to answer some questions. Two of the construction workers, Matthew and Kevin, noticed the children right away and came over to talk with the excited group of preschoolers.

Once back in the classrooms, the teachers could barely write fast enough to record all of the children's ideas and questions. The teachers thought there was a possibility that a project would grow from this observation opportunity. Much to my surprise and the surprise of the teachers, all three preschool classrooms and two toddler classrooms appeared to be interested in construction machines. The teaching teams were unsure how to move forward. Could they do a schoolwide project? Can all these children be interested enough in one topic to make it an authentic project?

Fortunately, the idea of one topic for all children did not last long. The children answered the teachers' questions. During a staff meeting teachers shared children's interests, and we discovered that the children in each classroom were interested in a different construction machine. So, following the lead of the children, *each* classroom began to investigate a different machine: the dump truck, the front-end loader, and the concrete mixer. However, as is typical of toddler projects, the toddlers were most interested in something they were already familiar with in their toys and what was closest to their eye level—the wheels.

FIGURE 4.13 • The toddlers in Katrina Larson's class watch the machines closely as the road is removed and replaced.

PHASE II: DEVELOPING THE PROJECT

Because the field site was adjacent to our campus, the teachers were able to bring their classes to the site for frequent, often daily, visits. There they could observe the machines and ask questions of the workers. This strategy of repeated visits deepened the experience. The children's questions moved from "What is that?" questions to more complex questions (see Figure 4.14).

Children in Catherine Price and Malerie Stickling's classroom were focused on the concrete mixer truck. As they observed the mixing and the pouring, the children became interested in the differences between concrete and cement. "What is cement?" "What makes concrete?" "How does the drum on the truck work?" "How quickly does it harden?" "Why does road construction need concrete?" Trish Deppermann, the church administrator, surprisingly knew a lot about concrete. In the process of interviewing her, the children discovered that her husband, Roger Deppermann, who is a farmer, owned a portable concrete mixer. "Could he bring it school?" "Could they make concrete?" To the teachers' and the children's delight, Mr. Deppermann was willing to come to school and show his concrete mixer (see Figure 4.15).

The children in Tracy Raab and Stephanie Randall's class focused on the front-end loader. During a class discussion, after one of the site observations, 3-year-old Owen exclaimed, "My dad knows about the tractor 'cause he builds them!" After school Mrs. Raab contacted Owen's dad and found out that he was a mechanical engineer at Caterpillar and designs some of the mechanics on front-end loaders. He promised to come into the classroom the following week and bring some artifacts. Corbin really wanted to know "how the digger part goes up and down" and Owen's dad was able to explain how the hydraulic system works on a front-end loader by bringing parts to school (see Figure 4.16).

The toddlers in Mrs. Larson's class returned again and again to the wheels of the machines. They were fascinated by how big the wheels were. Mrs. Larson recognized that

FIGURE 4.14 • Four-year-old Corbin wrote his own question to ask the expert: "Why does he have something to push the rocks?"

FIGURE 4.15 • **A.** Mr. Deppermann demonstrates how he mixes concrete. **B.** The children sketched what they observed during the demonstration.

narrowing the focus to wheels matched the developmental age of the toddlers and would be a good project topic for her 2-year-old students. She supported their initial investigations by bringing in artifacts, supporting their beginning questioning skills, and revisiting the field site daily (see Figure 4.17).

FIGURE 4.16 • Owen's dad, Evan, explains how a front-end loader bucket goes up and down.

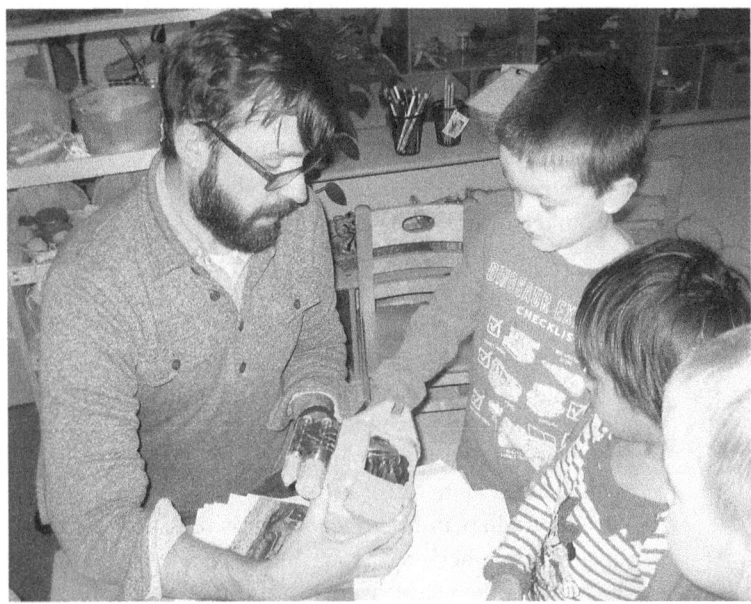

The children in Darlene Grant and Angela Pauli's classroom were very interested in the dump truck. They watched it day after day and were determined to figure out how the bed of the truck worked. A small group of children walked up the street one morning to find out if Mr. Matthew might be available to answer their questions.

Near the end of Phase I, as the children and teachers constructed webs and added new questions to their lists of questions, it became clear to me and to the teachers that in Phase II the children would need to investigate these machines *up close,* get inside them, study the engines and other components, and talk to the people responsible for running them. I called Sie Maroon, operations superintendent for the City of Peoria Public Works Department, and he agreed to bring the construction machines the children were studying to UPC Discovery and park them for the morning (see Figure 4.18). Mr. Maroon also provided experts at each of the machines to support the children's investigations. The teachers and children prepared for the field site visit by dividing into groups for sketching, interviewing, measuring, and photo-taking.

What an incredible morning! The children learned so much! Once back in the classrooms, the children shared and organized all

FIGURE 4.17 • Toddlers explore wheels by touching the various parts and comparing the size to their heights.

FIGURE 4.18 • With the construction machines in the school parking lot, the children were able to interview experts, measure, draw, and photograph to find answers to their questions.

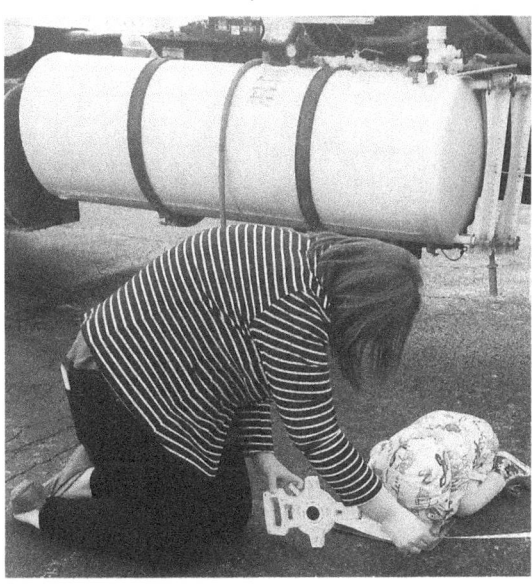

the information from the field site visit. Ideas for representing what they had learned and how to share it with others flowed naturally from those discussions.

In Mrs. Price and Mrs. Stickling's class, small groups began conducting concrete experiments—they were so interested in the properties of concrete. They had noticed that before Mr. Matthew and Mr. Kevin pour the concrete, they place strips of rebar on the road. Mr. Matthew said,

"This helps the concrete stay strong. It reinforces the concrete." The idea of reinforcing something to make it stronger fascinated a small group of children, and they spent days figuring out how to reinforce concrete in the classroom. Using small pieces of rebar, wire, and clay, they

FIGURE 4.19 • The children created a display showing how they experimented with different ways to strengthen concrete.

FIGURE 4.20 • Using data from the field site to write a book

FIGURE 4.21 • The toddlers enjoyed playing with the different wheels. Measuring tires with their bodies and measuring tools was a popular activity.

came up with a model that made sense to them (see Figure 4.19).

Mrs. Raab and Mrs. Randall's class took the information they had learned about front-end loaders and constructed models from found materials, using sketches, paintings, and field site photographs as a resource. Ryburn spent several days sketching the design of the front-end loader he was going to construct, using photos taken during the field site visit. Ayush decided he was going to make a book about front-end loaders and spent almost 2 weeks writing and drawing his book (see Figure 4.20).

In Ms. Grant and Mrs. Pauli's class, the children decided to build a model of the dump truck they had studied, but they wanted it big enough to play inside. They began by making a list of materials needed and sent the list home to their families to collect the pieces for the dump-truck construction.

The toddlers continued to be consumed with wheels and spent the next few weeks measuring wheels, painting wheels, collecting a wheel display, and playing with wheels in the block area (see Figure 4.21).

PHASE III: THE CHILDREN BECOME THE EXPERTS

Eventually, as the constructions were finished, the books written, and paintings and sketches displayed, the play waned. It was time to move into Phase III of the Construction Project. Teachers gathered the children once more to discuss how they would end their projects. The teachers asked, "How will you share what you have learned about the machines? What will you tell your families about your work?" As each teacher gathered the children's thoughts, they reported back to the other teachers. We decided to hold an exhibit and invite families to view all of the documentation and representations from all of the construction-related projects. As they wrote invitations, some of the children asked, "Can we invite Mr. Matthew and Mr. Kevin? They want to see our stuff too!" What a great idea! It took the children about a week to prepare their classrooms for the exhibit and then parents, grandparents, and City of Peoria road construction crews descended on UPC Discovery for the Construction Project exhibit (see Figures 4.22–4.24).

FIGURE 4.22 • Ryburn shows his mother his clay work in the Construction Project.

FIGURE 4.23 • Mr. Maroon, from Peoria Public Works, listens to Lily explain her photo documentation.

FIGURE 4.24 • Cooper explains to Mr. Matthew how his concrete-mixer construction works.

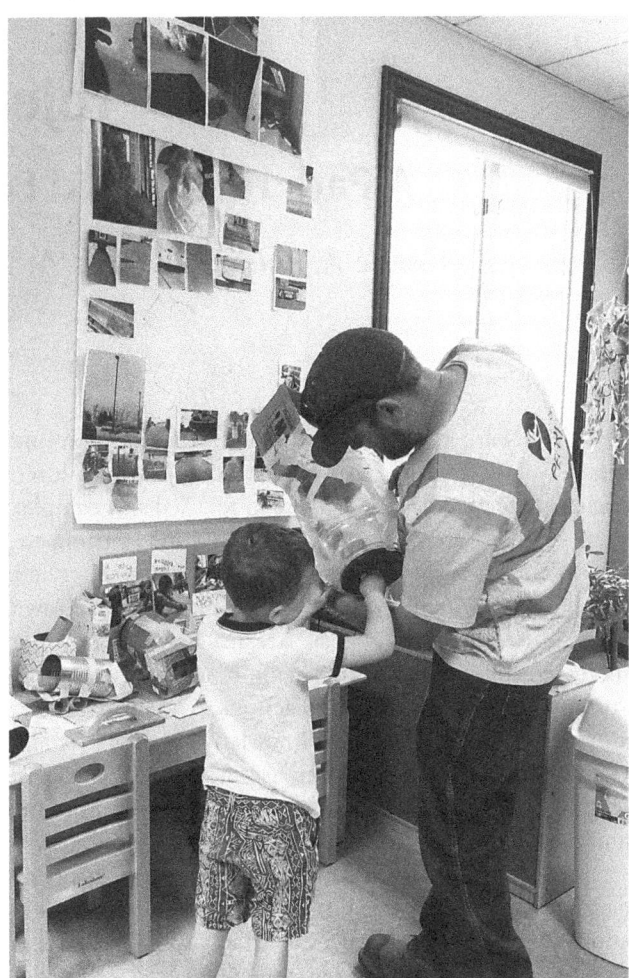

Although Phase III is sometimes a very short part of project work, I feel that it is so important. It gives children the chance to think about what they have learned and to see themselves as competent learners. Children learn to articulate concepts and define terms so others understand. Culminating events provide an opportunity for children to practice organizing their learning in a way that they can share. I have learned that the best culminating experiences are those that provide an opportunity for children to communicate with the people closest to them. During Phase III of the Construction Project, the children did exactly that; they planned and organized the exhibit and shared what they had learned about construction machines. They *were* the experts now, and they knew it!

CHAPTER 5

Project Work
A Path to Engaged Learning for All Children

Karrie A. Snider, Rebecca A. Wilson, Pegi Stamps, & Carol Bolz

CHILDREN are naturally curious about the world around them. Guided by their natural instincts, young children engage with curiosities to explore in focused and complex ways. As they enter an engaging teaching and learning environment, they are eager to talk, explore, touch, create, and play. When children are highly interested or drawn into authentic learning experiences, teachers observe their increased ability to maintain attention, use newly acquired vocabulary, focus on goals and actions, render their ideas, and use or reshape newfound knowledge as they play and test out ideas. In short, children in active and engaging learning environments learn to self-regulate their thinking and develop the capacity to learn.

Dewey (1916) believed children's development of the capacity for learning was profoundly central to the aim of education and, furthermore, viewed children's instincts as sources and tools for their learning. Much like the contemporary view of children's approaches to learning today, Dewey (1915) believed that children possessed natural instincts that propel them into learning and enable them to learn. These include children's desires to

- be social—engage with adults and peers using language and communication to develop meaningful conversation and connections;
- be constructive—make sense of thinking and learning, and represent understandings using constructive play;
- be investigative—explore real objects and actively research within concrete experiences; and
- be expressive—tell and represent ideas using art.

When caring adults create responsive learning environments that support children's natural instincts, all children gain confidence in themselves and competence in learning. In parallel to their use of learning instincts, children acquire greater control over strong feelings; that is, they develop self-regulation of emotions and behaviors. Yet, some children do not experience rich, authentically engaging early learning environments and experiences, or receive responsive adult–child interactions that support an efficient learner and create an efficient brain.

Diverse learners may encounter challenges or barriers for engaging in learning experiences, which are outside of their control. The teacher's role for fostering an inclusive learning environment becomes pivotal to their immediate and future success. For example, teaching and learning approaches that resemble traditional models may value individual, product-oriented work, where children are expected to follow the teacher's directions precisely or complete activities or seatwork in a predetermined, standardized way. Consider the Pumpkin Patch activity described in Chapter 1. For some children, but particularly for young diverse learners, this type of environment can lead to their developing negative feelings toward themselves and others and could impact their overall success and motivation to learn.

Children with diverse backgrounds may vary from mainstream learners based on individual familial factors: for example, the experience of poverty, which implies a difference in opportunity and exposure to early learning experiences, such as enriched vocabulary. Or children may vary in developmental needs of physical, cognitive, and health capacities; in speaking a language other than English; or in having a home culture, ethnicity, or religion different from the values predominant in schools today.

What the authors of this chapter and the teachers and children featured in the stories presented here have experienced is that project work provides a path for all children to engage in powerful learning experiences. The first two sections of the chapter look at enhancing teaching, thinking, and learning through projects for children who are dual language learners (DLLs) and for children with special needs. The concluding section focuses on supporting the development of the executive function of the brain and motivation in all children. Firsthand accounts and illustrations in this chapter depict programs and teachers working with diverse families and their children in toddler through primary classrooms across rural, suburban, and urban settings.

INTEGRATING RESEARCH-BASED STRATEGIES AND THE PROJECT APPROACH TO SUPPORT DUAL LANGUAGE LEARNERS

Rebecca A. Wilson

According to the National Center for Educational Statistics, 4.8 million students (9.5%) of the public school population in the United States are dual language learners. Higher percentages of young DLLs are found in kindergarten through 3rd grade (up to 16.5%) (U.S. Department of Education, 2017). Children who are learning a second language may receive instruction in a variety of classroom settings, including bilingual education (such as Dual Language or Transitional Bilingual Programs) in which content is provided to the children in both English and a home language, and English as a Second Language Programs in which all content instruction is provided in English.

Bilingual children can adapt their input to keep on pace with monolingual peers and even show signs of cognitive advantages in brain development (Bialystok, Craik, & Luk, 2012; Oates, Karmiloff-Smith, & Johnson, 2012). However, the U.S. Department of Education Policy Statement on DLLs in early childhood programs indicates

> DLLs in the U.S., on average, lag behind their monolingual English-speaking peers in academic achievement. This suggests that there is a mismatch between the learning experiences these children need to meet their potential, and the quality of experiences they are currently receiving. (Administration for Children and Families, 2016)

As the number of DLLs in early childhood classrooms continues to increase, it is critical that educators use a cohesive set of strategies for effectively teaching young DLLs while making learning meaningful for them.

Through my teaching experiences within a variety of DLL settings, including a public dual language elementary school program, a bilingual Head Start program, and a state-funded universal preschool program, I have been able to observe firsthand how deep project work ignited a spark in DLLs a multitude of times. At the same time, the Project Approach enabled teachers to joyfully connect academic content to children's experiences and introduce curriculum goals in multiple ways. Several frameworks with recommended practices for teaching DLLs strongly align and easily integrate with the Project Approach. In the following sections I present two such resources and their connections with project work.

World-Class Instructional Design and Assessment

The WIDA Consortium (formerly World-Class Instructional Design and Assessment) includes 40 states, territories, and federal agencies using research to collectively design high-quality, culturally and linguistically appropriate systems to support dual language learners (WIDA, 2017). WIDA Early Years provides standards for DLLs from 2.5 to 5.5 years of age, corresponding to state early learning standards, as well as recommended teaching practices. Each indicator contains the elements of language function, a content stem, and a language support.

WIDA Early Years maintains that early English language development should always be integrated with play-based content instruction and assessment through meaningful and authentic contexts (WIDA, 2017). This emphasis on play-based instruction and authentic contexts for language learning blends naturally with the teaching strategies of the Project Approach to support engaged learning. Figure 5.1 identifies recommended language supports from WIDA for early childhood classrooms and how they can be incorporated into project work.

Personalized Oral Language Learning

Personalized Oral Language Learning (POLL) (Espinosa, Matera, & Magruder, 2011) is comprised of specific strategies for increasing effective language and literacy instruction (Magruder, Hayslip, Espinosa, & Matera, 2013). Originally designed for the Los Angeles Unified School District, which serves the largest population of DLLs in the country, POLL was created to identify specific strategies beneficial for strengthening the oral language development of DLLs (Magruder et al., 2013). Three POLL components strongly align with the Project Approach: Families First, Environmental Supports, and Instructional Supports.

Connecting with Families. POLL recommends working with families early on and in person to establish common goals, build relationships, and learn children's interest areas (Magruder et al., 2013). Teachers also use information gathered to provide language supports in the classroom, such as possible cultural artifacts. During project work, families are invited and supported to be involved. Project activities provide numerous opportunities for family members to visit classrooms and participate in project activities.

FIGURE 5.1 • Crosswalk of WIDA (2017) language supports and Project Approach teaching strategies for dual language learners (DLLs) 2.5–5.5 years old

	Application of WIDA Supports to Project Work	Examples from Projects with DLLs
SENSORY SUPPORTS		
Real Life Objects & Models	During project work, objects are collected in the classroom for children to study and remember field site demonstrations, without having to rely on verbal information.	During a project on teeth, a dentist loaned a model of teeth for children to study. During a project on doctors, authentic doctor's tools, such as a real stethoscope, were incorporated into a child-constructed doctor's office.
Manipulatives & Artifacts	When selecting topics, teachers work to gather multiple concrete objects related to the project topic (up to 25 artifacts) that children study during project investigations.	During the Baby Project (Chapter 5), children examined real baby toys, supplies, and care items.
Pictures & Photographs	Real photos are paired with new vocabulary words to help make input comprehensible. Labeled photos may also be from informational texts above a child's reading level.	During a project on gardens, children loved to look at a flower field guide and became quite accurate in finding the names of specific flowers.
Illustrations & Drawings	Children's own observational drawings of objects can help them remember new words. Children can help create project word walls by copying words and pairing them with photos or their own drawings of objects related to the project topic.	During a project on pizza, children made their own word wall of objects they studied on their field site visit, such as mixer, pizza peel, and dough. They used the word wall to label sketches and make a class book about their visit to the pizza restaurant.
Costumes & Props	As mentioned by John Dewey (Dewey, 1915), children enjoy investigating the real roles of adults within the project topic, including what they wear and what tools they use.	During the Insect Project, the children were able to try on the beekeeper's protective gear.
Demonstrations	Within project experiences and demonstrations, project experts and field site hosts provide demonstrations using real equipment and objects.	During a project on farm machinery, the expert removed a head light from a tractor.
GRAPHIC SUPPORTS		
Charts	Project work involves lists of children's questions, charts depicting information being studied, or lists of new words in both languages.	During a project on construction, children dictated a chart with the recipe for concrete and cement. They also made a word chart to describe how concrete feels.
Graphic Organizers	Teacher Planning Webs and Child Topic Webs can be especially helpful if teachers make a drawing next to the word. Children are able to refer back to the web and use new vocabulary as they engage in other literacy activities or independent writing.	During the Power Lines Project (Chapter 2), DLL students referred to topic webs throughout their research and investigations.

FIGURE 5.1 • *Continued*

	Application of WIDA Supports to Project Work	Examples from Projects with DLLs
Diagrams	Children frequently are interested in diagrams of objects during project work. Use of diagrams is a strong motivator for writing.	Children copied the parts of a compass during a project on maps.
Graphs	Graphing activities, which involve children's collection of information and child-created tallies and surveys, frequently occur in project work.	Children collected data and created a graph depicting different colored vehicles in the school parking lot during an auto mechanic project.
INTERACTIVE SUPPORTS		
Partner Structures	Children can role-play asking their questions with each other before a field site visit or can plan their dialogue for hosting a culminating event.	For the culminating event in a project on doctors, children practiced asking their questions with peers before their field site visit and planned what to say to the families and guests in preparation for their culminating event.
Small Groups	Children engage in high levels of sociodramatic role-play during project work. DLLs have multiple opportunities to use new vocabulary in meaningful ways.	Role-play between English speakers and DLLs occurred as they pretended to report a fire, drive to the fire, and put out the fire during the Fire Station Project (Chapter 5).
Cooperative Group Structures	Children sign up for teams and choose to work cooperatively with monolingual peers as they create representations, often including dramatic play constructions during project work.	During the Reptile Project (Chapter 5), children worked collaboratively in teams to create "reptile movie posters" for their culminating event.
Use of the Home Language	Accepting children's contribution to webbing and questioning in their home language, providing print materials on the project topic in the home language, encouraging experts in the project topic who are bilingual.	Preschool children made signs for displays after conducting a project on veterinarians.
Adult Modeling	Teachers can role-play questions with DLLs prior to the field site visit.	In the Sign Project (Chapter 5), children practiced asking the state Department of Transportation guest their questions about signs.

At the beginning of the school year, teachers often have a Project Approach informational meeting with families. These can be held in both English and the languages spoken by DLLs. During these meetings, a list of possible ways families can be involved, including ways to help at home or school, is shared. While at the meeting, family members share hobbies, professions, and interests, better enabling teachers to seek them out as experts in projects later during the school year. This strategy values and respects families, while helping teachers learn about the expert areas, or funds of knowledge, that each family and child brings into the classroom (Moll, Amanti, Neff, & González, 2005).

Families participate in project nights and culminating event celebrations. Whenever possible, documentation can be posted in both languages. These informal nights can help families with DLLs feel at ease and network with other families. Children often help increase their families'

FIGURE 5.2 • AJ's family is bilingual and they speak English and Tagalog in their home. Here AJ and his mother work together on a field site visit to a bakery.

comfort levels as they show their families around during project nights and celebrate their learning together.

In my own classroom, the day before a project family night, children practice pointing out their contributions to the project so they can share their learning with their families. These are often power-packed moments for language development and sharing. Children can take turns taking home project history books that tell the story of the project in both languages. This is especially helpful if families' work schedules do not permit them to attend events.

Another way to involve families is to choose culturally relevant topics that draw support from DLLs families' strengths. Family members serve as experts, help with field site visits (see Figure 5.2), and contribute artifacts for the class to sketch. For example, during a project on a tortilla shop, a student's grandmother, visiting from Mexico, demonstrated how to make tortillas by hand. Families of DLLs also contribute by providing needed materials from home and share vocabulary words in the home language. For example, during a project on an auto-mechanic service station, the children decided they wanted blue shirts for the mechanics to wear, which were contributed by families. Another parent taught me the word for "hoist" in Spanish, which I was having a hard time finding in the dictionary.

Classroom Environments. POLL strategies emphasize the importance of creating "learning spaces that engage children's interest" as well as "support and promote conversations around exploration and discovery and are linked to study themes" (Magruder et al., 2013, p. 11). The learning or interest areas evolve as the children evolve. Center time is a wonderful opportunity for children to be highly engaged in sociodramatic play and discovery during project work. Teachers are given many opportunities to scaffold children's language learning as they interact meaningfully with their second language during project work.

During the Fire Station Project, children in my dual language kindergarten created a fire truck, complete with hoses. One day during center time, a mixed group of English and Spanish speakers were role-playing about putting out fires. Second language communication occurred frequently. A native English-speaking child was using the student-made computer and radio, calling out the name of the street with the fire to two children dressed up as firefighters (one a native English-speaker and one a native Spanish-speaker). As they fought the fire with their hoses, also created by students, I heard them communicating to each other, "Bring the hose over here," and "The fire's getting bigger!" As the native Spanish-speaking "firefighter" reported in English that the fire was getting bigger, the child on the radio said that it had moved, "All the way up to 15th Street now!" A fourth and fifth child, one a native Spanish-speaker and one a native English-speaker, alternated between driving the truck and making the fire on a nearby chalkboard "grow" by adding more lines and scribbles. This native Spanish-speaking child demonstrated growth in receptive language as he interpreted the English words *bigger* and *grow* by making more lines on the chalkboard as the firefighters reported the status of the fire. When the fire was out at last, the two firefighters reported it to the two drivers, who erased it from the chalkboard.

These high levels of sociodramatic play, which included more complex roles, language consistent with the roles, and more playmates interacting, came from the length of project work children experienced and the depth of children's interest levels. I do not believe this occurs to the same degree in more teacher-directed units. The high level of play occurring in project work aids DLLs as they interact with language and content in meaningful ways. The spontaneous nature of the play encourages children to continue to use their native language in addition to English. This language-rich play can help young children increase their oral language development in both home and school languages, which is an increased benefit for DLLs.

Instructional Strategies. POLL outlines instructional strategies to reinforce new concepts and vocabulary, while emphasizing the children's experiences (Magruder et al., 2013). Aligning with project work, these include intentional messages, anchor texts, and vocabulary imprinting.

Frequently, teachers using the Project Approach intentionally write morning messages to children that focus on project work. Messages may contain next steps for investigations or descriptions of new artifacts being introduced that day. By drawing a picture or using a photo to go with related project vocabulary words in the message, teachers reinforce dual language learning through visuals.

Recommended instructional practices for young DLLs all emphasize vocabulary acquisition and word knowledge (Meier, 2004). Research indicates that it is beneficial for DLLs to have instruction on a specific set of academic vocabulary words and to teach these across several days using a variety of materials, overlapping vocabulary development with content instruction (Baker et al., 2014). As the brain organizes words into webs of knowledge, tighter webs are formed through multiple exposure to words in different contexts (Whorrall & Cabell, 2016). POLL strategies include using photographs, images, and word walls to introduce new concepts in vocabulary and deepen comprehension (Magruder et al., 2013). These new words should be used in meaningful ways. Espinosa (2015) recommends providing daily opportunities for students to talk about content in pairs or small groups. This social aspect of language learning unfolds naturally in good project work, as children interact and discuss the topic with peers.

With repeated exposure to vocabulary, we have found that DLLs in project work are extremely motivated to write and use new words. For example, in Figure 5.3, Yuma, a native speaker of Japanese, has created a survey to the see which tomato-based food people like best. He copied the question and the choices, which were soup, salsa, ketchup, or juice. Over the course of the project, Yuma used the new vocabulary repeatedly, including during peer discussion to plan the Tomato Festival for a culminating event.

Word Knowledge and Vocabulary Building. To understand how word knowledge and vocabulary development occur for young children, it may be helpful to create a mental image of a bouncing ball and paint. Imagine a ball with paint on it. You bounce it. As the ball bounces, paint disperses onto the playground. The ball keeps bouncing, marking the playground. As the bouncing slows, smaller bounces continue making marks with more and more paint until, eventually, the ball stops. By the time the ball stops bouncing, paint has accumulated on the playground, leaving a trail behind. Left alone, the paint may fade or be

FIGURE 5.3 • Yuma, a native speaker of Japanese, was motivated to create a survey to see which tomato-based food was liked the most often.

washed away. If new paint is added and further bounces ensue, new paint accumulates on the playground, reinforcing the area already covered by paint.

When adults introduce new words to children, they give a "ball an initial bounce" by mapping new words onto familiar ideas and DLLs' home language. Using the new words in dialogue with children, while repeating and extending children's comments about the new words, builds vocabulary and word acquisition. As children use new words at school and/or at home, the ball makes subsequent bounces. If adults want the paint (the words) to stick to the playground (the child's mental vocabulary), adults must bounce the ball multiple times over a long course of time, and children must meaningfully engage in using and meaning-making with the new words.

How does this ball and paint analogy connect with the Project Approach? In project work when children interact with words repeatedly and *render* their own representations of the words, the vocabulary sticks (Helm, 2015). When teachers select topics that are culturally relevant, they can further strengthen children's connection to their newly acquired vocabulary. This "paint on the playground" is the vocabulary foundation in the brain that children need to build their future academic learning and reading capacities. If teachers bounce the ball just once, and children aren't engaged in multiple meaningful activities around the new vocabulary, then the ball stops bouncing, and the paint doesn't stick.

Back-and-forth exchanges as a language modeling strategy is especially critical for young DLLs. Because project work focuses children on an in-depth investigation of a meaningful topic over long periods of time, it is easy

FIGURE 5.4 • Gabriella points to and names the parts of the insect.

for a teacher to support repetition and extension of words and word patterns. In other words, the ball is bounced multiple times, with ample paint, and the words not only stick but create an interconnected map of captured movement (or in the case of words—a map of meaning and thinking). In fact, by the end of deep project work, teachers have, metaphorically speaking, covered entire playgrounds with paint.

When given the proper amount of instructional support, children's use of vocabulary in project work can be amazing. During an Insect Project in my preschool classroom, Gabriella, a dual language learner, started the school year speaking little English. She became very engaged and developed more and more command of new vocabulary words throughout the project. Early on, Gabriella was interested in butterflies and drew butterfly specimens. She drew the butterfly she intended to create when planning for representation. At the end of the project, we made a video in which children described their representations. Gabriella was demonstrating how her butterfly could fly for the video, when she suddenly stopped, placed her butterfly on a chair, and started singing a song our expert visitor had taught us, "Head, Thorax, Abdomen" while showing us the parts of the insect. Not only had Gabriella learned the word *butterfly* but she had learned and could correctly name and point to the parts of the insect (see Figure 5.4).

Project work results in DLLs' development of rich vocabulary for two reasons. First, as children become interested in certain parts of the project topic, they hear the pertinent words referred to again and again. Second, during project work *everyone* is involved in learning new vocabulary. Children are talking about different words, asking questions about what words mean, and writing or drawing pictures of newly acquired words that are meaningful to them. Children learning a second language are less likely to feel embarrassed or experience isolation about learning new words because there is increased involvement and interest in learning new words together. In other words, through project work, teachers can lower the affective filter (Krashen, 2003) and create a safe classroom climate for vocabulary development for *all* children.

In sum, the Project Approach shares strong connections with effective research-based teaching strategies recommended for young DLLs and optimizes their natural instincts for learning. The next section shows how project work supports families and their young children with special needs.

IMPLEMENTING PROJECTS IN SPECIAL EDUCATION CLASSROOMS

Pegi Stamps & Carol Bolz

In Kansas City, Missouri, the doors are open to possibilities at Ability KC and at the Early Childhood Center of Center School District. Both schools serve young children, including those with Individual Education Plans (IEPs), and both have made the decision to incorporate the Project Approach into their early childhood curriculum. Teachers see the Project Approach as an opportunity to grow each child's strengths and meet IEP goals. They have pioneered projects in their special education classrooms as ways to provide authentic and inclusive learning experiences for children.

The following stories from their classrooms highlight child development, teacher growth, and family experiences with projects. The stories offer evidence that all children are capable learners who can contribute to and grow from project work. All teachers are encouraged to follow the example of these early childhood special educators—who looked for possibilities to nurture diverse learners, saw opportunities for all children, and transformed their curriculum with the Project Approach.

How Experiences Inform Project Work

Deb Plumlee, Joan Williams, and Amanda Prater, the teachers in Room 417 at Ability KC, were introduced to the Project Approach and began looking for an opportunity to implement a project. Their first effort was a multisensory

FIGURE 5.5 • Ability KC teachers observed Dakotah's frequent engagement in dramatic play with a doctor's office theme.

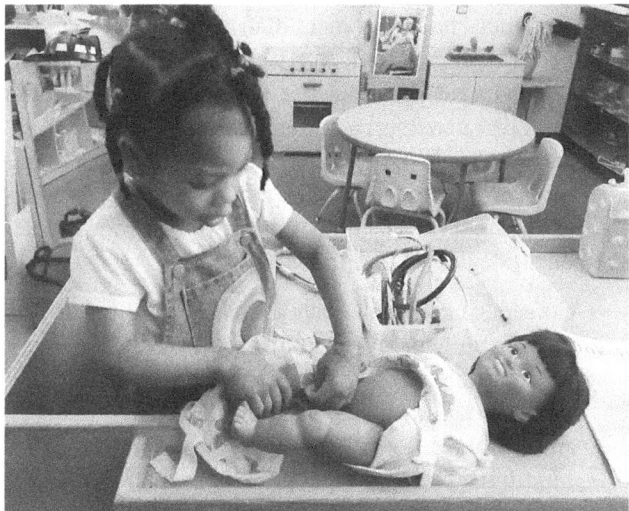

exploration of apples, which became foundational for classroom investigations. Then they facilitated their first real project after noticing the children role-playing their many experiences with doctors (see Figure 5.5). This project involved a parent who is a doctor and served as an expert visitor. X-rays and the X-ray machine were a focal point of investigation and representation. Children and teachers gained confidence in project skills and were eager for another project.

In the next program year, children's real-life experiences with visits to the doctor again appeared prominently in children's play. Teachers developed anticipatory plans, provided doctor artifacts, and asked parents to share doctor stories. They decided that another project on doctors was appropriate because it was so relevant to children's experiences.

This project included repeated field site visits to Ability KC's medical clinic. On one visit, preverbal children explored the drawers under the exam table, drawing the attention of other children. Some children investigated the working of the drawers and explored the medical equipment they contained. Other children asked questions of school nurse Jesse Merino about the table, the pillow, and the nearby IV pole. Eventually, the children made plans, gathered materials, and constructed an exam table with storage drawers in their classroom. They represented newly acquired knowledge about the clinic in play. Peer models were observed opening the drawers so that less mobile children could join the play.

The project culminated with an open house. Families and friends were treated to guided tours of the classroom clinic, displays of children's work, and free check-ups on the exam table.

Communicating Questions and Ideas

At the Early Childhood Center of Center School District, a crew began major road construction just outside the playground fence. Robyn Schreckenghaust, Amy Peterson, and Marley Baltz, the teachers from Room 10, accompanied 3- to 5-year-old children to the playground each day, only to see them bypass the playground equipment and rush to the fence to watch the backhoes, dump trucks, and construction workers. Clipboards were attached to the fence so children could draw as they observed the construction trucks (see Figure 5.6). Robyn recalled a key moment: "We were at the fence watching the construction trucks. Suddenly, Terry'ion ran over to the tallest playground structure, climbed to the top, and pointed at the large skid loader that was scooping and dumping pieces of asphalt." Robyn responded, "I've been wondering what that machine is called too! Do you want to know what it is

FIGURE 5.6 • Terry'ion and Andrew observe the road construction with teachers Robyn and Marley in front of the Early Childhood Center of Center School District.

FIGURE 5.7 • Through the action of lifting the truck onto a cube chair and crawling under it, Terry'ion shared his idea of fixing the truck with Andrew and the Center School District teachers.

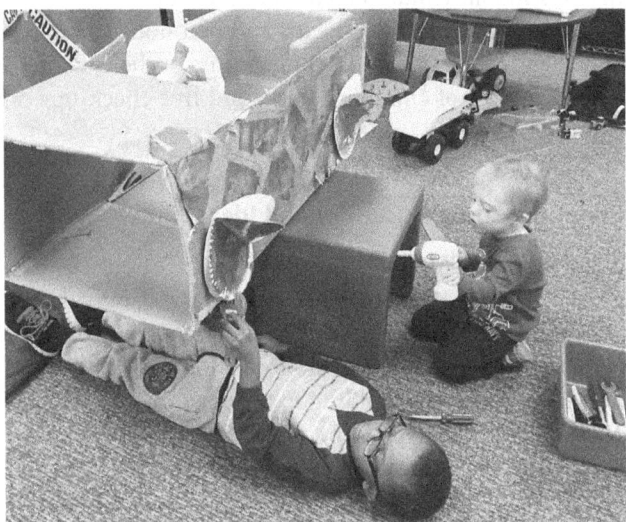

doing?" Helm (2015) asserts that questions are a key component of projects, determining their direction. With Terry'ion's implied question, Robyn knew they had their project topic.

After further investigation, the children represented what they had learned through a construction of their own. The teachers helped the children develop a list of parts they would need—wheels, doors, steering wheel, truck bed, and keys—and a large box was transformed into a green construction truck. Children pretended to drive the truck and talk on a toy cell phone while doing so.

The work on the road in front of the school ended. Robyn wondered if the project was winding down also, until a child communicated an idea by lifting the green truck to sit on top of two cube chairs. He crawled under the truck with tools in hands. Other children followed his lead—hammering, screwing, drilling, and "fixing it"—and the investigation was extended (see Figure 5.7).

Taking a Collaborative Team Approach

The Ability KC teachers Deb, Joan, and Amanda welcome children with differing abilities, including peer models, into their classroom each day. These special educators have participated in training, coaching, and communities of practice to grow their ability to include the Project Approach in the curriculum. They have been supported by their education coordinator, Kim Brooks, and community coaches involved in research initiatives.

Robyn, Amy, and Marley are the teaching team and Wendy Maupin the coach at the Early Childhood Center of Center School District. For more than 25 years, Robyn has offered experiences designed to help children in her low-incidence classroom meet their IEP goals. When she attended a Young Investigator training with Judy Harris Helm, Robyn realized that the Project Approach could offer an integrated approach to individualized education.

In both schools, the teachers collaborated with therapists on provision of learning experiences, including facilitation of the Project Approach. Together they implemented strategies such as the following:

- Considering general goals as well as children's IEP goals in anticipatory planning for projects
- Integrating sensory stimuli into investigations, while remaining aware of children's sensory tolerances and respecting their sensory boundaries
- Modifying children's speech and occupational therapies, such as adding project words to the Picture Exchange Communication System (PECS)® board, to allow full participation in project activities
- Describing details of artifacts and photo documentation to make project experiences visible
- Using alternative and augmented communication devices to include children in project-related discussions

Teachers and therapists supported children's progress toward IEP goals and encouraged transfer of learning from one setting to another. They observed for evidence of children generalizing their learning in the classroom setting. For example, the Center School District team tuned in to children's social interactions during their Construction Truck Project. Robyn noticed that the children increased their abilities to establish joint attention. From the time the children stood at the fence drawing the construction trucks through the time they built a green truck from a box and used it in play, the children were engaged in collaborative investigation and representation.

Helm and Beneke (2003) point out that "Classrooms in which the development of a caring community is a priority are beneficial for all children and even more so for children with special needs" (p. 51). At Ability KC, project work helped to bring children together and aided their abilities to function in group settings. Teachers noted that children on the autism spectrum increased their engagement in group play during project work, positioning themselves in closer proximity to peers. Teacher Amanda shared, "We watched the group of children transform from individual children playing in isolation, to a community of children who cared about each other and wanted to be together, play together, and investigate together." Children with varying abilities moved from being guests in the classroom to being capable peers who were a part of daily classroom experiences.

Enhancing Children's Learning and Development

The Ability KC teachers noticed the development of children's positive dispositions for learning, such as curiosity and initiative. The teachers observed children growing in their ability to ask questions during the Doctor's Office Project. Joan noted, "We had learned that it wasn't a project if children don't have questions about the topic." Deb added, "We were aware we needed to find ways to hear the silent questions being asked by our preverbal children, so we could uncover their thinking and include them in the project." The teachers believed all the children were curious about the doctor's office.

The Ability KC team began to refer to questions as Information Requesting Mechanisms (Chouinard, Harris, & Maratsos, 2007), and knew that these mechanisms included not only verbal questions but also expressions, gestures, and vocalizations. They observed children closely for possible questions. Joan watched one day as George, from his stander, turned his gaze to children playing with a stethoscope. Joan said, "I think George has a question about that stethoscope. He might be wondering how it works." (see Figure 5.8). Aaliyah helped George find an answer by coming over and including George in the play, listening to his heart.

Because the teachers frequently noticed and commented on questions, the children became more familiar with the concept of a question. One morning, Joan informed the children that a doctor would visit and asked, "What do you want her to tell us?" David raised his hand and asked, "Why do doctors check our bellies?" Joan wrote David's question on a chart before listening for questions from other children.

David shot his hand in the air again. Joan validated his enthusiasm before encouraging him to give other children an opportunity. David waited briefly and then looked at George sitting next to him with a therapist. He looked into George's eyes, looked at Joan, and back at George before grabbing George's hand and thrusting it into the air. "Ms. Joan," he exclaimed, "George has a question!" Joan smiled and asked, "What is George's question?" David proudly stated, "George wants to know why doctors give us Band-Aids." Joan added George's question to the list.

Questions and comments provided evidence of the vocabulary and communications skills that were cultivated during project work. During the Construction Truck Project, Center School District teachers and therapists listened with delight as their children, who were preverbal when enrolled, started to talk about trucks. Sentence length improved as children assumed the roles of drivers and construction workers in play. Children even helped write a song about trucks with lines such as, "The bed on the truck goes up and down."

At Ability KC, when children's language development was assessed, greater than usual increases in ratings from winter to spring were noted. Kim commented, "It was amazing to see their ratings and realize how much children's communication skills grew during project work."

Teachers and therapists from both schools observed enhanced motivation for learning when they embedded tasks related to children's IEP goals into project experiences. Math and literacy skills were promoted as children drew trucks and wrote letters of their names on their work, created eye charts, documented health checks, measured each other and charted growth, and wrote prescriptions. According to Helm and Katz (2016), project work provides reasons to learn academic skills and opportunities to apply them.

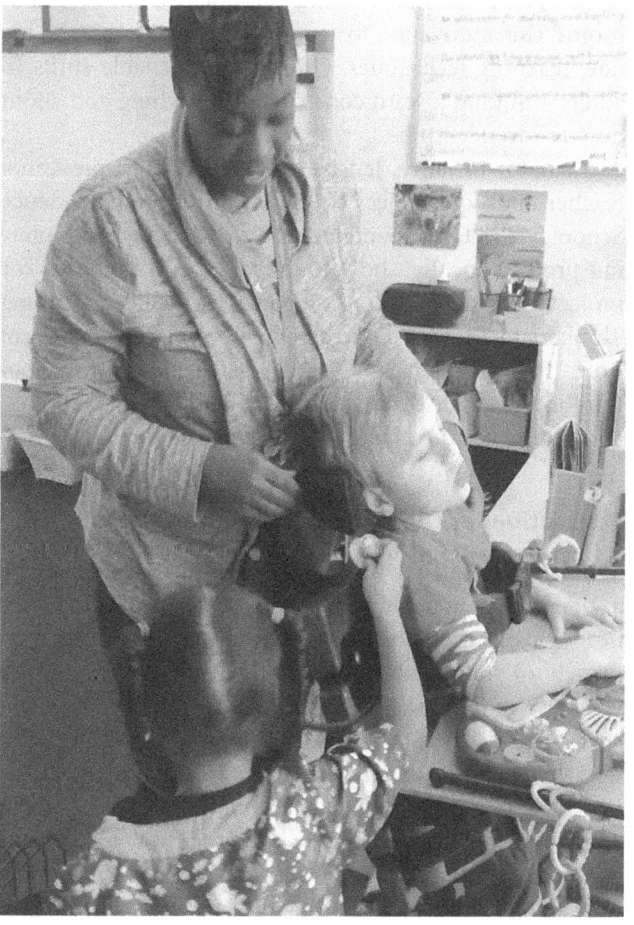

FIGURE 5.8 • Joan Williams from Ability KC notices and shares with Aaliyah that George has a question about the stethoscope.

Thoughts About Teaching and Learning with Projects

Educators. When the Ability KC teachers were asked to reflect on their professional growth, Joan said, "I realized after 20 years of teaching that I could give up control and let the children own the learning." Amanda added, "I saw so many changes in children over the time of the project, especially during center time. Children didn't wander the room anymore. They were fully engaged. I felt like children liked learning—they were serious about their work." Deb concluded, "We took risks in our teaching knowing we had to trust. We began to rethink our roles as teachers and developed an attitude of learning as a process."

When discussing the inclusion of the Project Approach in Center School District's curriculum, principal Tamara Sandage said,

> The work creates a joy-filled environment where children and staff are connected through learning. Project work deepens our students' experiences and opportunities. The authentic social interactions and language development observed in the classroom are powerful. We focus so much on these two areas and see so much growth in them during project work.

Families. "Our family's journey into a therapeutic preschool began when our oldest child, Kohanna, was born with a rare genetic condition. It's not a chosen path, but one that becomes reality," shared KoAnn Brass, an Ability KC parent. Given a grim prognosis, the Brass family found themselves attending endless doctor's office visits and diagnostic meetings. They were appreciative of the individualized services their child received but struggled with hearing her described in a fragmented manner.

Kohanna's enrollment at Ability KC changed the trajectory. The staff realized Kohanna's strengths and created opportunities for her to thrive. Kohanna shared in classroom discoveries and was included in all aspects of project work. KoAnn said, "Kohanna's enrollment at Ability KC gave our family hope. Teachers and therapists combined therapeutic goals with real-life experiences, which laid the foundation for Kohanna to now be included in a mainstream elementary classroom."

Kohanna's younger sister, Dakotah, is a peer model at Ability KC. She has been a strong leader during projects while providing empathetic support to other children. KoAnn concluded, "As parents, we yearn to see our children just be children. It has given me so much pride and a renewed optimism to see my girls grow and develop at Ability KC."

Including children with differing abilities in classrooms with typically developing peers is recommended practice for all children (Beneke, Ostrosky, & Katz, 2019). Lickey and Powers (2011) suggest that "as early childhood special educators, we have come to understand that the potential for children of all abilities to learn and develop successfully is dependent on our understanding and respect for these children's differences and strengths and how they affect the learning process" (p. 22).

Educators must be challenged to respond to this work—to discover authenticity in the powerful work that can be done through the Project Approach in special education and dual language learner classrooms. During a Young Investigators training in Kansas City, a teacher asked Judy Harris Helm, "Can I facilitate the Project Approach with the diverse learners in my classroom?" Without hesitation Judy replied, "It's not just that you can. It's that you must!"

UNDERSTANDING THE POTENTIAL OF CHILDREN'S CAPACITY TO LEARN

Karrie A. Snider

Many teachers, becoming inspired by stories of children's and teachers' journeys with the Project Approach, feel motivated by the observable benefits of project work and wonder, How can I incorporate this practice into my classroom? This motivation fosters teachers' willingness to try new teaching techniques. Often, stories enable shifts in adults' thinking toward constructivist teaching and about how children learn best.

Take, for instance, Jen Fletchall, Head Start preschool teacher and now project coach within the Independence School District, Independence, Missouri. After encountering projects locally, she saw the value and potential for project teaching. She then completed the Becoming Young Thinkers Institute and partnered with project coach Carol Bolz. Together, Jen and Carol started on a journey of thinking together that enabled Jen, her students, families, and staff to see the power of projects in action.

Distractions as Directions

The Baby Project, like most great projects, was not born by accident. Jen's first attempts at selecting a project topic for her inclusive preschool classroom began with a common preschool topic, caterpillars. When another preschool teacher was moving to the infant classroom, she gave Jen some mail-order caterpillars that she would not be taking with her. Jen's assistant teacher was also moving to the infant classroom (aka, the baby room to the preschoolers), which Jen's class passed every day on their way to the playground. It was early fall. Jen thought, *Why not try it out? Caterpillars might be interesting to the children.*

The children appeared very interested in caterpillars at first. However, Jen wondered and waited for the caterpillar topic to grow. But it was turning colder, and the children weren't finding many native caterpillars on their playground any longer. In fact, each day on their way out to the playground, Jen's preschoolers would pause and wave at their former teacher and at the babies in the infant room, stopping frequently to go in and say hello to the babies. Jen said that walking by the infant classroom was becoming a bit of a distraction.

Across the Kansas City metropolitan area from Jen's classroom sits United Inner City Services, home of St. Mark Family and Child Development Center, where recently "children's distractions" had become the center of conversation among teachers and their project coach, Merrill Hunt. Merrill, while assisting in a preschool classroom during cleanup time, noticed children excitedly watching and talking about squirrels running and jumping through the trees outside their windows. Merrill later learned this excitement happened frequently, to the point where children had names for the squirrels and told stories about where the squirrels lived and what they did.

Merrill soon realized that what was a distraction from the teachers' daily routines and expectations was actually the focus and interest of the children. Merrill reported to the communities of practice coaching group, "Children's distractions are really *directions* for us; if we slow down, we can really focus on children's interests." But she also realized, as not having been away from the classroom too long, that this is sometimes hard to do.

So, Merrill took the idea of distractions to the staff's next professional development day and asked teachers to brainstorm 10 things that distract their children. Monchell Mitchell, St. Mark toddler teacher, knew right away. During any portion of the day, when her toddlers heard the trucks coming down the adjacent drive outside their windows, they stopped and ran to see the trucks. Merrill and Monchell realized that "trucks" as a distraction to teachers was a *high child interest*, and the Truck Project began.

Just up the hill from Merrill's and Monchell's community-based program, Della Judie, Tara Edwards, and coach Mary Svoboda-Chollet at Woodland Early Learning Center, Kansas City Public Schools, described a similar phenomenon of children's focused attention that occurred in their diverse Head Start preschool classroom. Children had discovered signs during a community walk around their school. After this walk, children noticed the signs in their classroom. They spotted more signs in and around their school. The children would not stop talking about signs. The teachers knew this would be a project topic, and the Sign Project began. Throughout the project, Della emphatically noted, "They didn't think of anything else." As children engaged in finding out answers to their questions about signs—"Who makes signs?" "Can we make signs?" "What are signs for?"—their instincts and curiosities were directing their focused attention, goal-planning, and contributions to the community life of their school. These are features of critical brain-building processes called *executive function*.

Executive Function and Motivation to Learn

Executive function (EF) is a multidimensional construct comprised of many integrated cognitive processes: specifically, inhibitory control, working memory, and cognitive flexibility or planning (Meltzer, 2018; Raver & Blair, 2016; Zelazo, Blair, & Willoughby, 2016). EF encompasses interrelated skills that enable one's control of behaviors, understandings, thinking, and actions. EF develops throughout life, with rapid development early, at birth through age 7 (Rueda, Checa, & Combita, 2012). There is much interest in strengthening children's EF because of its value in supporting school achievement and social-emotional competence (Blair & Razza, 2007; Checa, Rodríguez-Bailón, & Rueda, 2008; Rueda et al., 2012).

Moran and Gardner (2018) propose three stages or topographies of EF strategies. They suggest all people experience the first *apprentice* stage, where EF strategies primarily keep a person on task. Some people experience the second *master* stage, as EF strategies join personal meaning with cultural beliefs in order to keep oneself focused on a goal. In the *contributor* stage, EFs focus the individual and keep the momentum on purposeful actions to impact one's own cultural development.

Most children will stay at the apprentice stage if learning in a teacher-oriented, teacher-directed classroom. To reach the master and contributor stages, Moran and Gardner (2018) suggest teachers must become guides, coaches, and facilitators and incorporate collaborative contribution-oriented learning experiences, where children experience freedom and responsibility during learning. A typical Project Approach environment shifts the attention from teaching skills to teaching children to strengthen their intellectual capacities for thinking.

"Hill, Skill, and Will." EF processes integrate what a learner wants to do (*hill*), can do (*skill*), and has the energy for (*will*), as described by Moran and Gardner (2018). *Hills* represent children's natural interests. Teachers follow children's interests during project work, while connecting interests to *skills*—concepts, learning standards, and activities. For example, in the Sign Project, children developed an understanding that signs inform and help people. One

FIGURE 5.9 • This child-created sign was posted in the bathroom to tell others to "Put the Trash in the Trash Can."

day, a child noticed trash all over the bathroom floor. She immediately said, "Ms. Della, we need a sign here, can you help me make a sign?" The child went right back to the classroom, made the sign, and wrote "Put the Trash in the Trash Can." She then went to the bathroom and taped it up (see Figure 5.9).

The emphasis for children's skill development in project work is not directly on isolated skills ("What letter is this?" "What shape is this?"). Instead, the emphasis is for children to acquire an intersection of process skills (e.g., asking, investigating, observing—"What is happening?") and thinking skills (e.g., analyzing, reasoning, evaluating—"What does this mean?"), which build a strong foundation for all academic, social, and emotional development. In short, they learn how to learn and how to contribute to the learning of others. The trash sign emerged because the child observed, "Here is trash all over the floor." The child reflected, "What can I do?" and determined, "I can make a sign to inform others." Hanging the sign in the bathroom validated the child's initiative and feelings of being a competent community learner.

When following their interests and incorporating their strengths, the teacher responds to the emotional and academic needs of individual children, which creates further motivation and access points to curriculum content and allows children to practice and strengthen important learning skills. Children in deep project work experience heightened emotions to drive their *will*—their motivation and persistence to continue through and complete challenging tasks.

During the Baby Project, *will* occurred spontaneously. The project was just getting started when one morning a DLL child cheerfully came into school waving a baby book (see Figure 5.10). Before the children could take off their backpacks and coats, Jen documented this exciting moment. Without any prompting from the teachers, the child had gone home, talked to her family in her home language, and found her birth picture to bring in. The motivation that the topic provided for this student (and all of the children) was really remarkable to concretely observe.

Motivation. Project work creates opportunities for intrinsic motivation in learning, because activities center around the children's interests, questions, ideas, and goals. Intrinsic motivation is either hindered or cultivated by environmental conditions (Cook & Artino, 2016). To foster intrinsic motivation, three basic needs must be met: "*autonomy* (the opportunity to control one's actions), *competence* (self-efficacy) and *relatedness* (a sense of affiliation with or belonging to others to whom one feels . . . connected)" (p. 1009). Intrinsic motivation is what drives children to

FIGURE 5.10 • Child bringing in baby book from home, unprompted

FIGURE 5.11 • Nearly every day, toddlers observed different trucks from their classroom and their playground.

want to learn and is associated with the interest, enjoyment, and inherent satisfaction in a task or activity.

Inhibitory Control. Internal and external stimuli flood the brain, and children develop increased inhibitory control as EF develops. Projects support children's ability to focus on information by using their desire to follow their interests. Children in Jen's classroom weren't distracted by the babies in the infant classroom. They were connecting with babies because of having baby siblings in their homes and sharing a real interest that focused their attention. Once Jen had realized the children weren't just gazing into the infant classroom every day as a distraction, and realized the children were intently focused on what the babies were doing, the Baby Project was born!

Likewise, once Monchell realized the distraction of the trucks was the interesting stimulus holding children's attention, she carefully planned learning activities to engage and increase this focus. As a result of her planning, Monchell's toddlers frequently stopped drivers who parked next to their playground fence, asked to see their truck, and talked to them. Some drivers who frequented the school provided repeat visits and explorations of their vehicles (see Figure 5.11).

Toddlers used gestures and words as they interacted with peers and adults. They learned to recognize their favorite trucks, such as the garbage truck and the Pepsi truck, which happened to be the work truck of the father of a child at the center.

During the Sign Project, teachers observed that children who sometimes struggled within more teacher-directed activities were focusing for long periods of time when in project work (see Figure 5.12). For example, Della described one child who was having difficulty learning academic skills, such as shapes, in isolation. The Sign Project was a natural tool for him to learn shapes in a meaningful way. Teachers noticed he had fewer behavioral outbursts, as he was less frustrated during project learning time. Della noted that during the period of time in which the majority of children created all sorts of signs, this boy persisted in working on his own sign, without getting frustrated, becoming upset, or giving up.

Working Memory. Another component of EF is working memory, which enables the simultaneous processing and storing of new information—an integral component for learning (Gray et al., 2017). Thought to be guided by focused attention (Engle, 2002), working memory involves *working with* information: that is, holding information in the mind while manipulating it and performing other mental tasks (Diamond & Ling, 2016). Working memory

FIGURE 5.12 • During the Sign Project, preschoolers spent long periods of time in Phase II exploring different materials to make a variety of signs.

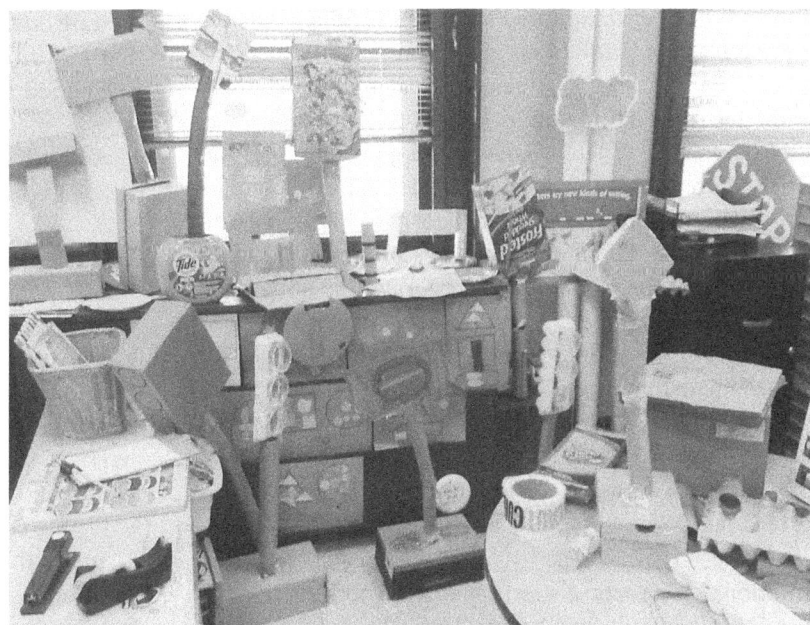

also assists in updating information that is relevant and needed for tasks in focus (Meltzer, 2018). It is critical for problem solving and reasoning (Diamond & Ling, 2016).

In the Baby Project children sustained long periods of activity as they explored questions, studied babies (real and pretend), and interviewed experts. Jen observed how DLLs grew in their autonomy. For example, several DLLs took initiative to coordinate the writing of baby books. They used working memory, took initiative using focused attention, and rendered pictures and labels that reflected their experiences during visits to the infant room.

Cognitive Flexibility. Cognitive flexibility is the ability to consider multiple ways to solve a problem (Zelazo et al., 2016) and "to adjust to changed demands or priorities" (Diamond & Ling, 2016, p. 35). In project work, children naturally experience goal-oriented actions. They participate in discussions and discourse, create plans, and test out ideas. The questions children ask in and out of project work represent their cognitive curiosities. By fostering this natural tendency of the thinking system within meaningful curriculum experiences, children's learning experiences mirror the way the brain functions.

Goal-Oriented Action. For instance, goal-oriented action or goal setting is a cognitive process working in both motivational theories and in executive function (Cook & Artino, 2016; Zelazo et al., 2016). Children in the Sign Project wanted to make signs. First, teachers Della and Tara assembled all sorts of materials with the help of parents. Any recyclable material you can imagine flooded their room. As a result of making plans, selecting and identifying needed materials, and following through to completion, children self-monitored their sign making by determining if it "worked" or served a real purpose for their school. For instance, Fatima, a 4-year-old preschooler, wanted to make a three-dimensional sign. She worked day after day, trying different amounts of glue and tape, and different configurations for getting the sign to stand. She remembered what the Department of Transportation expert told her about the meanings of sign colors and symbols, and she worked to incorporate this knowledge into her rendering (see Figure 5.13).

Fatima's efforts demonstrate a young child's use of higher mental process involving the ability to reflect, see the bigger picture, and make small incremental decisions to reach a desired end. This act of reflection incorporates EF skills such as using working memory, employing focused attention, and regulating behaviors and thinking.

Emotional Supports. A key influence on both motivation and EF is emotions. Researchers suggest that EF skills are

FIGURE 5.13 • Fatima creates her three-dimensional sign rendering.

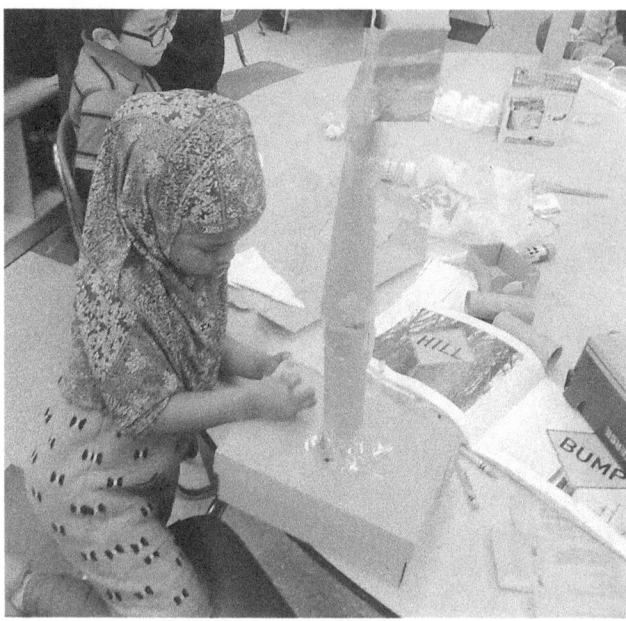

optimized when children learn within positive and emotionally supportive environments (Diamond & Ling, 2016). In Vartuli, Bolz, and Wilson (2014) and in a follow-up study (Snider, Holley, & Usman, 2017), Project Approach teaching practices have been found to be strongly correlated with emotional support teaching behaviors, among other instructional support practices. In other words, the Project Approach helped increase the observable teacher–child interactions that foster positive learning classrooms. Because children, like adults, are fundamentally social, EFs are boosted when learners feel a part of a group, working toward a common goal, and feel socially supported (Diamond & Ling, 2016).

THE POTENTIAL OF THE PROJECT APPROACH FOR TODAY'S YOUTH

Diverse learners, like all children, deserve to grow to their fullest potential. By using educational approaches that include children's strengths and their funds of knowledge, rather than seeing differences as deficits, teachers and programs create more thriving, interactive, and inclusive classrooms. With the Project Approach, teachers remove barriers and walls and promote high-level thinking in all children.

Young children are highly motivated by their interests. Using authentic, engaging projects, adults can harness children's interests and support the development of important thinking skills. We believe project work creates the optimal conditions under which all children, including diverse learners, can develop an efficient brain and the capacity for contributing to their present and future world.

REFERENCES

Administration for Children and Families. (2016). *U.S. Department of Health and Human Services, U.S. Department of Education policy statement on supporting the development of children who are dual language learners in early childhood programs* (Log No. ODAS, ECD-ACF-PS2017-02). Washington, DC: U.S. Department of Health and Human Services. Available at www.acf.hhs.gov/ecd/dual-language-learners

Baker, S., Lesaux, N., Jayanthi, M., Dimino, J., Proctor, C. P., Morris, J., et al. (2014). *Teaching academic content and literacy to English learners in elementary and middle school* (NCEE 2014-4012). Washington, DC: National Center for Education Evaluation and Regional Assistance (NCEE), Institute of Education Sciences, U.S. Department of Education.

Beneke, S. J., Ostrosky, M. M., & Katz, L. G. (2019). *The Project Approach for all learners: A hands-on guide for inclusive early childhood classrooms*. Baltimore, MD: Brookes.

Bialystok, E., Craik, F. I., & Luk, G. (2012). Bilingualism: Consequences for mind and brain. *Trends in Cognitive Sciences, 16*(4), 240–250.

Blair, C., & Razza, R. P. (2007). Relating effortful control, executive function, and false belief understanding to emerging math and literacy ability in kindergarten. *Child Development, 78*(2), 647–663.

Checa, P., Rodríguez-Bailón, R., & Rueda, M. R. (2008). Neurocognitive and temperamental systems of self-regulation and early adolescents' school competence. *Mind, Brain, and Education, 2,* 177–187.

Chouinard, M. M., Harris, P. L., & Maratsos, M. P. (2007). Children's questions: A mechanism for cognitive development. *Monographs of the Society for Research in Child Development, 72*(1), i–129.

Cook, D. A., & Artino, A. R., Jr. (2016). Motivation to learn: An overview of contemporary theories. *Medical Education, 50*(10), 997–1014.

Dewey, J. (1915). *The school and society* (rev. ed.). Chicago, IL: University of Chicago Press.

Dewey, J. (1916). *Democracy and education: An introduction to the philosophy of education.* New York, NY: Macmillan.

Diamond, A., & Ling, D. S. (2016). Conclusions about interventions, programs, and approaches for improving executive functions that appear justified and those that, despite much hype, do not. *Developmental Cognitive Neuroscience, 18,* 34–48.

Engle, R. W. (2002). Working memory capacity as executive attention. *Current Directions in Psychological Science, 11*(1), 19–23.

Espinosa, L. M. (2015). *Getting it RIGHT for young children from diverse backgrounds: Applying research to improve practice with a focus on dual language learners* (2nd ed.). Upper Saddle River, NJ: Pearson.

Espinosa, L., Matera, C., & Magruder, E. (2011, September 21). *Intentional planning for oral language and vocabulary instruction, planning for vocabulary routines personalized oral language(s) learning (POLL).* Paper presented at the meeting of the Advisory Committee on Head Start Research and Evaluation, Office of Planning, Research and Evaluation, Administration of Children and Families, U.S. Department of Health and Human Services, Washington, DC. Available at www.acf.hhs.gov/opre/resource/intentional-planning-for-oral-language-and-vocabulary-instruction

Gray, S., Green, S., Alt, M., Hogan, T., Kuo, T., Brinkley, S., et al. (2017). The structure of working memory in young children and its relation to intelligence. *Journal of Memory and Language, 92,* 183–201.

Helm, J. H. (2015). *Becoming young thinkers: Deep project work in the classroom.* New York, NY: Teachers College Press; Washington, DC: National Association for the Education of Young Children.

Helm, J. H., & Beneke, S. (2003). *The power of projects: Meeting contemporary challenges in early childhood classrooms—Strategies & solutions.* New York, NY: Teachers College Press.

Helm, J. H., & Katz, L. G. (2016). *Young investigators: The Project Approach in the early years* (3rd ed.). New York, NY: Teachers College Press.

Krashen, S. (2003). *Explorations in language acquisition and use: The Taipei lectures.* Portsmouth, NH: Heinemann.

Lickey, D. C., & Powers, D. J. (2011). *Starting with their strengths: Using the Project Approach in early childhood special education.* New York, NY: Teachers College Press.

Magruder, E. S., Hayslip, W. W., Espinosa, L. M., & Matera, C. (2013). Many languages, one teacher: Supporting language and literacy development for preschool dual language learners. *Young Children, 68*(1), 8–15.

Meier, D. R. (2004). *The young child's memory for words: Developing first and second language and literacy.* New York, NY: Teachers College Press.

Meltzer, L. (Ed.). (2018). *Executive function in education: From theory to practice* (2nd ed.). New York, NY: Guilford.

Moll, L. C., Amanti, C., Neff, D., & González, N. (2005). Funds of knowledge for teaching: Using a qualitative approach to connect homes and classrooms. In N. González, L. C. Moll, & C. Amanti (Eds.), *Funds of knowledge: Theorizing practices in households, communities, and classrooms* (pp. 71–88). New York, NY: Routledge. doi.org/10.4324/9781410613462

Moran, S., & Gardner, H. (2018). Hill, skill, and will: Executive function from a multiple-intelligences perspective. In L. Meltzer (Ed.), *Executive function in education: From theory to practice* (pp. 25–56). New York, NY: Guilford Press.

Oates, J., Karmiloff-Smith, A., & Johnson, M. (Eds.). (2012). *Developing brains. Early childhood in focus, 7.* Milton Keynes, UK: The Open University.

Raver, C. C., & Blair, C. (2016). Neuroscientific insights: Attention, working memory, and inhibitory control. *The Future of Children, 26*(2), 95–118.

Rueda, M. R., Checa, P., & Combita, L. M. (2012). Enhanced efficiency of the executive attention network after training in preschool children: Immediate changes and effects after two months. *Developmental Cognitive Neuroscience, 2,* S192–S204.

Snider, K., Holley, M., & Usman, A. (2017). *Final report: Project ABC²—Adults building capacities for young children.* Commissioned program evaluation report for Project ABC²—Adults building capacities for young children. Kansas City, MO: Greater Kansas City Community Foundation Grant.

U.S. Department of Education. (2017). *English language learners in public schools.* National Center for Education Statistics, EDFacts file 141, Data Group 678, extracted July 21, 2017; and Common Core of Data (CCD), "State Nonfiscal Survey of

Public Elementary and Secondary Education," 2015–2016. See *Digest of Education Statistics 2017*, table 204.27. Available at nces.ed.gov/programs/coe/indicator_cgf.asp

Vartuli, S., Bolz, C., & Wilson, C. (2014). A learning combination: Coaching with CLASS and the Project Approach. *Early Childhood Research & Practice, 16*(1), 1–13.

Whorrall, J., & Cabell, S. Q. (2016). Supporting children's oral language development in the preschool classroom. *Early Childhood Education Journal, 44*(4), 335–341.

WIDA. (2017). *WIDA Early Years guiding principles of language development*. Madison, WI: Board of Regents of the University of Wisconsin System. Available at wida.wisc.edu/resources/wida-early-years-guiding-principles-language-development

Zelazo, P. D., Blair, C. B., & Willoughby, M. T. (2016). *Executive function: Implications for education* (NCER 2017-2000). Washington, DC: National Center for Education Research, Institute of Education Sciences, U.S. Department of Education. Available at ies.ed.gov/ncer/pubs/20172000/pdf/20172000.pdf

---

VOICES FROM THE FIELD

The Reptile Project

Crystal Woodin, Kindergarten Teacher

Ensuring every child's success in school is what teachers strive for every day. We create lesson plans to help children achieve, collaborate, and dig deep into data, and we start each day with the determination to reach all children. Yet, I have observed that some young children struggle in school for a variety of reasons. For instance, I noticed that some children especially struggle when learning through teacher-directed or traditional district-required curriculum. Instead, I have found that for all children, but especially for children who learn differently, the Project Approach provides access to interesting topics, which increases children's engagement and motivation to learn, and builds important skills and confidence they carry into other learning activities.

A few years back, I had a truly inclusive kindergarten classroom in Prairie Branch Elementary School (Grain Valley, Missouri). I was a co-teacher with an early childhood special education teacher and a full-time paraprofessional. Several of the children came to us with individualized learning plans, which meant they needed specialized instruction or specific early learning strategies due to developmental delays, speech and language impairments, and other challenges such as post-traumatic stress disorder. Several children received related services that year, such as physical therapy and occupational therapy. With a room full of eager kindergartners, we were excited to integrate the Project Approach into our curriculum because we believed it to be a good fit for supporting the different ways in which individual children learn.

PHASE I: BEGINNING THE PROJECT

Project work began because of our classroom pet Echo the Gecko. Once the pet arrived, children's questions started rolling in, and that's when the Reptile Project started. At first, questions were specific to just the gecko, but then they branched out to the entire reptile family:

Gecko Questions

- Can geckos stick on walls?
- Why do they shed their skin?
- How do they eat big bugs with little mouths?
- Do geckos fly?
- How do their Mommies and Daddies leave them?

Alligator Questions

- Why do people shoot alligators?
- Can they change colors?
- Is an alligator and a crocodile the same?
- How do alligators know a predator is near?
- If an alligator flips over to his back and stays there, does he fall asleep?

Snake Questions

- How do they get away from predators who are trying to eat them?
- Are some snakes poisonous?
- Can they eat an egg?
- What snake is the biggest?
- How do they shed their skin?

Turtle Questions
- How do turtles walk?
- How long do they stay in their shells?
- How do the babies get out of their eggs?
- What is the difference between turtles and tortoises?
- Do they eat scorpions?

During this project, students kept asking more and more questions. Because of this, we had some unique experts help us answer questions and learn more about reptiles (see Figure 5.14). We met with one child's older brother in middle school and conservationists from the Missouri Department of Conservation, and we talked via Skype with two cast members from the television show *Swamp People* and with two different zoos. We even took a weekend field trip to the Kansas City Reptile Show.

The cycle kept going until a class of sixteen 5- and 6-year-olds had asked almost 50 questions. I was excited to see their really good questions. The questions led us to many different opportunities to accomplish numerous Missouri Learning Standards. For this project alone, we met 28 standards in an integrated way, which is how we know children learn best.

PHASE II: INVESTIGATION

One kindergarten boy started the year displaying physically aggressive behaviors; however, he found he had the ability to share with others during the Reptile Project. Learning many strategies during project work, he went from having daily outbursts to really looking forward to learning with others during our project time. Before the Reptile Project, he seldom wrote even his name. By the end of the Reptile Project, he was writing independently. In completing work for the culminating event, he used a full sentence to describe his illustration about a sea turtle. He was so interested in the topic and the classroom experiences that he literally could not wait for project work time. He displayed more appropriate and typical behaviors of a kindergartner and had found a way to become a whole different learner. When I asked him why he liked our Reptile Project so much, he said, "The other school stuff is too hard, and I am not good at it. But I am good at lizards." A project of high interest allowed him to take risks and engage appropriately with others, which increased his motivation to learn. As a result, he developed confidence that he had not had in other curricular experiences. He now believed in himself as a learner.

One really meaningful expert visitor was the older brother of one of our students who had speech and language challenges. The big brother had also struggled academically when he was younger. The brothers' parents shared that reptiles as pets were a huge motivator for their older son and an avenue that they would later use to help him succeed in school. It was a perfect match for our project, so he became one of our experts.

Armed with the children's questions, the older brother created his own presentation for our class. With his mom watching, he excelled in teaching her youngest son's kindergarten class about geckos. The study of reptiles had become an opportunity in which he, and now my kindergartners, had learned so much. Most important, the children had grown socially, emotionally, and intellectually as capable learners.

The younger brother with special needs could not have been prouder. He beamed from ear to ear to have his big brother and mother there in our classroom working with us on our project. He was a huge contributor to the questions and conversations during that specific guest expert visit. This child with speech and language challenges who typically did not raise his hand during other lessons, who appeared shy and soft spoken, had finally found his voice during investigations on a worthy topic.

PHASE III: CULMINATING THE PROJECT

To culminate this project the children decided to make a movie about reptiles and show it in a "movie theatre." They wanted our classroom to look like a real movie theatre, and each student took on a job for the grand opening. We had ushers, ticket takers, and a concession stand. To display their reptile knowledge, the children created representations of reptiles in a variety of media (see Figures

FIGURE 5.14 • Kindergartners created thank you cards for experts, showing the experts what they had learned from them.

FIGURE 5.15 • Children used iPads to research favorite reptiles and create reptile renderings in preparation for the culminating event.

FIGURE 5.16 • Clay reptile representations were shared with families at the culminating event.

5.15 and 5.16) and produced movie posters for the event (see Figure 5.17).

Our documentation covered all three phases of the project and detailed what standards we had met. We had more than 50 people in attendance, and the parents were thrilled by the children's attention to detail and all of their questions and work throughout the project.

The Project Approach lets every child shine. Children who learn differently in school find new opportunities to learn within projects. Featuring a team of child investigators, co-teaching support systems, and family engagement, our kindergarten classroom that year became a model of how inclusive classrooms can be a vital place to learn.

FIGURE 5.17 • Movie poster for *The Reptile Show*

CHAPTER 6

Professional Development Models to Support Teaching with the Project Approach

*Carol Bolz, Catherine Wilson, Erika Gray, Pam Scranton,
Lisa Roti, Pegi Stamps, & Liz Smith*

CHARACTERISTICS OF SUCCESSFUL PROGRAMS

Catherine Wilson & Carol Bolz

Reading about the Project Approach or attending presentations at conferences often inspires teachers, administrators, and families to think about how such intellectually rich classrooms might come to life in their communities. The children seem so capable, the teachers so engaged in thinking with the children, and the families and community so involved as valued participants in learning during project work. Teachers ask, "Could I do this in my classroom?" Administrators think, "What would it take to bring the Project Approach to our program?" And families and communities wonder, "Why not for our children?"

Yet, learning to support young children's intellectual development through the Project Approach can seem daunting. As shown in the Delphi study discussed in Part III, teachers might doubt their ability to make the Project Approach part of their curriculum or feel that their classroom is too large or diverse. Administrators might struggle with competing priorities. And families and communities might worry whether children will be prepared.

This chapter explores these concerns by describing four different programs of professional development in the Project Approach that are working. While each has its own history and context, all share the following characteristics:

- *An understanding that teachers need to build knowledge about the Project Approach.* The Project Approach has a definite structure that helps teachers plan and organize experiences with children. The programs described in this chapter each provide initial training for teachers and, often, administrators.

- *An ongoing support mechanism for teachers and administrators as they translate training into practice.* Structures and strategies have been developed to provide ample opportunities for teachers to refine, evaluate, and share their work with one another, ensuring that the work is sustained.
- *An appreciation of the importance of collaboration with the community.* Universities, nature groups, children's museums, churches, families, and foundations partner with early learning programs to bring the Project Approach to young children.
- *An emphasis on the critical role of making the work public.* It is sometimes challenging to explain and advocate for the Project Approach. The four programs described in this chapter have found that providing a platform for teachers to share stories of children's investigations is an effective strategy for contributing to knowledge in the field—and beyond. At the heart of making the work public is helping others to see children differently—to recognize their capabilities as collaborators, creators, problem solvers, and thinkers.

KOHL CHILDREN'S MUSEUM EARLY CHILDHOOD CONNECTIONS PROGRAM

Erika Gray

In 2001, the Kohl Children's Museum of Greater Chicago began an initiative titled Early Childhood Connections (ECC) that focused on professional development in implementation of the Project Approach. Participants were teachers of children in prekindergarten through 3rd grade in schools where more than 40% of the students receive free or reduced-price lunch. Research on the effects of poverty on both student learning and school resources in the Chicago Public School (CPS) System was the impetus for the program.

Overview of the Kohl ECC Program

The Kohl Early Childhood Connections Program is designed to achieve the following goals:

- To increase the use of Project Approach learning and developmentally appropriate practices in Chicago and Lake County public schools, prekindergarten through 3rd grade
- To increase the positive attitudes of public school teachers toward Project Approach learning
- To provide parents with opportunities to play an active role in their children's education

The underlying principles of the Kohl ECC program are grounded in the Museum's belief that children learn best when they are engaged, motivated, intrinsically curious, and, most of all, having fun. The program utilizes the Project Approach, which, as explained earlier in this book, encourages children to formulate questions, seek out and discover answers, consider their findings, and form conclusions. In this environment, teachers become the facilitators of learning rather than distributors of knowledge. The Project Approach also allows children to explore and learn in their own way and fosters the development of critical thinking, cooperation, and communication skills. The Kohl ECC program is supported by government, foundation, corporate, and individual donations.

Since the Kohl ECC program began in 2001, the Chicago Public Schools administration has taken an active role in identifying schools serving young children in underserved communities and working with the Kohl Museum to expand its ECC offerings throughout the entire city. In 2005, the Museum expanded the program to include teachers from Waukegan Public Schools, a suburb of Chicago, and in 2007 created a sister program for family- and center-based child care providers in Cook and Lake counties, Illinois. From 2001 to 2007, the Museum focused its ECC efforts specifically on training teachers to implement the Project Approach in their classrooms using the Kohl Children's Museum as a resource and learning laboratory.

Since 2002, the Kohl ECC school district program has served 42,687 public school children and parents and 1,099 teachers, including teachers in bilingual and special education classrooms. Since 2007, the Kohl ECC child care program has served 24,307 children and their families, and 784 family- and center-based child care providers.

Kohl ECC Training and Professional Development. The Kohl ECC training module consists of three professional development days. The first two days of training include foundational work for understanding the three phases of the Project Approach and how to support children in project work. Teachers learn to observe children's interests and provide a platform for them to learn how to ask questions and then investigate to find out the answers. Teachers learn about using experts, artifacts, and site visits to support children's learning. The third and final day of professional development takes place after participants have completed their projects during the school year. This is a time for teachers to share project work with colleagues, reflect on their journey, examine types of documentation, and share children's learning with various audiences.

Program Evaluation

To evaluate the success of the Kohl ECC program, ongoing research and evaluation have been conducted. Each year, participants in the program complete an attitude survey before and after the professional development training. This 11-item Likert-type attitude survey reflecting the principles of the Project Approach is used to determine participants' understandings and comfort levels with the implementation of project work in their classrooms.

As part of the research evaluation during 2001–2006, researchers conducted observations within intervention and control classrooms. The intervention group consisted of teachers in the Kohl ECC program who had received training and were actively conducting projects. The control group was made up of teachers who did not receive any services. Both groups were observed in their classrooms at the beginning and end of the Kohl ECC programming cycles. Observers used an observation instrument based on the Early Childhood Environment Rating Scale (Harms, Clifford, & Cryer, 1998) to observe selected items of interest. Observers also collected data regarding the teachers' abilities to align goals and standards set by the National Association for the Education of Young Children, Illinois State Board of Education, and Chicago Public Schools with the Project Approach.

Applying the data from surveys and observations, the research and evaluation team used a pre- and post-test control group design, which included controlling for differences between the intervention and control groups. Results included evidence that the Kohl ECC program is producing statistically significant and practically meaningful positive changes in the use of developmentally appropriate methods and strategies by early childhood teachers (Kohl Children's Museum, n.d.). The teacher surveys also showed positive changes in teacher attitudes toward the Project Approach. In sum, data analysis indicated the effectiveness of professional development provided through a collaboration between children's museums and public schools.

Participants also provide evaluations for each professional development workshop, the focused field trips, and the parent/child workshops. Feedback from teachers and parents has indicated that the professional development workshops remain valuable and that the field trips are positive experiences. Testimonials are anecdotal evidence of the participants' perception of the effectiveness of the Kohl ECC program.

Training of Trainers

In 2005, the Museum worked with Judy Harris Helm to design and conduct a Train-the-Trainer program for the Early Childhood Connections Program called the Early Childhood Connections Academy (ECCA). This 2½-year study program was intended for teachers who were interested in expanding their knowledge of project-based learning and sharing the value of this approach with others. Training modules focused on specific areas of content: Presentation Skills and Strategies, Family Involvement in Project-Based Learning, Documenting Children's Projects, and Evaluation and Assessment of Projects and Presentations. In the fall of 2007, ECCA teachers became the new trainers/facilitators for the Early Childhood Connections Program.

Over the next few years, results from pre/post observations and attitudinal surveys showed a pattern of positive increase in teacher behaviors, but teachers still wanted more training on deepening their understandings and use of the Project Approach. They inquired whether the Museum had additional resources to support that need.

So, in 2010, the Museum's education team and Judy spent time brainstorming ideas of what this next phase would be, and through that process they developed a Level 2 program for past participants that provided more in-depth training on teacher interactions and the elements of an entire project. In 2011, the Level 2—Deepening Project Work (DPW) program was offered to past participants. With the development of DPW, the Museum consulted with Douglas Powell and Judy Harris Helm on creating a fidelity scale as an observation tool designed to collect data on project work. The fidelity scale was used for four years, and through many drafts, and the developers concluded it was better designed for use as a coaching tool—the Kohl Project Approach Assessment and Coaching Tool (Powell et al., 2013).

To continue support efforts for their ECC program, in the fall of 2017 the Museum piloted an online community of practice website: www.projectapproachconnections.org. Through the use of newsletters, blog posts, and project boards, the website served as a platform for educators to post questions to colleagues and find resources in content areas focusing on phases of project work and project examples. Throughout the pilot year, data were collected on user visits to the website, pages visited, and surveys. At the end of the year, the Museum conducted a focus group to collect feedback from users. Since then the website has been adapted to make it easier for educators to use as a Project Approach resource to find project examples, support on topic selection, and other content related to phases of project, artifacts, site visits, and experts.

BECOMING YOUNG THINKERS SUMMER INSTITUTE

Pam Scranton

The Becoming Young Thinkers (BYT) Summer Institute began in 2013 at UPC Discovery, a Reggio-inspired, faith-based preschool, which is a ministry of the United Presbyterian Church (Peoria, Illinois). The preschool provides a setting for teachers to immerse their "teacher brain" in the Project Approach.

How BYT Began

The BYT Summer Institute was designed to be the kind of professional development program that the BYT leadership team would have wished to attend ourselves. The topics and activities were based on our own experiences of the challenges of learning to implement projects. We knew teachers would benefit from training that gives them opportunities to get into classrooms set up for project work, to view examples of really well-done documentation of projects, to practice skills presented by trainers, and to reflect on their own practice. The format at the institute is a series of learning experiences that follow a repeated sequence of *Focused Presentations, Hands-on Coached Practice,* followed by *Reflective Processing,* referred to as PPR.

The first institute provided training for teachers new to project work and was called Young Investigators. As beginning teachers became more confident implementing projects in the classroom, more questions emerged:

- How do we deepen and extend the children's questioning skills?
- How can we extend the children's understanding of the topic?
- What is the impact of project work on intellectual development as it relates to Mind Brain Education Science?

The Level 2 session, Deepening Project Work, was added to the institute in Year 2 and has continued every year since. Designed to support teachers who have had basic training and completed at least two projects in their classrooms, this session provides more advanced skills in facilitating project work such as teaching children how to ask questions, provoking student thinking, and guiding representations to deepen their project work. The participants from both BYT groups come together for some of the sessions, including updates on neuroscience applications to learning, visits to the Documentation Gallery (where documentation of projects from the last school year is displayed), and optional discussion groups on topics of interest that are offered during the 90-minute lunch break.

Unique Features of BYT

Every BYT participant completes an online survey from the Concerns-Based Adoption Model (CBAM) (www.air.org/resource/concerns-based-adoption-model-cbam) as applied to their work with the Project Approach, providing information on ages or grade levels of students they teach, years of teaching, context of teaching, previous training, and books read regarding the Project Approach. The CBAM survey samples beliefs, attitudes, and concerns about supporting project work. This information is analyzed and used to be sure that the participants are in the most appropriate level of training and is also used to form groups and match coaches to groups.

One of the components of BYT that ensures its success is the availability of experienced teachers-as-coaches. These coaches volunteer their time, their knowledge, and their energy to support teachers as they learn about project work (see Figure 6.1). The beginning level teachers actually do a project as an adult, going through the project processes from both the teacher and the child perspective. As these beginning teachers web their topics, conduct field site investigations, and represent the data collected in the art studio, the teacher coaches are beside them, mentoring and supporting their learning.

On the evening of the Institute's second day, the teacher coaches and other advanced training participants present their own project work in *Pecha Kucha*. Japanese for "a little chat," *Pecha Kucha* often takes place in other professions and gives architects, lawyers, engineers, and doctors an opportunity to present their best ideas, their best work. On *Pecha Kucha* project night, teachers share their best project work in presentations of 20 slides shown 20 seconds each.

FIGURE 6.1 • As participants complete projects in small groups, a coach observes, facilitates, and models the process of guiding projects.

FIGURE 6.2 • By working in the studio, participants experience the process of representation and what will make that process more effective for children.

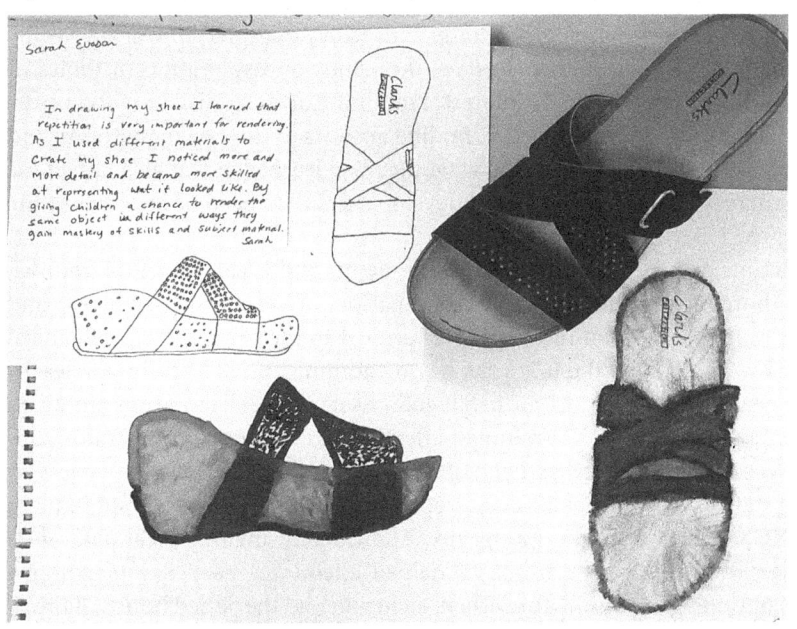

FIGURE 6.3 • Participants in the Moss Project found answers to some of their questions from their expert, Randy, the Nature Ranger.

Another unique feature of the Institute is access to the toddler and preschool classrooms at UPC Discovery, which remain set up from the last project completed during the school year. Participants have opportunities to study documentation and classroom arrangements specific to encouraging deep project work and are encouraged to bring cameras so they can "capture" these environments to share with colleagues at their home school or program.

One of the most popular activities for both beginning and advanced participants is time in the preschool studio, where participants experience a variety of media and learn how to support children's observational drawing and use of other materials to represent what they are learning (see Figure 6.2).

UPC Discovery has an Arbor Day Foundation-certified Nature Explore Classroom, and the school is committed to strengthening children's connection to nature, including focusing many projects on nature topics. BYT participants have opportunities to stroll the campus, hike on the trails through the woods, and observe children and Nature Rangers playing in the Nature Explore Classroom (see Figure 6.3).

The Becoming Young Thinkers Summer Institute is planned, organized, and hosted by the UPC Discovery teachers and administrators, the UPC Discovery Preschool committee, the UPC Nature Connections committee, the United Presbyterian Church office staff, and the church's congregation members. It truly takes a village.

NATURE CONNECTIONS: THE POWER OF COLLABORATION

Lisa Roti

In 2006, the seed of an idea sprouted on the shores of West Lake Okoboji, Iowa. This notion was planted when a small group of formal and informal educators at Iowa Lakeside Laboratory attempted to deliver nature-based professional development to early childhood teachers.

Responding to Concerns for Integration of Nature into Classrooms

Lakeside Lab, a 147-acre field research station, has been educating students for the past 110 years in northwestern Iowa. Having offered one-shot, fragmented bursts of teacher renewal credit summer after summer, the educators felt something was lacking. While the nature-oriented workshops were successful, teachers would often lament they had no time to implement what was learned due to the demands of required standards and curriculum.

Adding to the group's concern was mounting evidence regarding *nature deficit* in young children. According to author Richard Louv (2008), today's youth are spending less and less time outdoors. His research points to increasing levels of behavioral problems, obesity, and depression associated with children who do not spend enough time in nature. He goes on to express his worry over the "human costs of alienation from nature" (p. 36).

Determined to help with these two concerns, the Nature Connections (NC) team was formed with nearly a dozen committed agencies and organizations. Comprised of Lakeside Lab, Head Start, Child Care and Resource Referral, and Iowa Area Education Agency (AEA) staff, as well as college faculty and retired educators, the NC team went back to the drawing board in an effort to better train early childhood teachers. They reviewed countless options while hunting for a model that could provide effective nature-based professional development. The team was ultimately drawn to the compelling work of Judy Harris Helm on the Project Approach and brain-based learning. After much discussion with Judy and subsequent development, Young Investigators: Connecting Children with Nature Through Project Work was born.

Launching the Nature-Based Project Approach

The Young Investigators (YI) program began at Lakeside in the fall of 2012 with an invitation to the first cohort of participants. Each cohort's make-up would include seven teams from area school districts. These teams were required to include preschool teachers, their associates, and administrators. County naturalists were also encouraged to attend the trainings.

Program funding was secured from a number of sources. Course registration fees were received from the participating teams. Grants were obtained from Iowa's Department of Natural Resources REAP-CEP program, as well as from the Friends of Lakeside Lab, a nonprofit organization at Lakeside, and the Patrice Leary Foundation. A considerable amount of financial support also stemmed from in-kind donations of staff time from Upper Des Moines Opportunity's Head Start, Iowa Lakeside Lab, Prairie Lakes AEA, Northwest AEA, and others.

Each cohort would take part in three years of YI training led by Judy Helm: Year 1—four days, Year 2—two days, and Year 3—one day. The goal was to offer sustained deep learning for teachers across time, which is rare in today's professional development landscape. It was expected that a nature-based Project Approach would help teachers assist children in investigating, exploring, questioning, predicting, documenting, and deeply engaging in learning while in nature. Besides the hands-on exploration of topics of children's interest, examining artifacts, listening to nonfiction literature, finding answers to their own questions, and documenting what they had learned, it was also hoped the children would develop a desire to become stewards of the environment.

In addition to the depth and breadth of this training, the requisite combination of teachers, associates, and administrators was critical to the program. As evidenced in the first year, having administrators learn beside teachers was an invaluable asset. This collaboration amplified the YI training's effectiveness. Strong administrator support has been shown to bolster teacher effectiveness in initial teacher implementation and then in subsequent program longevity. Additionally, inviting local naturalists to the trainings helped encourage participants' comfort with nature. Their inclusion had the added bonus of introducing teachers to the naturalists who would later become the "experts" in their classrooms.

The first cohort's success led to the continued roll-out of several more: Cohort II in 2013–2014 and Cohort III in 2014–2015.

Adding a Coaching Component

After reviewing teacher post-attitude survey data, the NC team decided to add a coaching component. Starting in the fall of 2013, each early childhood teacher was paired with an NC team member as a coach. This was done in an effort to help support teachers throughout their training and facilitate the implementation of the nature-based Project Approach with fidelity. Evidence shows that coaching can increase the odds of application of newly acquired skills by educators from 25% to 90% (Joyce & Showers, 2002). This follow-up coaching concept proved to be an effective component within the YI program, as pre/post-attitude teacher surveys indicated. As one teacher remarked, "It does help to have a coach to bounce ideas off of and to answer questions as they arise, and just to be there for support when it gets frustrating."

As the YI program progressed, coaches began to observe a shift from teacher-directed to child-centered methodology. Rather than seeing classrooms filled with identical pumpkin themes each fall, NC team members observed child-driven, authentic projects on topics ranging from millipedes to beavers (see Figure 6.4). The impact of the YI training on teacher confidence with nature and outdoor learning was also apparent.

FIGURE 6.4 • Children investigating nature

As Sue Dietering, T–K teacher at Emmetsburg, Iowa, reflected:

> The children have a natural curiosity for nature, and, as teachers, we have grown in our comfort. It is fun when children first find worms and are so scared to touch them, but with encouragement from teachers and friends, end up loving the experience and learning so much through their investigations. This may never have happened without the Project Approach trainings. [see Figure 6.5]

Deepening the YI Program

With the graduation of Cohort I in April 2015, the NC team set to work to determine the project's future. A series of discussions ensued, including a virtual meeting with program stakeholders such as parents, teachers, and administrators. These conversations led to two conclusions. First, without continued support, teachers may not sustain the nature-based Project Approach in their classrooms. Second, the education community from area school districts to state universities had persisted in requesting additional opportunities for the YI training. With this in mind, the team decided to begin a fourth cohort and add a Year 4 for Cohort I in 2015–2016. The Year 4 curriculum was developed to further deepen and add rigor to the YI program.

The 2016–2017 school year continued as planned with two cohorts continuing their work, in addition to a second Year 4 group. In response to requests to deal with staff turnover in previously trained districts, the team chose to develop a Basics of Project Approach class for the fall of 2016. This solution provided a two-day training for any teacher, associate, or administrator who was replacing staff that had graduated from the YI program. While the two-day training was not nearly as extensive as the three-year version, it enabled new staff to have at least a rudimentary understanding of the nature-based Project Approach.

As 2017 wound to a close, so did the initial chapter in Lakeside Lab's Young Investigators teacher professional development program. Cohort IV completed their third and final year of the training. The Basics Class was offered for a second time. Head Start renewed their commitment to have teachers complete two projects a year in their classrooms (with at least one having to be nature-based). The NC team continued to meet on a monthly basis to ascertain the future of YI and to develop strategies for perpetuating this powerful approach to education.

Sustaining Nature-Based Learning

Moving forward, the NC team is committed to sustaining and promoting nature-based learning. Teachers continue to be supported with integrating nature and the outdoors into their classrooms through project work. This has been accomplished in a variety of ways, including offering an online college credit course, Early Childhood Nature-

FIGURE 6.5 • Where is the worm?

Based Learning through the Project Approach, at the University of Iowa, hosting the Basics of Project Approach class at Lakeside Lab each fall, and maintaining the NC website (www.natureconnections.org) as an ongoing resource for teachers. Finally, Facebook, Twitter, Zoom, and an annual "Project Sharing Celebration" in northwestern Iowa have enabled teachers to stay connected with the NC team, coaches, and each other.

Seven years ago, the Nature Connections group began a quest to bring the nature-based Project Approach into preschool classrooms. This has been accomplished as approximately 800 teachers, associates, and administrators in a series of four cohorts have each successfully completed the three-year training. The implementation of this child-centered, nature-oriented teaching method has impacted over 5,000 preschool students across Iowa to date. Without question, neither the Young Investigators program nor its success in classrooms would have occurred without collaboration. The cooperative efforts of the Nature Connections team along with teachers, associates, administrators, naturalists, and area experts have been instrumental in the delivery of a much-needed, long-overdue initiative focused on the health and well-being of young children.

COACHING WITH THE PROJECT APPROACH AND CLASS

Carol Bolz, Pegi Stamps, Liz Smith, & Catherine Wilson

For many years, a small group of Head Start leaders and education coordinators, along with partners from the higher-education community in Kansas City, Missouri, studied the cognitive development of young children and the professional development of their teachers. As we engaged and collaborated through coursework, conference attendance, and shared reading about children's thinking, we became increasingly committed to the Project Approach to curriculum (Helm & Katz, 2016; Katz, Chard, & Kogan, 2014). We learned to rely on the theories of John Dewey (1897, 1910, 1916, 1938) and William Kilpatrick (1918).

Although we hold no claim to being Dewey experts, we have been guided by the following ideas in particular:

- Central to thinking is an element of wondering, questioning, and feeling uncertainty that sets the stage for inquiry.
- Powerful thinking occurs when children and adults share the work of inquiry, and in the process build a sense of community.
- Learning flourishes when there is a connection between education and real-world experience. Projects are a method of investigating the real world.
- Children and teachers learn with opportunities to represent experiences (e.g., telling, drawing, dramatic play, writing, constructing).

These ideas are woven into the work of young children engaged in the Project Approach. They also informed our thinking and decision making as we sought to bring active, engaged learning to a larger number of young children and their teachers in our city.

Building Our Professional Community

In 2006, Sue Vartuli, University of Missouri–Kansas City, and Catherine Wilson, Park University, Parkville, Missouri, approached Mid-America Head Start education coordinators and offered support for teacher development. (Mid-America Head Start is a network of ten community-based and eight school district programs serving approximately 2,500 children across three counties of the Kansas City, Missouri, region.) The education coordinators, whose responsibilities included coaching and teacher development, gladly accepted the offer, and the group began meeting monthly. We built relationships by discussing readings about an inquiry approach to professional development (Catapano, 2005; Helterbran & Fennimore, 2004) and sharing examples of effective coaching strategies, such as sitting side by side with teachers to analyze videos of their practice. After this time spent in relationship building, thinking together, and discussion, we were on the lookout for shared work.

A Required Standard—An Unexpected Gift

In 2008, an opportunity for strengthening our coaching community of practice through shared work arose. The Office of Head Start identified the Classroom Assessment Scoring System (CLASS) Pre-K for federal monitoring of Head Start grantees and encouraged its use for teacher development. CLASS (Pianta, LaParo, & Hamre, 2008) is a classroom observation instrument validated to describe the types of teacher–child interactions that lead to enhanced social and academic outcomes for children. We felt sure that Mid-America Head Start classrooms, much like those rated in the national studies of CLASS, would need to improve the interactions described in the Instructional Support Domain. (The Instructional Support Domain is one of three CLASS domains, and it includes three dimensions: Concept Development, which describes interactions that support children's thinking and cognition; Quality of Feedback, which describes responsive interactions that lead to children's deeper understanding and expanded participation; and Language Modeling, which describes interactions that facilitate children's language and vocabulary acquisition.)

Our coaching community began to grapple with strategies for including CLASS in our support of teachers. We recognized that teacher–child interactions in our programs, as rated with CLASS, would need improvement and hoped that coaching could be an effective approach for doing so. We decided to request funding from the H & R Block Foundation for providing intensive coaching as well as researching and analyzing the results. We were beginning to appreciate that CLASS, in addition to setting new standards for our Head Start program, was offering us a useful perspective for our inquiry into children's thinking and teacher development.

Coaching with CLASS

We immersed ourselves in learning about coaching and the CLASS tool. Head Start education coordinators, eager to further define the role of coaching in teacher development, participated in Strengths-Based Coaching training (Humbarger, 2012). Sue and Catherine became certified as CLASS trainers and provided CLASS Pre-K Observer training to Head Start education coordinators, who would use CLASS as a framework for coaching.

Each education coordinator (coach) invited one or two teachers to be part of our inquiry, and the teachers were given introductory training on CLASS. Teachers began meeting weekly with coaches to analyze their own interactions with children through the lens of the CLASS tool. They identified goals and implemented strategies for improving their interactions with children. They reviewed progress toward such interactions as analysis and reasoning, creating, connections to the real world, and prompting thought processes. Seeking to engage in practices congruent with their work with teachers, coaches met monthly to share what they were discovering about coaching.

At the end of the 2008–2009 program year, coaches met with Sue, Catherine, and Mid-America Head Start leaders. Sue shared the results of her research, which showed modest but promising gains in CLASS ratings. As we discussed the results of the first year and planned for the second year, we acknowledged the value of the CLASS tool in pinpointing effective teacher–child interactions. However, we felt we had not supported teachers in grounding the interactions in the learning experiences of the classroom. The interactions seemed disconnected from experience, and therefore, less effective in promoting deeper thinking. This realization became the turning point for our shared work.

"Consideration of Some Solution for the Problem"

Reenter John Dewey (1910) and his description of how we think:

- The origin of thinking is some perplexity, confusion, or doubt.
- Given a difficulty or question, the next step is a suggestion of some way out, a theory, the "consideration of some solution for the problem." (p. 12)
- The source of suggestions is past experience and prior knowledge.
- To think, to reflect means to hunt for additional evidence and data.
- The difference between good and bad thinking (corroborating or refuting the theory) is found at this point.

We believed that deeper thinking was most likely to occur when there were interesting experiences and ideas for children and teachers to think about with one another. How would we connect effective teacher–child interactions with learning experiences to more fully support children's intellectual development?

Our suggestion of a possible solution was informed by our past experiences and previous knowledge of the Project Approach. We had experienced the Project Approach in a variety of ways. Some coaches had studied the Project Approach in graduate courses with Sue and Catherine and facilitated projects as teachers in Head Start classrooms. Some had attended Project Approach training at Kohl Children's Museum. Many had read the writings of Lilian Katz, Sylvia Chard, and Judy Harris Helm or attended presentations at national conferences.

We were convinced that the Project Approach to curriculum provided a structure for the types of learning experiences that promote the development of positive intellectual dispositions. Therefore, we decided to integrate the Project Approach into the coaching with CLASS and continue to research the results. Would our research corroborate or refute our thinking?

Coaching with the Project Approach plus CLASS

A critical element would be the research. We wanted to know if pairing the Project Approach with CLASS in our coaching for teachers would make a difference in CLASS scores. Beyond interest in benefits to our Head Start grantee, we saw the potential for providing much-needed research about the Project Approach to our field. If we were anticipating a broader audience for the research, the Project Approach would need to be implemented with fidelity. Sue set to work developing a Project Approach

Fidelity measure to accompany the measures she had selected to research coaching with CLASS. This was no small task.

Building Basic Knowledge

We knew that if we wanted teachers to implement the Project Approach with fidelity, and coaches to support their efforts, we needed to provide opportunities to build basic knowledge. Judy Harris Helm visited Kansas City to introduce the Project Approach in 3-hour trainings for Head Start teachers, coaches, and leaders. These presentations helped us become more mindful readers of *Young Investigators: The Project Approach in the Early Years* (Helm & Katz, 2016). Sue's Project Approach Fidelity form became a useful tool for describing what classrooms sound and look like when projects are under way. The focus for teachers and coaches in the second year shifted to facilitating the Project Approach with young children. Coaches helped teachers recognize opportunities for the interactions captured in the CLASS tool that naturally occur during project work.

Catherine assumed the role of consultant to coaches and teachers. She visited them at their sites—18 programs spread across three counties. She recognized that many of the ways of thinking together with children as they investigated real-world topics were unfamiliar to teachers and coaches. As Helm and Katz (2016) recommend, they initially focused on learning the structure and phases of projects to build their certainty.

Eventually, Catherine urged teachers and coaches to take the less certain step of studying what happened when they shared the decision making with children. For example, Catherine met monthly with George Garrett and Anita Gomes-Stewart, a teacher–coach pair from the YMCA of Greater Kansas City Head Start. During a Tree Project, George had asked children to count the trees at their homes and planned to graph the results. He wondered how to get the most thinking out of the experience of representing their findings. During an animated discussion, the three decided to turn a blank, chart-sized paper over to a small group of children and see what they would do. Back in the classroom, Mr. George observed as the children engaged in a lively discussion and process of their own, making decisions about the baseline of the graph and the size of the tallies. (See results in Figure 6.6.) In moments such as this, children stepped into the role of protagonist, showing the adults what capable thinkers they are. Their highly motivated activity helped persuade teachers and coaches to involve them directly in planning, problem solving, and decision making in the classroom.

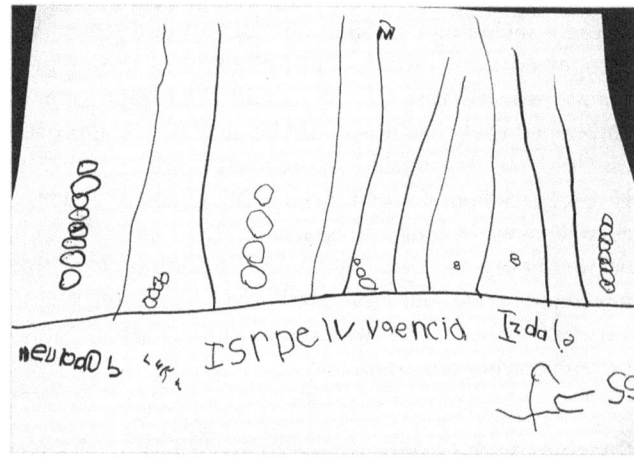

FIGURE 6.6 • At a monthly Mid-America Head Start coaches meeting, YMCA of Greater Kansas City Head Start teacher George Garrett and Coach Anita Gomes-Stewart made their work public, discussing the children's creation of the tree graph.

Making the Work Public

Catherine continued to consult with coaches and teachers, learning from and with them. She acted as a link among the programs, identifying work and discoveries that might be spotlighted. Based on our belief that we understand our work more fully when we help others to see it in action, teachers and coaches were invited to share their project work and coaching strategies at monthly meetings. We also gathered all teachers and coaches together at the end of each year to describe projects and celebrate young investigators.

We wished to contribute to knowledge of the Project Approach in our field, so we wrote articles and presented at national conferences. Some teachers and coaches were co-presenters and offered their firsthand accounts of thinking with children. Each time, we were reminded that learning occurs when we tell our stories, represent our experiences, and share our thinking with others.

Research Results Corroborate Our Thinking

At the end of the 2009–2010 program year, Sue again shared her research results. She found that greater fidelity of implementation of the Project Approach predicted higher CLASS scores, not only for the Instructional Support Domain but for all three domains. Our theory about the Project Approach being the curricular context for more effective teacher–child interactions was corroborated.

Encouraged by the results, we decided to continue our inquiry. We received funding from the Office of Head Start

Early Learning Mentor Coaches grant. Coaches working within a community of practice to support teachers, and the accompanying research, continued for 3 more years with similar findings. (See Chapter 3 for a discussion of the research.) After 5 years of inquiry, we felt confident that coaching with the Project Approach and CLASS was an effective strategy for supporting children's thinking and teacher development.

Reinvigorating the Work

There was a break in the work from 2013 to 2015. However, focus on the Project Approach returned in 2016, when St. Mark Center, a community-based program from the Mid-America Head Start network, formed a partnership with Karrie Snider from University of Central Missouri and obtained a research grant from the Greater Kansas City Community Foundation. Additional coaches, who would support teachers with implementation of the Project Approach, were hired and placed at five centers in the Mid-America Head Start network. The new additions reinvigorated our coaching community. The research replicated the earlier findings that Project Approach Fidelity predicts higher CLASS ratings. Importantly, new findings indicated that child, family, and coaching outcomes were enhanced when coaches supported teachers' implementation of the Project Approach (Snider, Holley, & Usman, 2017).

Sustaining the Work: Two More Gifts

Along with the rest of our profession, we had been attempting to emphasize the essential role of coaching in teacher development. Having collected nationwide data on the effectiveness of coaching, the Office of Head Start gave us new program performance standards requiring that teachers receive coaching. The Mid-America Head Start coaching community developed a policy to meet the new standards, recommending the number of hours that education coordinators should spend on coaching and identifying the number of classrooms coaches could be assigned. The number of coaches would increase, so existing coaches made plans for integrating new members into our coaching community. We decided to present to them our experiences and discoveries before immediately involving them in planning for the work of the expanded group.

The enthusiasm of veteran members of the coaching community for project work was contagious, and new members expressed eagerness to join the work. A second gift arrived in the form of a timely opportunity, when Judy Harris Helm convened a group of Project Approach aficionados for Certified Young Investigators Training. Four people from Kansas City, including two Head Start leaders, became certified, and would therefore be able to provide introductory on-site training to teachers and coaches.

During the 2018–2019 program year, the coaching community and certified trainers offered two days of training on the Project Approach to teachers—expanding to include toddler teachers and home visitors—followed by intensive coaching as projects were conducted with children. They brought teachers, home visitors, and coaches back together several months later for a morning of presenting and reflecting on project work, and an afternoon of experiences targeted to teacher–coach pairs. At the end of the program year, the larger community was invited to celebrate our young investigators as teachers and coaches made the work public. Examples of projects shared at the celebration are shown in Figures 6.7 and 6.8. More about our community can be found at www.projectapproachkc.org/

FIGURE 6.7 • Parent educator Hannah Vanderpool shared the Fish Project she facilitated with mother Andrea and child Thomas from the Lee's Summit R-7 School District's Early Head Start home-based program. Andrea reflected, "Tommy has really responded to the Project Approach. He notices fish wherever we go, and it has definitely sparked a curiosity for learning in him."

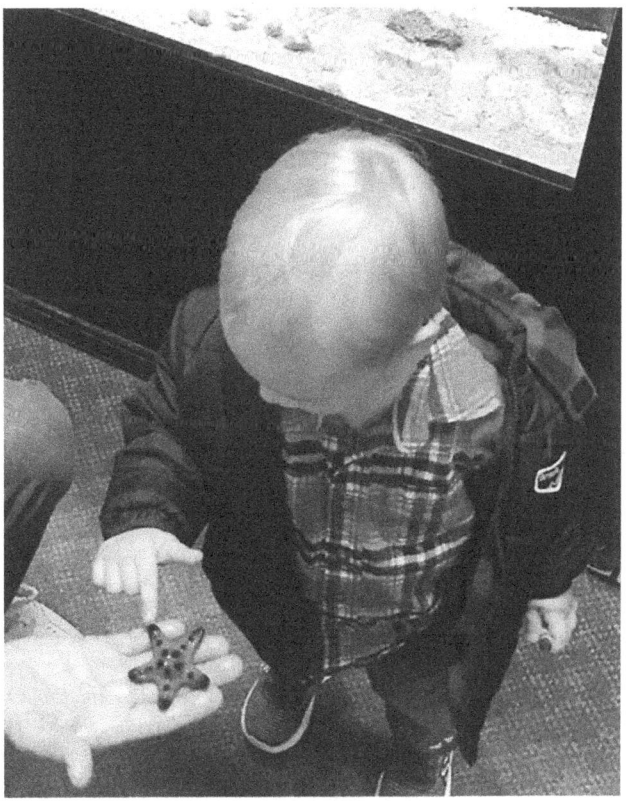

FIGURE 6.8 • Guadalupe Centers Early Childhood Center teacher Claudia Davis and coach Ann Camey shared the Bones Project with Mid-America Head Start Program director Liz Smith.

CONCLUSION

Each of the four professional development initiatives described in this chapter involved partnerships between early education programs and community agencies or individuals. Notably, the community partners and programs formed collaborative relationships based on shared views of children and teachers *as thinkers*. The partnerships led to successful initiatives involving training, follow-up support, and research as well as making project work public. Early childhood educators received intellectual and social support so that engaged teaching and learning, which are both thoughtful and thought-provoking, could thrive.

REFERENCES

Catapano, S. (2005). Teacher professional development through children's project work. *Early Childhood Education Journal, 32*, 261–267. doi: 10.1007/s10643-004-1428-2

Dewey, J. (1897). *My pedagogic creed*. Washington, DC: Progressive Education Association.

Dewey, J. (1910). *How we think*. Boston, MA: Heath.

Dewey, J. (1916). *Democracy and education: An introduction to the philosophy of education*. New York: Macmillan.

Dewey, J. (1938). *Experience and education*. New York, NY: Collier MacMillan.

Harms, T., Clifford, R., & Cryer, D. (1998). *Early childhood environment rating scale* (Rev. ed.). New York, NY: Teachers College Press.

Helm, J. H., & Katz, L. G. (2016). *Young investigators: The Project Approach in the early years* (3rd ed.). New York, NY: Teachers College Press.

Helterbran, V. R., & Fennimore, B. S. (2004). Collaborative early childhood professional development: Building from a base of teacher investigation. *Early Childhood Education Journal, 31*, 267–271. doi: 10.1023/B:ECEJ.0000024118.99085.ff

Humbarger, J. A. (2012). *Strengths-based coaching & facilitator guide* [registered curriculum]. Kansas City, MO: Francis Institute for Child and Youth Development, Community College District of Metropolitan Kansas City, Missouri.

Joyce, B., & Showers, B. (2002). *Student achievement through staff development* (3rd ed.). Alexandria, VA: Association for Supervision and Curriculum Development.

Katz, L. G., Chard, S. C., & Kogan, Y. (2014). *Engaging children's minds: The Project Approach* (3rd ed.). Santa Barbara, CA: ABC-CLIO.

Kilpatrick, W. H. (1918). The project method: The use of the purposeful act in the education process. *Teachers College Record, 19*, 319–335.

Kohl Children's Museum. (n.d.). *Early Childhood Connections*. Available at www.kohlchildrensmuseum.org/outreach-programs/early-childhood-connections/

Louv, R. (2008). *Last child in the woods: Saving our children from nature-deficit disorder*. Chapel Hill, NC: Algonquin Books.

Pianta, R. C., LaParo, K. M., & Hamre, B. K. (2008). *Classroom Assessment Scoring System (CLASS) manual: Pre-K*. Baltimore, MD: Brookes.

Powell, D., Bynum, S., Gray, E., Helm, J. H., Knable, P., & Trieschmann, M. (2013). *Kohl PAACT: Project Approach assessment and coaching tool*. Glenview, IL: Kohl Children's Museum.

Snider, K., Holley, M., & Usman, A. (2017). *Final report: Project ABC²—Adults building capacities for young children. Commissioned program evaluation report for Project ABC²—Adults building capacities for young children*. Kansas City, MO: Greater Kansas City Community Foundation Grant.

VOICES FROM THE FIELD

Bringing Project Work to an Elementary School

Tricia DeGraff, Executive Director

In 2015, I became the school leader of a small, but growing, arts-integrated elementary charter school, the Academy for Integrated Arts (AFIA; Kansas City, Missouri), with a stated philosophical framework grounded in constructivism. As I set out to determine the best way to unite our instructional team around a shared vision for constructivist teaching and learning, with an emphasis on integrating the arts, the Project Approach just made sense. Luckily, I had previously spent time with other teacher educators in a higher education consortium that supported beginning teachers' use of project work.

BUILDING INFRASTRUCTURE FOR PROJECT WORK

My first priority as the school leader was to build an inquiry stance into planning and implementing professional development: that is, working to set the conditions for teachers to have time to reflect, collaborate, and deepen their ability to implement project work. One of the key structures we decided to put in place was time for weekly intentional teacher professional development. Each Wednesday, we end our instructional day early to allow for 150 minutes of professional development. During this time, teachers collaborate together on practices such as planning, engaging in structured protocols to analyze student work, and documenting projects.

Another decision our leadership team made was to be intentional about supporting teachers with resources, such as access to training, mentor-coaching, and a materials center. We also encourage teachers to bring in field experts and go on field experiences with their students. Additionally, because it is critical to be an advocate for projects, we invite many visitors to our school so they can witness the power of projects firsthand.

When we first started implementing projects schoolwide, parents asked many questions about what their children were doing at school, because the children were not coming home with completed worksheets. We have gotten better over time at communicating student learning to our families through newsletters and the displays of student work in our school. The student-created work is always grounded in individual classroom projects connected to standards. Our families see the power of projects through the school's Celebration of Learning held twice a year. During these events, all of our students share their learning with their families and our community through student-created songs, plays, dances, and even video productions (see Figures 6.9–6.11).

The Project Approach has opened the door for our teachers and children to engage in powerful, productive learning. However, because teaching and learning is com-

FIGURE 6.9 • Colleen White's 3rd-grade students' project on animals culminated with student-created Claymation videos. When making their videos, students paid close attention to their animal's physical features and explored their animal's mechanics (e.g., How does it move? Is it fast or slow?).

plex, our teachers and school leaders have learned that they need to support one another when challenges arise. For example, there are times when professional development time, intended for project work, is pushed aside for competing priorities, and we need to brainstorm solutions to that problem. Other times, we realize we need a concentrated effort on one part of project work.

Recently, we have intensified our focus on documentation. This focus on documentation not only allows us to make learning visible for families and visitors but also has helped teachers see and reflect on the deepened thinking and achievement of their students, as well as to be able to learn from colleagues and create goals and action steps to move forward in their own project journey.

One of the challenges as a school leader is finding a way to balance all of the moving pieces, while not letting go of those pieces that matter the most to children and teachers. I believe that it is possible to teach in this way—making learning authentic, relevant, and meaningful. We have observed that this is the learning that not only is memorable and engaging for our students but also motivates and inspires educators.

REFLECTIONS ON OUR JOURNEY

My focus as an administrator is on long-term outcomes for children's learning. Recently, our 4th-grade class engaged in a project related to the Troost Divide in Kansas City, which references Troost Avenue, a main thoroughfare, that is viewed as the most prominent racial and economic dividing line in our city. Students in Keyonia Cobbins's class presented on sophisticated topics such as structural racism, and organizations in Kansas City that are making a change in our community. Many of these 4th-grade students have engaged in project work since kindergarten, so I have been able to see the growth in their skills and intellectual dispositions. Through project work they have learned how to ask important questions and have had the opportunity to learn how to answer their questions through interviewing field experts and conducting research. As I watched the 4th-graders present their research to invited community members, I reflected on how confident they were. Students dressed up. Some wore ties. Watching these young people get up in front of an audience of more than 50 people and share their research was inspiring. These are the moments when you see this hard work pay off. Great teaching is truly life changing.

FIGURE 6.10 • Kindergarten students in Erica Stevens's class take apart a keyboard during a music project that started after Ms. Erica noticed that the students turned the dramatic play area into a stage each day.

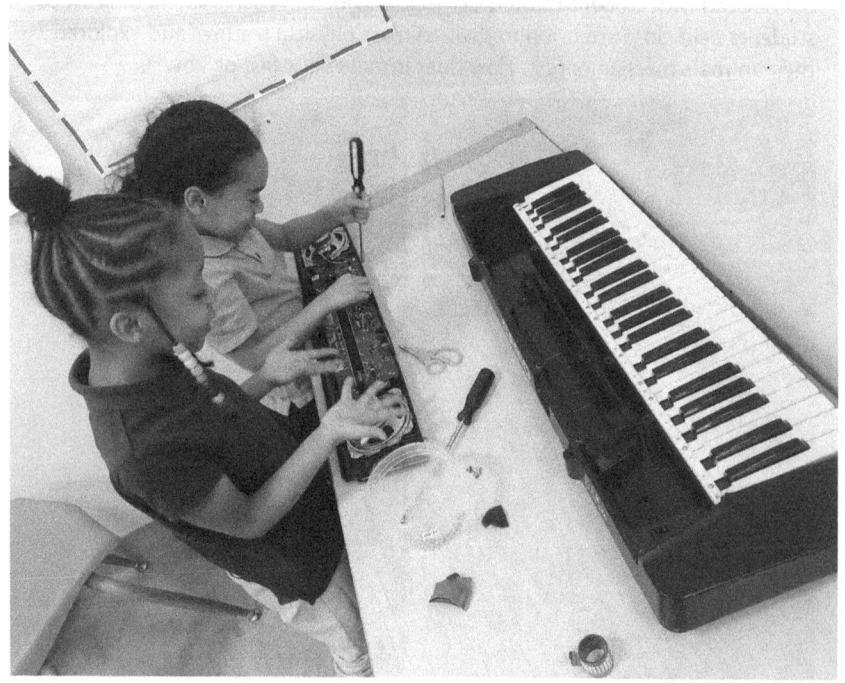

FIGURE 6.11 • In collaboration with experts during the Music Project, Allison Doerr's 1st-graders created a music video entitled "AFIA Rocks and Rolls." Children asked numerous questions about how people make money related to music, music and video production, as well as other related fields.

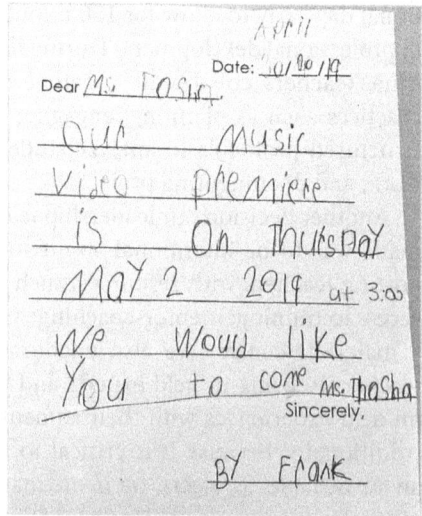

PART III

The Manifesto on Active, Engaged Learning Through the Project Approach

CHAPTER 7

Moving Forward with the Project Approach

Karrie A. Snider, Sue Vartuli, & Judy Harris Helm

BRINGING the intellectual classroom deserts to life is a responsibility we all must share. In Chapter 1, we began our journey of thinking together about the limitations and potential of early childhood education by examining the contrasts between the Pumpkin Patch lesson and the Path Project. These classroom examples represent the ongoing challenges educators face in shifting their philosophical teaching beliefs and practices to include more appropriate, authentic, and intellectual opportunities to learn.

In the chapters throughout Parts I and II, and in the six Voices from the Field, teachers, administrators, and researchers shared stories of how project work fostered deep child thinking. These stories were selected to provide a vision of what joyful, thinking-rich classroom environments and teaching interactions look like, sound like, and feel like, *for all children*, in toddler through primary grade settings. Further, mentor-coaches, teacher educators, and consultants illustrated how they have approached teacher education, training, and ongoing support for successful implementation of project work within their communities.

Clearly those who have experienced and researched the Project Approach see it as a way to meet standard curriculum requirements and accomplish the same goals as mandated curriculum. The Project Approach provides a way to meet accountability requirements through a structure that teachers can use to bring authentic and active, engaged learning into their classrooms. It is effective in meeting Mind Brain Education Science instructional guidelines for high-quality teaching (refer to Figure 2.1). It is practical and, most importantly, welcomed by family members, administrators, and policy makers.

For some educators the Project Approach has provided a pathway back to authentic, child-centered teaching. However, those who have experienced and researched the Project Approach also see it as a vehicle to develop child intellect, to create children who are thinkers, and to build children's sense of self-efficacy, so that they can be self-directed learners and independent problem solvers. In turn, teachers and program leaders who conduct deepened project work engage themselves in thinking together more deeply about children, about their own teaching practices, and about how to solve implementation challenges.

In order to support thinking deeply and to provide meaningful, timely suggestions to education stakeholders, we now share the Manifesto Delphi study. As introduced in Chapter 1, this study was conducted in conjunction with assembling and writing the stories shared in this book. The Delphi study first informed the development of *The Manifesto for Engaged Learning* and then identified challenges and suggestions-as-solutions for all education stakeholders to successfully support or implement the Project Approach. In this chapter, we describe how the study was conducted and highlight the results. Then we present *The Manifesto for Engaged Learning*, a statement that pronounces the clear vision of why active, engaged classrooms are needed and what they look like.

THE MANIFESTO DELPHI STUDY

Assembling Experts

As introduced in Chapter 1, the Delphi research method uses a group communication process to enable a consensus of opinion. Primarily, the process creates an information-rich feedback loop where experts contemplate, reflect on, and evaluate their collective ideas about a real-world issue. The method is widely useful in educational research (Avella, Kebritchi, Nunn, & Kanai, 2016; Hsu & Sanford, 2007).

A total of 17 experts, who have demonstrated expertise in teaching with, leading, or researching the Project Approach, were recruited for the study. Delphi panelists had 11–50 years of experience in various aspects of the early education field (e.g., teacher, leader, teacher educator, researcher; age- and grade-level teaching experience; program-based vs. university-based; family child care; community agency). Biographical sketches for the Delphi panelists are provided in Figure 7.1. While there was international representation, numerous experts were located in the Midwestern United States, which is consistent with locations of research sites in publications.

Conducting the Delphi Research

Karrie and Sue, as researchers, engaged with experts anonymously through written formats within four different response rounds. There were approximately 2 weeks between each round for data analyses. To conduct each round of analysis, we separately reviewed panelists' responses and individually created codes and themes and made interpretations, and then conferred with one another to reach consensus. Further, the panelists' responses were summarized, creating documentation for redistribution in the next round. We wanted the documentation to deeply represent the individual yet collective group responses, and as such, maintained data as close as possible to the panelists' exact words using a qualitative content analysis approach called manifest analysis (Bengtsson, 2016). Before the documentation was finalized, we conferred with one other researcher for feedback and verification of results.

During round one, the panel identified challenges for Project Approach implementation. In round two, they ranked these challenges in order of importance and then provided suggestions as possible solutions. During round three, suggestions were reviewed and expanded, or new suggestions were made. In the last round, panelists assigned roles of responsibility to each suggestion. Roles included administrator, community member, families, funders, mentor-coach, teacher, teacher educator, policymaker, researchers, or "other." The panel also reviewed suggestions for when the actions can take place (i.e., immediately, ongoing, recurring, etc.). In these last two rounds, panelists provided a member check of information. This is a process where participants review and verify the researchers' interpretations of their recorded statements. Member checking strengthens the validity of the study and the achieved agreement among study participants and ensures accuracy of analysis and confirmation of coding (Burnard, 1991; Creswell & Miller, 2000).

After all of this, we compiled a master list of challenges and suggestions, which included statements of expert advice, specific actions, who is responsible, and when to take action. We quantified the assignment of roles to each action item. We determined three levels of responsibility for taking on action steps: primary, secondary, and support. For example, the panel assigned almost all of the challenges that addressed teaching with the Project Approach to "teacher" and the secondary and support roles were interchangeably "administrator" or "mentor-coach."

Delphi Results: What We Learned About How We Can Move Forward

Two overarching ideas for understanding implementation challenges emerged from the Delphi study: (1) general challenges for the field of early childhood education; and (2) specific challenges to implementing the Project Approach. We explore each of these below.

General Challenges. General challenges from school and society include those associated with school mandates, policies, and priorities; differences in philosophical views between traditional and developmentally appropriate practices; and the need to advance cultural diversity and equity. All statements in italics in the following section are the exact words of the expert panel.

Panelists ranked "curriculum and assessment mandates" as the most important general challenge, stating: *Traditional school philosophies require contact time with core curriculum and implementation of assessment mandates. This creates a challenge for early childhood educators including primary teachers (K–2) especially, to work diligently at weaving in project activities across the daily schedule, routines and subject-specific time blocks.* (See supplemental material at tcpress.com/growingchildintellect for challenge summaries.)

The second most important general challenge focused on societal values. *Societal, cultural and parental educational values may emphasize a more traditional philosophical approach to teaching and learning in schools. Teaching with the Project Approach requires a shift from the behavioral-transmission style to constructivist teaching. The required shift and the current societal pressure lead to a lack of congruency among stakeholders within programs.*

Specific Challenges. Challenges specific to the Project Approach addressed the following areas:

- Education, training, and experience in the Project Approach
- Beliefs and dispositions about the Project Approach
- Knowledge, skills, and strategies for teaching with the Project Approach
- Support of, commitment to, and involvement in the Project Approach

Delphi panelists overwhelmingly agreed that access to quality trainings and ongoing professional development is paramount for cultivating deep insight into project teach-

FIGURE 7.1 • Delphi panel participants: Biographical sketches

JOLYN BLANK, Ph.D., is associate professor of early childhood education at the University of South Florida. Her research explores the ways arts and inquiry—integrated processes of investigating and representing meaning using multiple modes of communication—are enacted within the diverse social and ideological complexities of contemporary early schooling. She teaches graduate and undergraduate courses on play, arts in early learning, and qualitative research.

CAROL BOLZ, M.A., is the education manager for Mid-America Head Start in Kansas City, Missouri. As a teacher in a Head Start classroom in 1995, Carol was introduced to the Project Approach and has never looked back! She facilitated many projects with young investigators. She currently provides training and coaching to educators on implementation of the Project Approach, coordinates research, and presents at national conferences.

DeCARLA BURTON, B.A., director/owner of Jump Smart Learning Academy for 20 years, has been a trainer for Kohl Children's Museum's Early Childhood Connections Program since 2005. DeCarla founded the Supporting Professionals Network Association, a not-for-profit home-based and center child care advocacy organization representing 75 business owners in Chicago and South Suburbs. In 2001, DeCarla received the Kohl McCormick Teaching Award.

MEREDITH BURTON, M.A., director and lead teacher of the Furman University Child Development Center in Greenville, South Carolina, has taught using the Project Approach in public and private schools for the last 18 years and currently teaches a graduate level practicum in the Project Approach at Furman University. She is also a Master Certified Trainer for the Center for Child Care Career Development in South Carolina.

SYLVIA C. CHARD, Ph.D., professor emeritus of early childhood education, University of Alberta, Canada, was director of the Child Study Center. She taught at various levels in schools from preschool through high school in England. Sylvia has many publications on the Project Approach and presents on the Project Approach, interdisciplinary learning, and young children representing their understanding through drawing, in Canada, the United States, and around the world.

ANN-MARIE CLARK, Ph.D., retired associate professor from Reich College of Education at Appalachian State University, designed and directed an afterschool service-learning lab for students to tutor children who were learning the English language through participation in the Project Approach. Her research interests included literacy development through telling, writing, and reading personal stories and the effects of service-learning practices on her students' perceptions of the other.

TRICIA DeGRAFF, Ph.D., is the executive director of the Academy for Integrated Arts, a prekindergarten through 6th-grade public school in Kansas City, Missouri. She has over 20 years of experience in urban schools as a teacher, teacher educator, and school leader. Tricia's research interests involve professional development processes for teachers that are meaningful, inquiry-based, authentic, and teacher-centered, leading to transformative learning for children and teachers.

MAUREEN COSTELLO DWYER, M.Ed., teaches preschool at Duke School, an independent project-based preschool through 8th-grade school in Durham, North Carolina. She is a member of the Project Approach Teacher Education Network, was trained in the Project Approach by Lilian G. Katz and Sylvia C. Chard, and presents on project work in a variety of settings. She loves the excitement and synergy that develop among children as they explore project work together.

ERIKA GRAY, B.S., director of education for Kohl Children's Museum, Chicago, Illinois, oversees Kohl's education department, which creates and facilitates all public programs, outreach, professional development grants, and workshops for children, caregivers, and teachers. Erika has been involved in Kohl's Early Childhood Connections Project Approach professional development program since its conception in 2001 and has been a coach-mentor to home-based and school district educators.

YVONNE KOGAN, M.A., cofounder of Eton School in Mexico City and current principal of the early childhood and elementary departments, is also a bilingual international education consultant and presenter. She has coauthored *Picturing the Project Approach: Creative Explorations in Early Learning,* which was awarded the Academics' Choice Award; *Engaging Children's Minds: The Project Approach,* third edition; and *From My Side: Being a Child.*

KATRINA LARSON, B.A., was a teaching assistant in a special education classroom and a 2nd-grade teacher. In 2008, she started the toddler program at UPC Discovery, Peoria, Illinois. She attended project training with Lilian G. Katz and Judy Harris Helm and presented projects at Illinois Project Day and Project Night at the National Association for the Education of Young Children. One of her projects with toddlers is published in *Young Investigators: The Project Approach in the Early Years,* third edition.

NICK PETTIT, M.A., is a Kansas City, Missouri, based educator/principal who has worked with hundreds of students and teachers in Kansas City's urban core. Beginning his career in early childhood education, Nick has taught multiple grades and is now a building principal at Maplewood Elementary in the North Kansas City School District. Engaging students in student-centered learning experiences and creating impactful relationships drives his approach to leading.

PAM SCRANTON, M.Ed., is the founder of UPC Discovery and adjunct professor at Bradley University in the teacher education department. Pam coaches teachers and undergraduate students in documentation and the Project Approach, and she provides leadership in the programs of UPC Discovery. She is co-author with Dr. Helm of *Teaching Your Child to Love Learning and Teaching Parents to Do Projects at Home.*

PEGI STAMPS, M.A., has a diverse career in the field of early childhood education, with experiences in teaching, training, coaching, and leadership. She was a Head Start director of Education, Inclusion, and Mental Health; taught post-secondary education; and is currently the director of Early Learning for Constructive Playthings. Pegi is a Certified Young Investigator Trainer on the Project Approach.

LORA TAYLOR, M.A., director at UPC Discovery in Peoria, Illinois, has taught in a variety of programs for over 20 years, including an a preschool for at-risk children; a private, faith-based, Reggio-inspired preschool; and a Catholic preschool—all of which implemented the Project Approach. Lora is a Certified Young Investigators Consultant and has presented on many topics, including the Project Approach, literacy development, nature experiences, room environments, and spiritual development.

REBECCA TEALL, B.A., has been working in early education for over 20 years and is currently a curriculum coach and prekindergarten teacher at St. George's Episcopal School in New Orleans, Louisiana. Rebecca has been an enthusiastic proponent for the Project Approach since joining the St. George's faculty in 2012.

REBECCA A. WILSON, M.S., current director and lead teacher of Van Meter Community Pre-Kindergarten in Van Meter, Iowa, has taught in a variety of programs using the Project Approach from preschool through 1st grade. These include dual language and bilingual Head Start programs. Rebecca is the author of several publications, including a chapter in *The Power of Projects* and co-author of *Teaching Parents to Do Projects at Home.*

ing and learning processes. *Teachers and leaders need guidance on quality trainings and access points for getting started with project work.* Further, panelists identified that for some teachers in some programs, the project journey can be lonely. These types of challenges produced suggestions for supporting adults' education, development, and experiences through professional learning communities and by creating a Project Approach Network.

Teachers naturally encounter the most challenges as they live out the teaching of project work in their classrooms. It was no surprise to us that the greatest number of perceived challenges focused on teaching with the Project Approach. For example, sometimes it is hard for teachers to shift their beliefs to be more child-centered or to trust themselves that all children can learn through projects. Teaching with projects also means that teachers must learn new teaching techniques, and that teachers and administrators have both knowledge and experience with project work. The first half of the specific challenges related to teaching with the Project Approach included anticipatory planning, topic selection, gathering children's questions, observing and listening to children, and guiding learning with intentional teaching.

The final area of challenges focused on the stakeholders, who must develop an attitude of support, commitment, and involvement toward the Project Approach. Ten challenges addressed the need for infrastructure and administrative support; the need for buy-in and commitment from program stakeholders, administrators, and teachers; and the need to facilitate family and community involvement and commitment. Infrastructure support, the challenge ranked highest in this section, described structures needed to support the financial, professional development, and tangible resources teachers need for implementing quality project work.

What We Noticed. Patterns emerged as to who is primarily responsible for addressing challenges and taking the next steps. Teachers, followed by administrators and then mentor-coaches, shared the majority of primary roles across all action steps. Stakeholders, such as teacher educators and researchers, had a moderate amount of responsibility. Finally, families, policymakers, community agencies, and funders were mentioned, but have limited primary roles in solving implementation challenges (see Figure 7.2).

Teachers were assigned the most responsibilities. These results reminded us that the teacher has the most influential role in the child's immediate classroom context. Teachers also had the most immediate and practical steps to take. The administrators and mentor-coaches were mentioned frequently, representing the next levels of support to teachers and children in the classroom. This also made

FIGURE 7.2 • Rank order of primary, secondary, and support responsibilities assigned to various early childhood stakeholders

Role	Primary	Total Assigned
Teacher	99	158
Administrator	70	155
Mentor-Coach	19	154
Teacher Educator	20	54
Researcher	12	21
Policymaker	3	16
Family	2	14
Community Member	1	6
Funders	0	5

practical sense, as these roles, by function, lend ongoing support and resources to the teachers. It is also important to remember that the panelists have served in these roles themselves, often in several roles, and have worked with many programs observing what works. It may be that their understanding of the value of a strong teacher–administration–coach partnership influenced their ratings.

The group of support roles with fewer primary responsibilities included researchers, families, policy makers, community members, and funders; yet they all had actions to take. These individuals are important to the classroom, but in this study may have been either targets of the action items, such as families (i.e., provide education to families, involve families in documentation processes); had specific job functions related to action items, such as researchers (i.e., researchers can create methods and measures); or the items simply had fewer suggestions directly connected to these more indirect roles. This suggests the different levels of influence that stakeholders can make in the life of the classroom. It is important to remember, however, that even though possible action items may be fewer the farther we go from the classroom, these groups may have extreme power for change. For example, through legislation or funding they can take actions that have a powerful impact, such as requiring standardized testing, funding only programs with a commercial curriculum, or specifying time allocations for isolated content instruction.

How do we take the next step? First, as the Delphi panel emphatically stated, we must maintain a clear mission and vision for project work and know how to communicate this important work to teachers, administrators, families, and communities. Following this guidance, *The Manifesto for Engaged Learning* was developed as a stand-alone tool for advocacy in advancing the Project Approach, and is presented on the pages that follow.

THE MANIFESTO FOR ENGAGED LEARNING

High-quality early childhood education is undoubtedly an important factor in the development of young children's academic skills and their dispositions for learning. Currently, educational initiatives seek to improve the quality of young children's learning environments in order to "prepare" children for the next age or grade level. All indicators suggest that the 21st century skills needed in our future global society include critical thinking, collaboration, communication, and creativity. Yet, many initiatives simply end up reducing the teaching and learning experiences to discrete isolated activities, which are often removed from the children's immediate world or cultural context. We believe this has resulted in the creation of classrooms that are like intellectual deserts, where thinking is not encouraged and dies from lack of nurturance. In these classrooms, children have fewer opportunities to actively and authentically engage in learning and develop the intellectual dispositions needed to be prepared for the future world. In contrast, all of these 21st century skills can be attained through the Project Approach and its real-world focus.

We believe instead of "preparing" children we should prepare a pathway for optimal learning. To do that, we need a collective vision that considers how adults can best prepare the learning environment—that is, the curriculum and instructional choices made every day. We believe the focus of traditional teaching is on learning isolated skills, rather than the application of skills to think, solve problems, and be creative. These kinds of executive function skills are fundamental components of project work and essential to children's social, behavioral, and academic achievement.

The need to take a stand for active, engaged learning arises from the latest neuroeducation research about what children need from their early environments. It also arises from observing the status quo of education-as-usual and its outcomes. We believe this traditional approach limits child agency, diminishes child motivation to learn, and minimizes children's ability to choose, plan, and think. In addition, these intellectual desert classrooms characteristically reduce the scope of rich, accessible content topics down to mere facts and rote learning tasks.

With the Project Approach, which includes both an approach to curriculum and instructional practices, teachers and other key educational agents can find a very important and practical guide for making the most out of teaching, thinking, and learning every day. We have no more time to waste on drill-and-skill lessons that isolate skills like shapes, colors, and letter recognition; instead we believe a better use of time is focusing on building skills and mastering content within a meaningful context and deepened thought-provoking investigations on topics of interest. We believe we are at a crucial time in early education when we must *make* time to move forward and implement the Project Approach.

This *Manifesto for Engaged Learning,* the statement of our beliefs and values, is drawn together from a myriad of ideas shared with experts from across the country. The Project Approach was most likely first inspired by John Dewey's (1910) insights on thinking and then Lilian Katz and Sylvia Chard's *Engaging Children's Minds: The Project Approach* (1989) and clarified for young children in *Young Investigators: The Project Approach in the Early Years* (Helm & Katz, 2000). This Manifesto symbolizes the zeal and energy many communities experience year after year when teacher and school networks and communities celebrate the amazing thinking of young children and adults. The ideas presented here have been percolating among a variety of education change agents for years, and after countless hours of shared thinking are now brought forth through the Manifesto Delphi study.

We recognize everyone might not agree with us, but we invite you to challenge yourself to think about children's learning and their thinking, and to consider the possibilities that come alive in classrooms for all children when adults, equipped with project-minded teacher-thinking, are ready for children. We acknowledge the importance of teacher intellectual development and ask that you too position thinking as an important learning goal for every child and every teacher.

Advancing the Project Approach

1. We recognize that the Project Approach, a unique approach to teaching young children, has a sound theoretical basis as well as distinct features that complement brain development and how children learn best. To advance the value of this child-centered, emergent curriculum approach, all stakeholders must share the benefits of the Project Approach in

relation to children's early brain development and learning.
2. We recognize that philosophical differences exist between societal views of teaching (status quo education) and the required curriculum and assessment mandates at all learning levels versus the need for more invigorating and responsive educational approaches, like the Project Approach.
3. We recognize the need to build a coalition of teachers, administrators, mentor-coaches, teacher educators, researchers, funders, policy makers, and other educational and community stakeholders by establishing national Project Approach networks with regional communities of practice groups to provide a system of support and a clearinghouse of information.

Every Child Has a Right to Learn in an Active, Engaged Learning Environment

4. Schools need to be forward-thinking, providing opportunities for developing creative thinkers and problem solvers. One strength of the Project Approach is the context it provides for the children to appreciate the value and purpose of academic skills. Children can see the value of writing in real-world communication, the value of number skills in the business world, the value of scientific knowledge in the practice of medicine or agriculture, to name just a few examples.
5. Advancing equity in early childhood education means utilizing diverse approaches to teaching and learning rather than a homogeneous approach. The Project Approach is inclusive of all children who differ in abilities, interests, and decision making. The strong emphasis on collaboration in project work can be helpful in integrating strengths that children with different cultural, linguistic, and intellectual backgrounds bring to the classroom community.
6. An active, engaged learning environment includes authentic assessment practices to best determine and demonstrate how all children are learning. Teachers must align assessment goals to project work through observation- and documentation-generated data, and then use authentic assessment to inform instruction, to link to curriculum standards, and to advocate to families and for teacher professional development.

Teacher Beliefs and Practices for Active, Engaged Learning

7. Project work is built on the foundation of constructivism. Therefore, teachers must shift from instructor to facilitator and collaborate alongside children. Collaborative learning means that teachers are respectful and responsive to the children's contributions and decisions throughout project work.
8. Teaching with projects is intentional. Teachers must believe in the importance of guiding children in learning intentionally yet responsively, while being accountable for meeting educational goals.
9. Unlike traditional teaching and learning, children in project work are active rather than passive learners. This requires teachers to believe in the power of children's capabilities. Teachers then must have the disposition to use all of their senses in observing, noticing, listening, wondering about children, and wondering with children.
10. The Project Approach requires teachers to hone their skills to select co-constructed, researchable topics for the age of their learners, to gather children's ideas and questions, and to integrate their program's required learning standards into projects through anticipatory-teacher-planning and child-webbing processes.
11. Teachers need the disposition of flexibility to navigate the open-ended nature of projects, to be responsive to children's questions and interests, and to trust children as they try things that teachers may think are too hard for them.
12. High-quality documentation is critical to project work. It involves assessment and evaluation and is proof of the teacher's knowledge about what and how children are learning, and includes the pedagogical documentation method, which intentionally relaunches experiences with children after reflecting together on documentation gathered throughout project investigations.
13. Teachers gain confidence with project work through practice, experience, and seeing children's curiosity for learning grow. Teachers' knowledge of child development and developmentally appropriate practice supports their confidence to take risks in teaching through projects.
14. Teachers and administrators need clear examples of how the Project Approach can fit with their daily schedules, grade-level learning expectations, and standards.

15. Teachers and school leaders need access points for getting started with project work, but also need a firm understanding of Project Approach fidelity, that is, adherence to the Project Approach structure and its components, as they are intended to be implemented.
16. The field needs access to mentor-coaches with experience in the Project Approach, who can effectively guide teachers through implementation.

Funding

17. In order to build and sustain the infrastructure support needed for implementing quality project work, funding is needed for the initial and ongoing access to project-related resources (materials, transportation to field site visits, documentation, etc.), human resources (education, training, networking, conferences), and structural resources (time for planning, adequate space, etc.).
18. To help support the widespread implementation of the Project Approach, stakeholders should commit start-up and expansion funding through teaching grants that support innovative teaching and learning.
19. Project work needs a well-funded research community in which researchers and practitioners collaborate in developing shared knowledge, and whose teaching practices are informed by up-to-date research.
20. Research funding is needed to create methods and measures, including authentic assessment of children, to demonstrate the positive outcomes of the Project Approach.
21. Funding is needed for supportive technologies. The Project Approach research and information must be shared via professional organizations, websites, applications, and media that are accessed by the general public, as well as in professional educational journals.

Transformative Leadership

22. Leaders need access to current research in order to clearly communicate the philosophies, practices, and benefits of teaching through projects.
23. Leaders are best equipped to lead, support, and guide program implementation when they have deep insight and knowledge of the change in paradigm concerning project teaching and learning processes.
24. Leaders need to collaborate *alongside* their teachers during trainings. Leaders also need to get into the classrooms regularly, participate in the phases of the Project Approach, and share and celebrate the work of their young investigators as a way of advocating with other teachers, families, and administrators.
25. Leaders need to understand that children are more motivated and experience deeper satisfaction in school when they engage in project work.
26. Leaders should commit to providing teachers time to plan project work and protect this prioritized time when competing priorities arise.

Policies

27. Programs must create strategic long-term action plans to prioritize implementation of the Project Approach and to be intentional with the professional development needed at each grade level to sustain project implementation and to address teacher attrition.
28. Various levels of decision makers (grade-level, building-level, district-level, state-level, etc.) should work diligently to demonstrate the congruence between early childhood and primary grade curriculum and assessment mandates and the Project Approach.
29. Because educational policies or priorities (state, regional, district, program, classroom) may compete with or limit the support teachers need when implementing the Project Approach, policy makers and program administrators should set clear policies to expect projects in early learning classrooms, which will guide teachers' decision making and increase their autonomy.
30. Early education lobbyists and legislators can affect the current societal view of educational practices through effective policy change.

Professionalism

31. Quality education and research on the Project Approach, for teachers and administrators, must be embedded in higher education programs and coursework, and must be initiated by qualified, experienced Project Approach instructors. The field should have access to dialogue between practice and research, which should be facilitated by colleges, universities, and professional organizations.
32. The field needs guidance on quality Project Approach training with clearly identified training stages, such

as beginning, novice, experienced, and expert, and fidelity structures to guide pre/post training activities (i.e., training checklists, practice profiles, and identified fidelity training tools).
33. The field needs increased access to initial and ongoing quality training and professional development that includes job-embedded follow-up trainings, networking, and collaborative professional learning communities.
34. Teachers benefit from collaborating when planning, implementing, and reflecting upon project work. This can lead to discussing experiences, raising questions to investigate, and presenting project outcomes to professional learning community groups and at conferences, at the local or national level.
35. Teachers, administrators, family members, teacher educators, and researchers can advocate for the Project Approach through presenting and publishing their experiences and stories.

It takes a dedicated team to implement the Project Approach. Commitment and involvement come from many places inside and outside of the classroom. Teachers must receive support from colleagues, administrators, families, and community volunteers and experts. Programs must collaborate with businesses, agencies, universities, and advocates. As adults actively engage in what is happening in education, all stakeholders can make conscious decisions about the changes that need to be made to ensure that children learn and grow to their fullest potential.

References

Dewey, J. (1910). *How we think*. Boston, MA: Heath.
Helm, J. H., & Katz, L. G. (2000). *Young investigators: The Project Approach in the early years*. New York, NY: Teachers College Press.
Katz, L. G., & Chard, S. C. (1989). *Engaging children's minds: The Project Approach*. Greenwich, CT: Ablex.

CALL TO ACTION: HOW WE MOVE FORWARD

We hope you are now getting a clear vision of what classrooms can be like when the necessary strategies, structures, and supports are in place. The individuals who develop success with project work for all children believe that their personal growth in thinking and learning about best practices actually translates to better learning for children and more fulfilling teaching experiences. All of the Delphi panelists themselves, or through their current work with teachers, have had to overcome barriers to implementing project work every day.

As we conclude this book in the next chapter, we invite you, as a teacher, to keep listening and thinking, but also to see yourself overcoming implementation challenges. This kind of teacher commitment is a key ingredient for believing that you can do project work too, and that you must! We also hope that if you are beginning or renewing your own journey with projects, you will stand with us now by responding to the Manifesto Call to Action in Chapter 8, for your role is paramount.

REFERENCES

Avella, J. T., Kebritchi, M., Nunn, S. G., & Kanai, T. (2016). Learning analytics methods, benefits, and challenges in higher education: A systematic literature review. *Online Learning, 20*(2), 13–29.

Bengtsson, M. (2016). How to plan and perform a qualitative study using content analysis. *NursingPlus Open, 2*, 8–14. Available at doi.org/10.1016/j.npls.2016.01.001

Burnard, P. (1991). A method of analyzing interview transcripts in qualitative research. *Nurse Education Today, 11*(6), 461–466.

Creswell, J. W., & Miller, D. L. (2000). Determining validity in qualitative inquiry. *Theory into Practice, 39*(3), 124–130.

Hsu, C.-C., & Sanford, B. A. (2007). The Delphi technique: Making sense of consensus. *Practical Assessment, Research & Evaluation, 12*, 1–8.

CHAPTER 8

Manifesto Call to Action

Growing Child Intellect Through the Project Approach

Karrie A. Snider, Sue Vartuli, & Judy Harris Helm

IF YOU, like the educators represented in this book, have come to the point where you believe that project work can be the pathway toward enhanced teaching, thinking, and learning, then a natural outcome is to think of your own self-efficacy. You may be thinking about your own ability to change the outcomes for the development of intellect for the children in your classroom, in your school, and in the thousands of schools where classrooms seem to be intellectual deserts. You might then be wondering, "What can I do to get started or improve my own teaching, leading, or coaching?" "What suggestions will help me overcome the potential obstacles I may face in my classroom or program?" or "What can I as an administrator do to make this happen in my school?"

In order to address those questions and move project work forward, we now conclude this book with the Manifesto Call to Action, a direction from the Delphi study for what each of us can do, no matter our position or program, to nurture children's intellectual development in our early childhood classrooms. The Delphi recommendations are specific strategies to overcome issues with Project Approach implementation that can be undertaken immediately and in a recurring manner. Some suggestions will need to be developed. We invite you to continue to think about teaching and learning with the Project Approach, and join with us now, for your effort is critical.

CALLING TEACHERS TO ACTION

The Delphi study illustrates directions, actions, and the significance of moving the Project Approach forward through collective action. The Delphi study results indicate that the primary responsibility lies with teachers, followed by those who support them (refer to *The Manifesto for Engaged Learning* in Chapter 7).

Becoming Skilled in Project Planning

Delphi panelists believe that the first step in effective project work is to take the time during Phase I to plan and identify the state or program learning standards within the Topic Selection and Teacher Anticipatory Planning processes, as specified in the following recommendations:

- During anticipatory planning, brainstorm with other teachers and consider resources, artifacts, and experts available to teach the topic within the school or community.
- Connect the standards, learning goals, and skills that need to be explicitly taught into the Teacher Anticipatory Planning Web. *Then*, generate possible investigations children can do to answer their questions. The last step is to connect your anticipatory planning web with what the children know and wonder about the topic. This process will help you communicate to educational decision makers and families how the Project Approach accomplishes goals and standards through the children's experiences.
- Practice webbing, getting children's questions, and leading inquiry-based activities planned from and for investigating the children's own questions.

Remember that authentic teaching and learning comes from the children's interests and experiences. Recall Jen Fletchall's scenario in Chapter 5. She could have used the mail-order caterpillars to develop a project topic. Instead, she recognized that the children's real interests were with human babies. From this example, you can learn to trust yourself with testing out topics, and you can feel confident to trust that children can lead you to valuable learning opportunities.

Working with Children

In project work, teachers offer children choices and follow their interests, ideas, and questions rather than having them follow preset plans. Co-teaching with children is very effective in responding to the needs and interests of each child individually. To cultivate a collaborative climate of inquiry among the children, teachers can model language that supports collaborative thinking and actions, and that fosters children's abilities to help one another, to give suggestions, and to discuss and argue possible outcomes with peers. Teachers also support collaborative learning when they demonstrate that children's ideas are important, help children talk with and interview experts, teach children to conduct surveys, prompt children to share their findings at group time, and help children work collaboratively together in play and project work investigations. The Delphi panel recognizes that a key ingredient to a climate of inquiry, which is also a common challenge for teachers, is identifying children's questions, and the experts offer the following recommendations:

- Use teacher observation techniques to gather questions. Children can ask through actions and interactions, not just through words. For example, dual language learners and younger children often display their questions through nonverbal actions and in play.
- Spark interest with objects, artifacts, and photos while modeling wondering, and turn children's wonderings into questions. Say, "Let's look at this," and model a few questions and then refer back to the child, "Do you have any questions?" "What do you want to know about the bird's nest?" "I wonder what this part of the fire truck is for."
- Rather than using traditional structures, such as sitting in a large circle and asking children for their questions about a topic, try the following:
  - Documenting questions that emerge naturally while children are engaged in an investigation or that emerge on field visits
  - Observing and listening more closely to a particular child during project work, rather than thinking about the interests and needs for the whole class at one time
- Journal once a week about an activity or child, and then gradually build to recording daily observations as they pertain to assessment collections.
- Use a voice recorder or video to capture full interactions and conversations.
- Once the questions begin to flow from the children, enable discussion of each question by the small group or larger group involved so that the wording can be improved, if necessary, and that answers sought will provide useful information.

Documenting the Project and the Learning

Recall, from Chapter 4, Pam Scranton's examples for how children, teachers, and administrators create meaningful documentation displays. In planning for project work, teachers must include authentic assessment practices and documentation. Teachers should plan to gather authentic assessment evidence during project experiences, such as observations of children's actions and interactions, and collections of children's work samples. These artifacts provide some of the best examples of children's learning that occurs in the context of a project.

Well-planned documentation displays include children's thinking and learning during project investigations, the explicit connections to required standards, and highlights of project processes. When moving documentation to pedagogical documentation, teachers may also include reactions from children and family members about project stories, artifacts, and experiences. It is critical to remember that documentation is often the best tool teachers can use to advocate and explain the value of the Project Approach. Following are the Delphi panel recommendations for documenting:

- Ensure that your documentation educates families about the Project Approach by explicitly communicating how the project enabled children's learning and the development of children's intellectual dispositions.
- Document both in-process and final child representations to capture the full range of experiences, development, thinking, and learning.
- Reproduce children's dialogue and quotes as a large part of the documentation.
- Include family participants in documentation. Ask families to react to the documentation through written comments or online communities.

Working with Administrators and Families

It is clear that teachers need supportive administrators who are involved and attentive to the learning happening in project classrooms. Delphi panelists recognize that teachers need to know how to engage with administrators, families, and other members of their school and community throughout the three phases of project work. This helps build support and expand children's learning. For example, children learn from people who work in the community. Many of the community people children encounter in their pursuit of real-world questions through fieldwork will also be family members and grandparents themselves. Teachers must ask members of the school community to assist as experts or connections to field sites.

When working with families and administrators in particular, teachers need to know how to clearly communicate the philosophies, practices, and benefits of teaching and learning through projects. They need to insightfully interpret, explain, and share observation data using well-selected documentation; this enables teachers to build strong, supportive relationships with other adults. Effective communication often leads to administrator and stakeholder involvement and commitment, and solidifies their advocacy efforts. Teachers may also need to communicate their needs for specific resources such as funding for field site visits, including transportation, for a different classroom space, or for access to materials and space outside of their classroom space. Following are Delphi panel recommendations for teacher communication:

Communicating with Your Administrator

- Use the Project Planning Communication Form for Teachers and Administrators developed by Judy Helm, in which teachers share project updates and requests to administrators in an organized, systematic way. (See supplemental material at tcpress.com/growingchildintellect for the Project Planning Communication Form for Teachers and Administrators.)
- Become involved and have a voice in educational decision making through different groups: grade-level, building-level, and district-level curriculum groups, and state cadres.
- Team with other teachers in learning communities to build collective support and excitement around project work. Excitement and high-quality documentation often lead to increase in advocacy.
- Share files using technology that enables communication within the school building or through network-wide resources.

Communicating with and Engaging Families

Good communication with families enables them to support and engage in project work.

- Inform families about project teaching and learning regularly, but especially at the beginning of the year and during curriculum nights.
- Communicate and engage with room parents or parent organizations to support project work. Ask them to create a database of school community expertise and resources.
- Use technology, such as applications, social media, websites, and blogs to share photos, individual children's learning, and video documentation—creating a "buzz" about project work.

Families need to experience projects so they can see and experience their value.

- Ask families to be involved, contribute to project work, and coordinate resources in various ways: from sending in artifacts, sharing a story or experience, serving as an expert, or attending events.
- Give families and expert visitors an example of what to expect when they visit your classroom. This helps them feel comfortable to share their knowledge with young children.
- Assist children in showing family members what they are learning and involve them in the project processes (i.e., surveys, resources, expert interviews, field site visits, culminations).

Family education and advocacy can be facilitated through family-to-family sharing.

- Use family book clubs or workshops, along with family–teacher book clubs.
- Offer suggestions and provide family members with open-ended materials to do projects at home (i.e., plastic containers for each family that include art materials, scissors, disposable camera, clay, etc.).

Working with Colleagues to Reflect

Teacher reflection is an important part of implementing the Project Approach, especially due to the fluid nature of this curriculum approach. The inevitable challenges encountered through lived experiences in project work really draw teachers in to think more deeply about their teaching beliefs and practices, and about why they commit to professional growth. Teachers need to feel confident in their undertaking of the Project Approach, and they need to know they will hit bumps along the way, but that's the part of the learning. As a result of learning through project work themselves, teachers change their own schema and gain new understandings from which to build on book knowledge and trainings experienced.

Reflecting on project experiences (both teaching and learning) will help develop increased teacher self-efficacy, which in turn helps teachers commit to the Project Approach. When experiences lead to feelings of success, confidence builds. Several strategies, as recommended by the Delphi panel, can help immediately and in the future:

- Use a journal; spend time reflecting with other professionals to focus in on practices.
- Join a book club led and organized by a Project Approach teacher.
- Self-identify at different levels of experience—such as beginning, novice, experienced, or expert—to discern the type of training support needed.
- Attend trainings in schools where successful implementation of the Project Approach occurs; this is invaluable.

- Be available for other teachers to ask questions about project experiences.
- Seek out and connect with other Project Approach teachers in the community to ask questions and share successes.

CALLING ADMINISTRATORS TO ACTION

The Delphi study results emphasized the important role supportive administrators serve, second only to that of teachers, in making project work a reality amidst the intellectual deserts of classrooms. This was evident in the examples presented in Chapter 6. Recall how leaders from diverse communities and programs created structures and pathways to support adult and child learning. The field needs more transformational leaders like these to cultivate the institutional commitment that drives long-term implementation of the Project Approach, so that project work becomes business-as-usual. Although many practitioners may be on an independent journey with project work in their program or school, when teachers can partner with leaders, everyone benefits.

Transformational leaders, as outlined in the Manifesto, are able to effectively create the infrastructure to sustain project work and, perhaps more important, can clearly make visible to all stakeholders how the Project Approach applies to the lives and society our children live in. Delphi panelists suggested several immediate and ongoing actions for advancing the Project Approach through leadership, as specified below:

Program-Level Leadership

- Provide infrastructure for project work to be successful, such as training, time, funding, mentor-coaching, materials, and equipment.
- Complete cultural diversity training to enhance one's reflective skills for addressing issues of inequity across the types of instruction, curriculum, and experiences offered to children with diverse backgrounds.
- Create structures for professional learning communities (PLCs) with a consistent time and space to meet, and knowledgeable facilitators to guide group meetings.
- Avoid asking teachers to work with incompatible curricula or initiatives at the same time.
- Adopt authentic assessment systems in which curriculum standards, instruction, and assessments are linked.

Classroom-Level Leadership

- Provide, attend, and participate in quality trainings with teachers.
- Identify teachers for vertical PLCs; that is, when possible include teachers in other early childhood education programs, family child care providers, single teachers working alone, and elementary and middle school teachers in the same PLCs.
- Build time into the day or week for reflection with others around documentation, either in a community of practice or a staff meeting.
- Identify teachers' different strengths and allow teachers to present throughout the year to support in-service learning.

Community-Level Leadership

- Attend board meetings and serve on committees. Attempt to effect policy change, particularly when policies inhibit teacher decision making in context.
- Invite school leaders, board members, and legislators into classrooms that are doing high-quality project work to see the model firsthand.
- Connect and network with others outside of your program, such as family child care educators, community leaders, and agency professionals.
- Share about the Project Approach with other administrators at conferences (i.e., Association for Supervision and Curriculum Development, National Association for Elementary School Principals, National Association for the Education of Young Children).

CALLING OTHER STAKEHOLDERS TO ACTION

Teachers and administrators cannot succeed by doing this work alone. As the Delphi responses indicated, it takes all stakeholders to make the necessary change to shift long-standing beliefs about what young children can do and should learn, and how best to teach them. Project work is the answer, and the following recommendations of the Delphi panel will support the work of specific categories of stakeholders. The first group of strategies may be done immediately and on an ongoing basis. The final group are strategies for advancing project work that need to be developed.

Immediate Actions for Stakeholders

Mentor-Coaches

- Facilitate job-embedded professional development for initial and novice-level project implementation.
- Act as cheerleaders who help teachers identify and reflect upon successes.
- Help teachers develop ideas and solutions for how to integrate Project Approach skills into the school's required curriculum experiences: critical thinking,

observing, making predictions, collaborating, collecting data, communicating, using graphic organizers, and representing ideas.

Teacher Educators

- Use quality Project Approach publications as college texts.
- Teach project teaching and learning processes, such as webbing, getting children's questions, and leading inquiry-based activities planned from and for investigating the children's own questions.
- Teach the spectrum of child agency in curricula, as discussed in Chapter 2, to help preservice and in-service teachers and administrators to think critically about the kinds of experiences they are observing in schools and where these fit on the continuum (refer to Figure 2.2).

Researchers

- Share the benefits of the Project Approach in relation to children's early brain development and learning to advance the value of child-centered, emergent curriculum approaches.
- Take more opportunities to highlight project work in publications and at state, regional, and national conferences (e.g., ACEI, AERA, ASCD, NAEYC, etc.).

Other Stakeholders

- As members of the school and larger communities, assist as experts in classrooms or provide connections to field sites.
- As trainers, adapt training and forms to fit the public school primary grade level (i.e., provide training tracks for primary grade teachers and publications on primary school project work).

Work and Actions to Be Developed by Stakeholders

Teachers and Administrators

- Engage in a highly collaborative effort to create professional Project Approach networks. Stakeholders need an international professional organization with networks of Project Approach teachers, leaders, and researchers, with regional, state, and area subgroups. This organization can provide support, education, policy, advocacy, and access to funders.
- Provide an orientation video or workshop specifically designed to explain the Project Approach in a way that anyone could understand and is easily accessible to wide audiences.
- Write opinion essays about projects that impact a community and display high-quality project documentation in public places (i.e., banks, stores, etc.).
- Seek out other Project Approach teachers in the community, region, or state through a unified Project Approach network.
- Share about curriculum philosophies, project success stories, and documentation—tying philosophy to specific learning goals being met—in public forums such as district principals' meetings, school board meetings, websites, newsletters, and podcasts or radio shows.
- Create and organize discussion or study groups of new and experienced teachers, led by a teacher-leader who can help with Project Approach fidelity. Groups can agree to hear project stories from different classroom teachers weekly as critical friends who support one another's professional growth by giving honest, yet constructive, feedback to encourage reflective thinking practice.

Teacher Educators

- During instruction, clearly articulate the critical impact project work has on brain development.
- Include the Project Approach in courses that address emergent curriculum and show how it connects to required learning standards.
- Pair undergraduates and graduates with Project Approach schools and/or cooperating teachers that value child-centered learning and best practices.
- Advocate for the Project Approach in publications and presentations, and share about curriculum philosophies in public forums.
- Make the Project Approach needs visible to school leaders and future/current teachers. Develop and require undergraduate and graduate degree program coursework in emergent curriculum models and inquiry-based learning for education and educational leadership studies.
- Create small video clips or webinars that could be viewed at different times, linked to a portal or discussion board, for teaching staff to engage with one another.

Researchers

- Apply methodologies to identify where research information needs to be shared, and the outlets for research dissemination across stakeholder groups (i.e., interviews, focus groups, surveys, etc.).
- Conduct qualitative or mixed-methods research studies that describe and explain the Project Approach in context and highlight its value and the ways stakeholders have observed the Project Approach working.
- Expand interactions research and examine the relationship between Project Approach implementation and interactions as measured by standardized

observation and evaluation methods such as the Classroom Assessment Scoring System (CLASS) and the Environmental Rating Scale.
- Conduct research (i.e., graduate action research) to examine the cognition of children during project work in comparison to daily activities.
- Conduct research collaboratively between early childhood education researchers and economists, and include examples that represent a variety of age ranges and communities, as well as diverse teachers, families, and children.
- Extend the publishing of research-based Project Approach information to media beyond educational journals—media accessed by the general public.

Other Stakeholders

- Identify and develop paid lobbyists and connect with community agencies, lobbyists, legislators, civic organizations, and charities who support early childhood education and the Project Approach.
- Encourage businesses that allow field visits to share the experience with their corporate offices in order to increase awareness and potential resources, and to create funding opportunities.
- Build collaborations among family child care centers, partners, agencies, associations, charity groups, and early childhood education center-based programs for coordination of implementation effort.

IMPLICATIONS FOR THE FUTURE

The Delphi panelists represented pockets of national and international interest and implementation of the Project Approach. Their reflective work now becomes a collective vision for the field and for the future through *The Manifesto for Engaged Learning*. We invite you to share the Manifesto with others as a part of your advocacy efforts, and to critically examine your own knowledge and thinking about active, engaged learning. We also suggest that you use the immediate and ongoing Delphi recommendations to further your practice and work with communities, families, and children.

Most important, we invite you to respond to future calls for engaging with Project Approach networks, which will require funders, leaders, advocates, and members. We invite you to respond to and participate in calls for research, education, training, and leadership. We must now create a movement by putting these ideas into action.

Thinking, teaching, and learning through the Project Approach is an answer for enriching children's and adults' intellectual capacities and for bringing early learning classrooms to life. Armed with comprehensive suggestions, strategies, and work to be developed, we now have a clear vision and mission to use in acting on our beliefs and creating a stronger world for our children.

OUR BELIEFS: THE MANIFESTO CREED

- We believe that many children in early childhood settings spend their days where they are not encouraged to think.
- We believe that all children have a right to an authentic, engaging learning environment.
- We believe that project work enhances children's development of skills, knowledge, and learning dispositions, but most profoundly, enables child intellect.
- We believe that Mind Brain Education Science provides a solid justification for active, engaged, integrated, and meaningful learning experiences.
- We believe that high-quality early childhood programs are threatened by curriculum mandates, lock-step teaching schedules, and cumbersome assessment systems that consume learning time.
- We believe project work provides a way to meet accountability requirements through a structure that brings authentic, engaged learning into classrooms.
- We believe that projects, investigations of topics children care about, can provide a lifeline—a way to develop active, authentic curriculum experiences for prekindergarten and primary classrooms.
- We believe adding project work to prekindergarten through primary grade classrooms is both practical and effective, and once the benefits for children's learning are clearly communicated, is welcomed by families, administrators, and policy makers.
- We believe that we, as those responsible for the care and education of young children, must make a conscious decision to take action, to stand up and be counted as advocates for the Project Approach in the early years.

Index

Ability KC (Kansas City, MO), project implementation in, 69–74
Academy for Integrated Arts (Kansas City, MO), 53
   Plant Project in, 54–55
   professional development of teachers in, 95–96
Accountability, 53, 99
   in curriculum requirements, 47–48
ACEI (Association for Childhood Education International), 111
Active learning, 6, 104
   assessment of, 47, 50, 57
   capacity for learning in, 64
   in constructivism, 31
   curriculum research on, 29, 31, 33
   Manifesto for Engaged Learning on, 99, 103, 104–105
   MBE instructional guidelines on, 18, 19
   neuroeducation research on, 103
   in Path Project, 20
   professional development of teachers on, 23, 33, 90, 104–105
Administration for Children and Families, 65
Administrative support of Project Approach, 54, 56
   challenges in, 102
   Delphi study recommendations on, 108–109, 110, 111
AERA (American Educational Research Association), 111
Agency, sense of, 20, 24, 103
   in behaviorism, 20, 21
   in constructivism, 20, 21, 22, 23
   in documentation and assessment, 23
   teacher training on, 23, 111
Aguiar, C., 20
Alfaya, E., 32
Amanti, C., 67
Amaro, F., 20
American Educational Research Association (AERA), 111
Animals as project topic, 95
Anticipatory planning
   administrative support of, 56
   challenges in, 102
   collaborative team approach to, 72
   Delphi study recommendations on, 107
   in Ice Cream Project, 39, 40
   on learning standards, 50, 52, 107
   Manifesto for Engaged Learning on, 104
   MBE Science instructional guidelines on, 17, 18
   professional development and collaboration of teachers on, 23, 57
   Teacher Anticipatory Planning and Tying Standards in a Bow, 39, 40, 47
   Teacher Anticipatory Planning Web, 52, 57, 107

Apprentice stage in executive function development, 75
Aral, N., 31, 32, 35
Artifacts
   in Construction Project, 59, 60
   Delphi study recommendations on, 108
   in documentation of learning, 23
   for dual language learners, 65, 66, 68, 69
   in Plant Project, 54
   in Power Lines Project, 25, 26, 28
   in prop box, 39
   in Restaurant Project, 39
   in special education classrooms, 71, 72
Artino, A. R., Jr., 76, 78
ASCD (Association for Supervision and Curriculum Development), 110, 111
Assessment
   authentic, 48, 50, 108, 110
   in behaviorism, 23
   Classroom Assessment Scoring System (CLASS) in, 35, 46, 90–91, 112
   in constructivism, 23
   Delphi study recommendations on, 108, 110
   mandates on, 100
   qualitative studies on, 34
   standardized testing in, 56
Association for Childhood Education International (ACEI), 111
Association for Supervision and Curriculum Development (ASCD), 110, 111
Associative memory, 17
Attention
   and instructional guidelines in MBE Science, 18
   and working memory, 77
Authentic activities, 22, 23, 48
   in Construction Project, 58
   for diverse learners, 78
   for dual language learners, 65
   research on, 29, 30
Authentic assessment, 48, 50, 108, 110
Autism spectrum, 72
Auto-mechanic services as project topic, for dual language learners, 68
Autonomy, 34
   and motivation, 76
Avella, J. T., 99
Ayhan, A. B., 32

Baby Project, 74, 76, 77, 78
   with dual language learners, 66, 76
Background knowledge from prior experiences, 23, 53
Baker, S., 69
Baltz, Marley, 71, 72
Bandura, A., 20, 22
Barnett, Mac, 53

Becoming Young Thinkers Summer Institute, 74, 85–87
Behavioral-Transmission Model, 20, 29, 100
Behaviorism, 20–23, 24
   and challenges in transition to constructivism, 100
   classroom interactions and relationships in, 22
   curriculum planning in, 22
   documentation and assessment in, 23
   teacher learning and training in, 23
   teaching environment and educational materials in, 22
Beneke, S. J., 29, 30, 31, 32, 33, 48, 72, 74
Bengtsson, M., 100
Bialystok, E., 65
Bilingual children, 64, 65–70
Bıçakçı, M. Y., 31, 32, 35
Blair, C. B., 5, 75
Blank, Jolyn, 101
Bolz, Carol, 32, 35, 74, 78, 83, 101
   on coaching, 90–93
   on special education classroom projects, 70–74
Bones Project, 94
Bonwell, C. C., 19
Boss, S., 5
Bracken Basic Concept Scale-Revised, 35
Brain development
   in dual language learners, 65, 69
   executive function in, 5, 75–78
   experiences affecting, 15, 16, 23
   functional areas in, 15–16
   imaging studies of, 14, 15, 16
   in Mind Brain Education Science, 14–20
   neuron networks in, 15, 16, 22, 23
   pruning process in, 16
Brass, KoAnn, 74
Braun, A. R., 15
Bredekamp, S., 48
Brewer, R. A., 32, 34
Brigance Early Development Inventory II, 35
Bronfenbrenner, U., 30
Brooks, Kim, 72, 73
Brooks, M., 32, 34
Buldu, M., 34, 35
Burnard, P., 100
Burton, DeCarla, 101
Burton, Meredith, 101
Butterflies as project topic, with dual language learners, 70

C3 Social Studies Standards, 46
Cabell, S. Q., 69
Çabuk, B., 32, 33, 34
Caldwell, L. B., 34
Call to Action, 9, 107–112
Camey, Ann, 94

113

Camilo, C., 20
Case studies on Project Approach, 33
Catapano, S., 90
Caterpillars as project topic, 74–75, 107
Cement as project topic, 59
   with dual language learners, 66
Chard, Sylvia C., 5, 6, 30, 31, 51, 90, 91, 101, 103
Charner, C., 48
Checa, P., 75
Chen, J. J., 32, 33
Child Care and Resource Referral, 88
Child-centered approach, 5, 6, 30, 52
   challenges in transition to, 102
   in constructivism, 22
   Delphi study recommendations on, 107–108
   executive function development in, 75
   in Nature Connections, 90
   in Young Investigator program, 88
Chouinard, M. M., 73
Chrispeels, J., 33
Chun, E. J., 32, 34
Claas, Mackenzie, 39, 40–41
Clark, Ann-Marie, 30, 101
Classroom Assessment Scoring System (CLASS), 35, 46, 90–93, 112
Classroom environment, 4–9, 52, 64
   in behaviorism and constructivism, 22–23
   as intellectual desert, 4–8, 103
   MBE Science instructional guidelines in, 17–19
   in Personalized Oral Language Learning, 68
   of special education classrooms, 72, 74, 82
Clifford, R., 84
Coaching, 35, 36, 90–93, 105
   Delphi study recommendations on, 110–111
   Strengths-Based, 91
   in Young Investigator training program, 88–89
Cobbins, Keyonia, 96
Cognitive flexibility in executive function, 75, 78
Cohrssen, C., 32, 34
Collaboration, 8
   among teachers, 57, 96, 106
   with community, 83
   Early Childhood Framework for 21st Century Learning on, 45–46
   in Nature Connections, 90
   of teachers and children, 23, 104, 108
   of teachers and leaders, 105
   of teachers and therapists in special education classrooms, 72
Combita, L. M., 75
Common Core State Standards, 46, 53
   in Plant Project, 54–55
Communication
   with administration, 108–109
   documentation in, 108, 109
   Early Childhood Framework for 21st Century Learning on, 45
   with families, 109
   in special education classrooms, 72, 73
Communities of Practice Model, 35
Community participation
   collaboration in, 83
   Delphi study recommendations on, 108, 110
   leadership in, 110
Competence and motivation, 76, 81
Computed tomography scans of brain, 14
Concept Development Domain in CLASS, 90–91
Concerns-Based Adoption Model, 86
Concrete as project topic, 59, 60, 61
   with dual language learners, 66
Conductor Project, 50
Construction Project, 58–63
Construction Truck Project, in special education classroom, 71–72, 73

Constructivism, 8, 20–23, 24, 104
   challenges in transition to, 100
   classroom interactions and relationships in, 22, 30
   curriculum planning in, 22
   documentation and assessment in, 23
   research on, 31
   teacher learning and training in, 23
   teaching environment and educational materials in, 22, 30
Contributor stage in executive function development, 75
Convergent thinking, 20
Cook, D. A., 76, 78
Copple, C., 48
Correia, N., 20, 22
Council of Chief State School Officers, 54
Craik, F. I., 65
Creativity, Early Childhood Framework for 21st Century Learning on, 45
Crestview Elementary School (Kansas City, MO), Power Lines Project in, 25–28
Creswell, J. W., 33, 100
Critical thinking, Early Childhood Framework for 21st Century Learning on, 45
Cronley, Madison, 39, 40, 41
Cryer, D., 84
Culminating events and activities, 7
   in Academy for Integrated Arts, 95
   in Construction Project, 63
   with dual language learners, 67–68, 69
   in Plant Project, 54, 56
   in Power Lines Project, 28
   in Reptile Project, 81–82
   in special education classrooms, 71
Cultural relevance/responsiveness, 8, 17, 29, 56, 65, 68–69, 75
   in leader training, 110
   in Manifesto, 103–104
Cummings, R., 32
Curriculum, 4
   in behaviorism and constructivism, 20, 21, 22
   components of, 21–23
   integration of project work into, 5, 6, 8
   planning of, 21–22
   requirements on, 47–48, 53, 100
   research on, 29–36
   role of children in, 20–21
   supporting intellectual development, 14–24
   teacher-centered, 20

Dallas, K., 32
Danby, S., 22
Danielson, C., 46
Danielson's Framework for Teaching, 46
Davis, Claudia, 94
Dawson, G., 16
Deepening Project Work (DPW), 85–86
Defending the Early Years, 6
DeGraff, Tricia, 52–57, 95–96, 101
Dekker, S., 16
Delphi study, 9, 83, 99–102, 107
   Call to Action based on, 9, 107–112
   experts in, 9, 99–101
   on Mind Brain Education Science, 16–17
   panelists in, 100
   process in, 9, 100
   results of, 9, 100, 102
Deppermann, Roger, in Construction Project, 59, 60
Deppermann, Trish, in Construction Project, 59, 60
DeVries, R., 21
Dewey, John, 9, 90
   on capacity for learning in children, 64
   on constructivism, 20

   on experience, 30
   on learning process for teachers, 23
   on natural instincts of children in learning, 64
   project concept of, 5, 30, 31, 33, 103
   on thought process, 91
   on use of costumes and props, 66
Diamond, A., 77, 78
Dichtelmiller, M. L., 47, 50
Dietering, Sue, 89
Disposition of children and teachers, 5, 23, 30, 34
Distractions as direction, 74–75, 77
Diverse learners, 8, 64–79
   leadership training for, 110
   in Reptile Project, 80–82
Doctors as project topic, 66
   in special education classrooms, 71, 73
Doctor's Office Project, in special education classroom, 73
Documentation, 104
   in Academy for Integrated Arts projects, 96
   in accountability for curriculum requirements, 47–48
   in behaviorism, 23
   in constructivism, 23, 34–35
   content and process of, 34
   Delphi study recommendations on, 108, 109
   of learning, 50–52
   pedagogical, 34–35, 45, 108
   professional development and collaboration of teachers on, 57
   project timeline in, 50, 51, 52
   value of, 50, 51, 57
Doerr, Allison, 96
Donegan, M., 32, 33
Dresden, J., 32
Dual language learners, 64, 65–70, 108
   working memory of, 78
Duarte, V., 32, 33
Duck Project, 48–50, 52
Duman, H. G., 32
Dwyer, Maureen Costello, 101
Dymond, S. K., 32

Early Childhood Center of Center School District (Kansas City, MO), 70, 71–72
Early Childhood Connections Academy, 85
Early Childhood Connections Program of Kohl Children's Museum, 36, 83–85
Early Childhood Environment Rating Scale, 84
Early Childhood Framework for 21st Century Learning, 45–46
Early Childhood Nature-Based Learning, 89–90
Ecological research model, 30
Edutopia, 5
Edwards, C., 22, 23
Edwards, Tara, 75, 78
Eison, J. A., 19
Emotional development, documentation of, 50
Emotions
   and executive function, 78
   and memory, 15, 17, 22
   and motivation, 78
   and neurotransmitter release, 15
Empowerment of children, 22
Engaged learning, 6–8
   assessment in, 47, 50
   background knowledge in, 53
   in behaviorism and constructivism compared, 20, 22, 23, 31
   curriculum research on, 29, 33, 36
   of dual language learners, 65, 68, 69, 70
   and engaged teaching, 29
   Manifesto on, 9, 99, 102, 103–106, 112
   memory in, 22
   neuroeducation research on, 103
   neuron connections in, 15, 22

professional development of teachers on, 84, 90
in special education classrooms, 72, 74
standards met in, 54–55, 56, 57
Engaging Children's Minds: The Project Approach (Katz & Chard), 6, 103
Engle, R. W., 77
English as Second Language Programs, 65
Espinosa, L. M., 65, 69
Executive function, 5, 64, 75–78
Exercise, and mind-body connection, 18
Experience
and background knowledge, 23, 53
and brain development, 15, 16, 23
Dewey on, 30
Experts, 8, 23, 45
brain development in, 16
in Construction Project, 60, 61, 62–63
in Delphi study, 9
in Doctor Project, 71
in Duck Project, 48
in Path Project, 11
family of dual language learner as, 68
in Manifesto Delphi study, 9, 99–101
in phase II of projects, 7
in Power Lines Project, 25
in Reptile Project, 81
in Sign Project, 78

Family
beliefs on Project Approach, 34
communication with, 109
Delphi study recommendations on participation of, 108, 109
frustration with standards and mandates, 6
in Personalized Oral Language Learning, 65–68
in special education classroom projects, 74
Farm machinery as project topic, with dual language learners, 66
Farrell, A., 22
Fennimore, B. S., 90
Finkelstein, C., 32
Fire Station Project, with dual language learners, 67, 68
Fischer, K. W., 16
Fish Project, 93
Fletchall, Jen, 74, 75, 76, 77, 78, 107
Forman, G., 22, 23
Foulger, T. S., 32
Fowler, R. C., 6
Frameworks, 45–46
Danielson's Framework for Teaching, 46
Early Childhood Framework for 21st Century Learning, 45–46
Frandsen, Abby, 39, 40
Functional magnetic resonance imaging, 14
Funding for Project Approach, 105, 112

Gaffney, J. S., 32
Galbraith, J., 35
Gandini, L., 22, 23
García, M. A., 32
Gardens as project topic
with dual language learners, 66
in Plant Project, 53–55, 56
Gardner, H., 75
Garrett, George, 92
Gencer, A. A., 32, 35
Gillogly, Faithia, 39
Giovannini, D., 35
Glassman, M., 5, 30
Goal-oriented action, executive function and motivation in, 78
Goal-oriented professional development and collaboration, 56–57

Golinkoff, R. M., 48
Gomes-Stewart, Anita, 92
Gonen, M., 32, 35
González, N., 67
Grant, Darlene, Construction Project in class of, 60, 62
Gray, Erika, 83–85, 101
Gray, S., 77
Great Beginnings Early Learning Center (Lee's Summit, MO), 39
Greater Kansas City Community Foundation, 93
Griebling, S., 32
Gronlund, G., 48
Groups, social nature of learning in, 18
Guadalupe Centers Early Childhood Center, 94
Gürsoy, F., 31, 32, 35
Guven, Y., 32

Haktanır, G., 32, 33, 34
Hamre, B. K., 21, 35, 46, 90
Han, H., 32, 33, 34
Harms, T., 84
Harris, P. L., 73
Harte, H. A., 32, 34
Hassinger-Das, B., 48
Hayslip, W. W., 65
Head Start, 35, 36, 65, 74, 75
Classroom Assessment Scoring System (CLASS) in, 90–93
coaching in, 35, 36, 90–93
Early Learning Mentor Coaches grant, 92–93
Mid-America, 36, 90–93, 94
in Nature Connections program, 88, 89
Heidemann, S., 48
Helm, Judy Harris, 91
on anticipatory planning, 47, 57
on caring community in special education classrooms, 72
on Common Care State Standards, 46
on documentation, 48
Early Childhood Connections Academy, 85
on guidelines in Project Approach, 30
on Mind Brain Education Science, 14–20, 54
Project Planning Communication Form developed by, 109
on project work, 5, 73, 90, 103
on questions as component in projects, 72
on teacher development, 35, 39, 40–41, 92
on vocabulary development in dual language learners, 69
Young Investigators training program, 72, 74, 88–89, 93
Helterbran, V. R., 90
Heroman, C., 47, 50
Hertzog, N. B., 32, 33, 34
Hewitt, D., 48
Hierarchical Linear Model, 36
Hill, C., 35
Hirsh-Pasek, K., 48
Holley, Maggie, 20–23, 35, 78, 93
Holm, M., 31, 33
Hong, S. B., 22, 23
Hong Kong, 33
Hooks, L., 32, 33
Houen, S., 22
Howard-Jones, P., 16
Hsu, C.-C., 99
Humbarger, J. A., 91
Hunt, Merrill, 75
Hurst, Haley, Plant Project of, 53–55

Ice Cream Project, 39, 40
Illinois Early Learning and Development Standards, 48, 49
Illinois State Board of Education, 48, 84
Immordino-Yang, M., 16

Inan, H. Z., 32
Individual Education Plans (IEPs), 70, 72, 73
Information Requesting Mechanisms, questions as, 73
Inhibitory control in executive function, 75, 77
Inquiry-based learning, 46, 52
Insect Project, with dual language learners, 66, 70
Instructional strategies
in MBE Science, guidelines on, 17–19, 54, 99
in Personalized Oral Language Learning, 68–70
Instructional Support Domain in CLASS, 90, 92
Intellectual, concept of, 5
Intellectual desert, classroom as, 4–8, 103
Intellectual development
curriculum supporting, 14–24
dispositions in, 5
neuroscience research on, 5, 16
in Project Approach, 6, 99, 107–112
sense of agency in, 20
Intentional teaching and learning, 104
International Mind, Brain, and Education Society, 16
Iowa Area Education Agency, 88

Jablon, J. R., 47
Jennings, Carolyn, 39
Johnson, M., 65
Johnson, Tiffany, 39
Jolles, J., 16
Joyce, B., 88
Judie, Della, 75, 77, 78

Kamii, C., 21
Kanai, T., 99
Kandir, A., 32
Kansas City Coaching Project Mid-America Regional Council Head Start., 36
Kansas City Community Gardens, 53, 55
Kantor, R., 32
Karmiloff-Smith, A., 65
Katz, Lilian G., 31, 35, 51, 91, 92
on challenges implementing Project Approach, 8
on dispositions, 5
on diverse learners, 73, 74
on guidelines in Project Approach, 30
on intellectual goals, 5
on metacognitive strategies, 46
on project work, 5, 6, 73, 90, 103
Kebritchi, M., 99
Kilpatrick, William H., 41, 90
Kinach, B. M., 31
Klarin, S., 32
Knauf, H., 35
Kogan, Yvonne, 5, 30, 32, 34, 90, 101
Kohl Children's Museum (Chicago, IL), 91
Early Childhood Connections Program of, 36, 83–85
Kohl Project Approach Assessment and Coaching Tool, 85
Koralek, D., 48
Krashen, S., 70
Krauss, J., 5
Kutcher, Jessie, 10

Lakeside Laboratory, Nature Connections program of, 87–90
Language and literacy, 5, 53
assessment requirements on, 47
background knowledge and prior experiences affecting, 23, 53, 64
of dual language learners, 64, 65–70
in Duck Project, 48, 49, 52
in Plant Project, 54–55, 56
qualitative studies on development of, 34

Language and literacy (*continued*)
 quantitative studies on development of, 35
 in Restaurant Project, 41
 in special education classrooms, 73
Language Modeling in CLASS, 91
LaParo, K. M., 35, 46, 90
Larmer, J., 5
Larson, Katrina, 101
 Construction Project in class of, 59–60
Latendresse, Janet, 39
Leadership
 classroom-level, 110
 community-level, 110
 program-level, 110
 transformative, 105, 110
Learning, 14
 active. *See* Active learning
 age-appropriate activities in, 19
 in behaviorism, 20, 21
 brain development in, 16. *See also* Brain development
 capacity of children for, 64, 74–78
 collaboration of teachers and children in, 104, 108
 connections to prior experiences in, 15
 in constructivism, 20, 21, 23
 dispositions in, 5, 23, 30, 34
 of diverse learners, 8, 64–79
 documentation of, 50–52
 emotions affecting, 15, 17
 engaged. *See* Engaged learning
 functional areas of brain in, 15–16
 inquiry-based, 46, 52
 in lifespan, 19
 MBE Science instructional guidelines on, 18
 memory in, 15, 77
 in Mind Brain Education Science, 16–19
 natural instincts of children in, 64
 nature-based, 89–90
 in play, 48
 in professional learning communities, 35, 36, 110
 qualitative research on, 34
 quantitative research on, 35
 roles of children in, 20–21, 30
 as service, 34
 social nature of, 18, 46, 69, 78
 sociocultural influences on, 20
 of teachers. *See* Teacher learning and training
 in 21st century, 45–57
Lee, K., 32
Lee, M. Y., 31
Lee, N. C, 16
Legislative policies on Project Approach, 105, 112
Levin, D. E., 6
Li, H., 32
Lickey, D. C., 74
Limb, C. J., 15
Linder, S. M., 32
Ling, D. S., 77, 78
Lippard, B., 32
Literacy. *See* Language and literacy
Long-term memory, 17, 22
Louv, Richard, 88
Luk, G., 65

MacDonald, M., 35
Machinery as project topic
 in Construction Project, 58–63
 with dual language learners, 66
 in special education classroom, 71–72
Magnetic resonance imaging of brain, 14
Magruder, E. S., 65, 68, 69
Maguire, E. A., 16
Malaguzzi, Loris, 22
Manifesto, definition of, 9

Manifesto Call to Action, 9, 107–112
Manifesto creed, beliefs in, 112
Manifesto Delphi study, 9, 99–102. *See also* Delphi study
Manifesto for Engaged Learning, 9, 99, 102, 103–106, 112
Maple, T. L., 32
Maratsos, M. P., 73
Markhan, T., 5
Maroon, Sie, 60, 63
Marsden, D. B., 47
Marszalek, J., 35
Master stage in executive function development, 75
Matera, C., 65
Materials, educational, in behaviorism and constructivism, 22–23, 30
Mathematics, 33–34, 53
 in Duck Project, 48, 49, 52
 in Plant Project, 55
 in Restaurant Project, 41
 in special education classrooms, 73
Maupin, Wendy, 72
Mawson, B., 32
Mayer, S., 35
MBE Science. *See* Mind Brain Education Science
McGaha, C. G., 32, 34
Meier, D. R., 69
Meisels, S. J., 47
Meltzer, L., 75, 78
Memory
 consolidation of, 18, 19
 emotions affecting, 15, 17, 22
 in executive function, 75, 77–78
 and instructional guidelines in MBE Science, 17, 18, 19
 long-term, 17, 22
 neuron connections in, 15, 22
 primacy-recency principle on, 18
 short-term, 15
 working, 75, 77–78
Mentor-coaches, 110–111
Merino, Jesse, 71
Merritt, J., 31
Meta-analysis of Project Approach research, 31–33
Metacognition, 46, 47
 MBE instructional guidelines on, 19
Metin, S., 32, 35
Mid-America Head Start, 36, 90–93, 94
 Classroom Assessment Scoring System in, 90–93
 coaching in, 90–93
Miller, D. L., 100
Miller, Jackie, 10, 11
Mind-body connection, 18
Mind Brain Education Science, 14–20, 23
 and Becoming Young Thinkers Summer Institute, 85
 instructional guidelines in, 17–19, 54, 99
 Manifesto creed on, 112
 principles of, 46
Missouri Learning Standards, 81
Mitchell, Monchell, 75, 77
Mitchell, S., 32
Moll, L. C., 67
Moran, M. J., 32, 33
Moran, S., 75
Moss Project, 87
Motivation, 81
 and executive function development, 75, 76–77
 intrinsic, 76–77
 in Kohl ECC program, 84
 in Reptile Project, 81
Musatti, T., 35
Music Project, 96

NAECS/SDE (National Association of Early Childhood Specialists in State Departments of Education), 36
NAEYC (National Association for the Education of Young Children), 36
Nariman, N., 33
Narrative inquiries on Project Approach, 32, 33
National Association for the Education of Young Children (NAEYC), 36, 84, 110, 111
National Association of Early Childhood Specialists in State Departments of Education (NAECS/SDE), 36
National Center for Educational Statistics, 65
National Association for Elementary School Principals, 110
National Council for Social Studies, 46
National Governors Association for Best Practices, 53–54
Nature-based Project Approach, 87–90
Nature Connections, 87–90
Nature deficit in children, 88
Nature Explore Classroom, 87
Neff, D., 67
Neurons, 15
 networks of, 15, 16, 22, 23
Neuroscience research, 5, 9
 brain imaging in, 14, 15, 16
 on engaged learning, 103
Neurotransmitters, 15, 22
The New Science of Teaching and Learning: Using the Best of Mind, Brain, and Education Science in the Classroom (Tokuhama-Espinosa), 19
Next Generation Science Standards, 46
 alignment with Project Approach, 47
 in Power Lines Project, 26
Nunn, S. G., 99
Nutrition, and mind-body connection, 18

Oates, J., 65
Oral language development for dual language learners, 65–70
Orchestrated immersion, MBE Science instructional guidelines on, 18
Ostrosky, M. M., 29, 30, 31, 32, 33, 74
Owen, P. M., 32, 33, 34

Page, J., 32
Pajares, M. F., 21
Partnership for 21st Century Learning, 45, 46
Path Project, 4, 6, 10–13
 compared to Pumpkin Patch activity, 5, 99
 engagement in, 15
 intellectual goals in, 5
 and Mind Brain Education Science, 17
 sense of agency in, 20
Patton, M., 33
Pauli, Angela, Construction Project in class of, 60, 62
Pecha Kucha, 86
Pedagogical documentation, 34–35, 45, 108
Personalized Oral Language Learning (POLL), 65–70
 classroom environment in, 68
 family connections in, 65–68
 instructional strategies in, 68–70
 word knowledge and vocabulary building in, 68, 69–70
Peterson, Amy, 71
Pettit, Nick, 6, 25–28, 101
Phase I of projects, 7
 in Construction Project, 58
 Delphi study recommendations on, 107
 learning standards and goals mapped in, 46–47
 Next Generation Science Standards in, 47

in Path Project, 10–11
in Power Lines Project, 25–26
in Reptile Project, 80–81
Phase II of projects, 7
in Construction Project, 59–62
Next Generation Science Standards in, 47
in Path Project, 11–12
in Power Lines Project, 26–27
in Reptile Project, 81
Phase III of projects, 7
in Construction Project, 62–63
curriculum goals met in, 52
in Duck Project, 52
Next Generation Science Standards in, 47
in Path Project, 12–13
in Plant Project, 54
in Power Lines Project, 27–28
in Reptile Project, 81–82
Piaget, Jean, 20
Pianta, R. C., 30, 35, 46, 90
Picchio, M., 35
Picture Exchange Communication System, 72
Pig Project, 52
Pin, J., 32, 34
Pizza as project topic, with dual language learners, 66
Planning, 21–22
anticipatory. *See* Anticipatory planning
cognitive flexibility in, 78
in Ice Cream Project, 39, 40
Plant Project, 53–55, 56
Common Core State Standards in, 54–55
Play, 6
for dual language learners, 65, 68
learning in, 48
sociodramatic, 68
in special education classrooms, 71, 72, 73
Plumlee, Deb, 70, 72, 73, 74
Poverty, experience of, 64
and Kohl ECC program, 83
Powell, Douglas, 36, 85
Power Lines Project, 6, 25–28
collaboration in, 45
dual language learners in, 66
engagement in, 15
and Mind Brain Education Science, 17
Powers, D. J., 74
Powers-Costello, B., 32
PPR format in Becoming Young Thinkers Summer Institute, 85
Prairie Branch Elementary School (Grain Valley, MO), 80
Prater, Amanda, 70, 72, 74
Prefrontal cortex in executive function, 5
Preservice teachers, 39–41, 111
research on, 32, 33–34
Price, Catherine
Conductor Project in class of, 50
Construction Project in class of, 59, 61
demonstration of documentation, 51
Problem solving, 5, 6, 8, 21, 99
cognitive flexibility in, 78
in constructivist classroom, 22
critical thinking in, 45
MBE instructional guidelines on, 19
and memory, 78
in Power Lines Project, 25, 26, 28
Professional development, 83–94. *See also* Teacher learning and training
Professionalism, 105–106
Professional learning communities, 35, 36, 110
Program evaluation, 36
of Kohl ECC program, 36, 84–85
Project Approach, 5–9
adherence to guidelines on, 33, 35, 36, 92, 93, 105

administrative support of, 54, 102, 108–109, 110, 111
anticipatory planning in. *See* Anticipatory planning
challenges in, 6–8, 100, 102
Classroom Assessment Scoring System in, 90–93
connections across content areas in, 56
Delphi study of, 9, 99–102, 107–112
distractions as direction in, 74–75, 77
for diverse learners, 64–79
executive function in, 75–78
family participation in, 65–68, 74, 108, 109
funding for, 105, 112
intellectual development in, 6, 99, 107–112
leaders in, 105, 110
learning standards in, 45–57
legislative policies on, 105, 112
and *Manifesto Call to Action,* 9, 107–112
and Manifesto creed, 112
and *Manifesto for Engaged Learning,* 9, 99, 102, 103–106
MBE Science instructional guidelines in, 17–19
nature-based, 87–90
nature of, 30
phases in, 7
preservice teachers in, 32, 33–34, 39–41, 111
professionalism in, 105–106
public recognition of projects in, 83
research on, 29–36. *See also* Research on Project Approach
scheduling and time use in, 53–54, 56
teacher learning and training in. *See* Teacher learning and training
teacher reflection in, 109–110
use of term, 6
Project Approach Fidelity measure, 92, 93, 105
Project Planning Communication Form, 109
Projects
Baby Project, 66, 74, 76, 77, 78
Bones Project, 94
Conductor Project, 50
Construction Project, 58–63, 71–72, 73
Construction Truck Project, 71–72, 73
Doctor's Office Project, 73
Duck Project, 48–50, 52
Fire Station Project, 67, 68
Fish Project, 93
Ice Cream Project, 39, 40
Insect Project, 66, 70
Moss Project, 87
Music Project, 96
Path Project. *See* Path Project
Pig Project, 52
Plant Project, 53–55, 56
Power Lines Project. *See* Power Lines Project
Reptile Project, 67, 80–82
Restaurant Project, 39, 41
Sign Project, 67, 75–76, 77, 78
Tree Project, 92
Truck Project, 75, 77
Project timeline, 50, 51, 52, 57
Prop box, 39
Provocations, 39
Pruning process in brain development, 16
Pui-Wah, D. C., 32, 33, 34
Pumpkin Patch activity, 3, 4–5, 14
compared to Path Project, 5, 99
as teacher-directed experience, 4–5, 14, 20, 64

Quadros-Wander, B., 32
Qualitative studies, 31, 33–35
on child learning and development, 34
on pedagogical documentation, 34–35
on teacher learning and development, 33–34
Quality of Feedback Domain in CLASS, 91

Quantitative studies, 32, 35–36
on child learning and development, 35
in program evaluation, 36
on teacher learning and development, 35–36
Questions as component of projects, 90, 104
Delphi study recommendations on, 107, 108
as Information Requesting Mechanisms, 73
in Reptile Project, 80–81
in special education classrooms, 72, 73

Raab, Tracy
Construction Project in class of, 59, 62
Duck Project in class of, 48–50, 52
Randall, Stephanie, Construction Project in class of, 59, 62
Rathkey, C., 32
Raver, C. C., 75
Ravitz, J., 5
Razza, R. P., 75
Reading, 53
in Plant Project, 55, 56
Reflection
by students, MBE Science instructional guidelines on, 19
by teachers, 109–110
Reggio Emilia schools, 22, 31
Relatedness and motivation, 76
Rendon, T., 48
Reptile Project, 80–82
with dual language learners, 67
questions of students in, 80–81
Research on neuroscience, 5, 9
brain imaging in, 14, 15, 16
in engaged learning, 103
Research on Project Approach, 29–36
call to action on, 111–112
challenges in, 29–31
on child learning and development, 34, 35
with Classroom Assessment Scoring System, 91–93
funding of, 105
international studies in, 31, 32, 33, 34, 35
limitations of, 36
Manifesto Delphi study in, 9, 99–102
meta-analysis of literature on, 31–33
methods in, 31–36
on pedagogical documentation, 34–35
program evaluation in, 36, 84–85
qualitative studies in, 31, 33–35
quantitative studies in, 32, 35–36
on teacher learning and development, 33–34, 35–36
Restaurant Project, 39, 41
Reunamo, J., 35
Richner, Nikki, 39
Rights of children
to active, engaged learning environment, 104
to participate, 22
Rillero, P., 31
Rimm-Kaufman, S. E., 30
Rintakorpi, K., 35
Rodríguez-Bailón, R., 75
Rohs, J., 29
Role-playing, 67
costumes and props in, 66
with dual language learners, 67, 68
in special education classrooms, 71
Roosevelt Prekindergarten, 3
Roti, Lisa, on Nature Connections, 87–90
Rueda, M. R., 75

St. George's Episcopal School (New Orleans, LA), Path Project in, 10–13
St. Mark Family and Child Development Center (Kansas City, MO), 75, 93
Sam and Dave Dig a Hole (Barnett), 53

Sandage, Tamara, 74
Sanford, B. A., 99
Scaffolding with dual language learners, 68
Scheduling issues, 53–54, 56
Schreckenghaust, Robyn, 71, 72
Science, in Duck Project, 52
Scranton, Pam, 102, 108
  on Becoming Young Thinkers summer Institute, 85–87
  on Construction Project, 58–63
  on preschool standards, 48–50, 52
Second language learners, 64, 65–70
Self-efficacy, 99
  and motivation, 76, 81
Serrano, R., 32, 33, 34
Short-term memory, 15
Showers, B., 88
Sign Project, 75–76, 77, 78
  with dual language learners, 67
Sleep, and mind–body connection, 18
Smith, Liz, 94
  on coaching, 90–93
Snider, Karrie A., 35, 93
  on capacity of children for learning, 74–78
  in Manifesto Delphi study, 100
  on teacher candidates in project work, 39–41
Social development, documentation of, 50
Social nature of learning, 18, 46
  for dual language learners, 69
  emotional support in, 78
Social studies, 53
Sociodramatic play, 68
Socrates, 20
Soil as project topic, 53–54
Souto-Manning, M., 32
Spain, 34
Special needs, teaching children with, 64, 70–74
  anticipatory planning on, 18
  Reptile Project in, 80–82
  sense of efficacy of teachers in, 33
Stakeholder actions, call for, 110–112
Stamps, Pegi, 101
  on coaching, 90–93
  on special education classroom projects, 70–74
Standardized testing, pressures of, 56
Standards, 45–57
  alignment with Project Approach, 84
  anticipatory planning on, 50, 52, 107
  Common Core, 46, 53, 54–55
  for dual language learners, 65
  Illinois Early Learning and Development Standards, 48, 49
  in Mind Brain Education Science, 16
  Missouri Learning Standards, 81
  Next Generation Science Standards, 26, 46, 47
  in Power Lines Project, 26
  in preschool, 48–50, 52
  in Reptile Project, 81, 82
  in Restaurant Project, 41
  Teacher Anticipatory Planning and Tying Standards in a Bow, 39, 40, 47
Stegelin, D. A., 32
Steiner, D., 29
Steinhardt, Katie, 10
Steinheimer, K., 48
Stevens, Erica, 96
Stickling, Malerie, Construction Project in class of, 59, 61
Strengths-Based Coaching, 91
Sudan, power lines and villages in, 25–28
Survival-value memory, 17

Svoboda-Chollet, Mary, 75
Swann, A. C., 32

Tabors, P. O., 47, 50
Taylor, Lora, 101
Teacher Anticipatory Planning and Tying Standards in a Bow, 39, 40, 47
Teacher Anticipatory Planning Web, 52, 57, 107
Teacher candidates, 39–41, 111
  research on, 32, 33–34
Teacher challenges in Project Approach, 6–8, 102
Teacher-directed activities, 4–5, 20, 21
  in behaviorism, 29
  executive function development in, 75
  in Pumpkin Patch experience, 4–5, 14, 20, 64
Teacher learning and training, 83–94, 105–106
  at Academy for Integrated Arts, 95–96
  in Becoming Young Thinkers Summer Institute, 74, 85–87
  in behaviorism and constructivism, 23, 24
  Classroom Assessment Scoring System in, 90–93
  coaching in, 35, 36, 90–93, 105, 110–111
  Delphi study recommendations on, 109–110, 111
  goal-oriented, 56–57
  importance of, 100, 102
  in Kohl Children's Museum Early Childhood Connections program, 36, 83–85
  learning dispositions in, 30
  models on, 83–94
  in Nature Connections, 87–90
  on nature of Project Approach, 30
  of preservice teachers, 32, 33–34, 39–41, 111
  in professional learning communities, 35, 36, 110
  reflection in, 109–110
  research on, 32, 33–34, 35–36
  in Young Investigator program. See Young Investigator training
Teacher reflection in Project Approach, 109–110
Teaching Strategies GOLD, 47, 50
Teall, Rebecca, 10–13, 101
Teeth as project topic, 66
Thorpe, K., 22
Tokuhama-Espinosa, T., 16, 17, 19, 46
Tomato-based foods as project topic, with dual language learners, 69
Topic selection
  Delphi study recommendations on, 107
  MBE Science instructional guidelines on, 17
Transformative leadership, 105, 110
Tree Project, 92
Trepanier-Street, M., 32
Troost Divide in Kansas City as project topic, 96
Truck Project, 75, 77
Trundle, K. C., 32
Turkey, 32, 35, 36
21st century learners, 45–57
Tye, Natalie, on teacher candidates in project work, 39–41

University of Central Missouri, 39
UPC Discovery Early Learning Center (Peoria, IL)
  and Becoming Young Thinkers Summer Institute, 87
  Conductor Project in, 50
  Construction Project in, 58–63
  Duck Project in, 48–50
U.S. Department of Education, 65
Usman, A., 35, 78, 93

Vanderpool, Hannah, 93
Van Hoorn, J. L., 6
Vartuli, Sue, 32
  on curriculum approaches, 20–23, 29
  on emotional support, 78
  in Manifesto Delphi study, 100
  on professional development, 33, 35, 90
Veterinarians as project topic, with dual language learners, 67
Vocabulary development, 34
  in Personalized Oral Language Learning, 68, 69–70
  in special education classrooms, 73
Voices from the Field, 6, 99
  DeGraff, Tricia, 95–96
  Pettit, Nick, 6, 25–28
  Scranton, Pam, 58–63
  Snider, Karrie A., 39–41
  Teall, Rebecca, 10–13
  Tye, Natalie, 39–41
  Woodin, Crystal, 80–82
Vygotsky, Lev, 20

Wang, J.-Y., 32
Wang, X. C., 32
Wangmo, T., 32, 34
Wastin, E., 32, 33, 34
Watson, John, 20
Webbing process
  Delphi study recommendations on, 107
  MBE Science instructional guidelines on, 19
  in Path Project, 11
  in Power Lines Project, 25, 26
Wetzel, K., 32
Whaley, K., 5, 30
White, Colleen, 95
Whorrall, J., 69
WIDA Consortium, 65
  Early Years, 65
  support for dual language learners, 65, 66–67
Williams, Joan, 70, 72, 73, 74
Willoughby, M. T., 75
Wilson, Catherine, 32, 35, 78, 83
  on coaching, 90–93
Wilson, Rebecca A., 32, 101
  on developing 21st century learners, 45–48
  on dual language learners, 65–70
Wong, J. M. S., 32
Woodin, Crystal, 80–82
Woodland Early Learning Center (Kansas City, MO), 75
Word knowledge, in Personalized Oral Language Learning, 69–70
Working memory, 75, 77–78
Work Sampling System, 47, 50, 52
World-Class Instructional Design and Assessment, 65
Writing, engagement in, 53, 56

Yaşar, M. C., 32
Young Investigators: The Project Approach in the Early Years (Helm & Katz), 92, 103
Young Investigator training, 88–89, 90, 93
  and Becoming Young Thinkers Summer Institute, 85
  coaching component in, 88–89
  on diverse learners, 74
  Schreckenghaust attending, 72
Yuen, L. H. F., 32, 33, 34

Zan, B., 21
Zelazo, P. D., 75, 78

About the Editors and Contributors

EDITORS

JUDY HARRIS HELM, Ed.D., helps teachers of preschool through 3rd grade to integrate research into their curricula through her consulting company Best Practices Inc. She is a national and international speaker and trainer on implications of Mind Brain and Education Science, project work, engaged learning, documentation, and school design. Dr. Helm served as the educational planner for three early childhood centers and two birth through 8th-grade community schools. Included among the nine books she has authored or co-authored are *Becoming Young Thinkers: Deep Project Work in the Classroom*; *Young Investigators: The Project Approach in the Early Years*; *The Power of Projects*; *Teaching Your Child to Love Learning: A Guide to Projects at Home*; *Windows on Learning: Documenting Young Children's Work*; and *Teaching Parents to Do Projects at Home*.

KARRIE A. SNIDER, Ph.D., is currently assistant professor of early childhood education at the University of Central Missouri. She has held several roles in early childhood and elementary education settings, including teacher, administrator, mentor-coach, teacher educator, and researcher. Dr. Snider's passion is working to support preservice and inservice teachers, coaches, and leaders in examining effective teaching beliefs, practices, and curriculum approaches in their classrooms and programs. Her most recent presentations and publications featured her research as well as the stories of teachers, coaches, and children teaching and learning together with the Project Approach. Dr. Snider received the 2018 University of Central Missouri Faculty Research Award for her research on the Project Approach.

CONTRIBUTORS

CAROL BOLZ, M.A., is the education manager for Mid-America Head Start in Kansas City, Missouri. As a teacher in a Head Start classroom in 1995, Carol was introduced to the Project Approach and has never looked back! She facilitated many projects with young investigators. She currently provides training and coaching to educators on implementation of the Project Approach, coordinates research, and presents at national conferences.

TRICIA DeGRAFF, Ph.D., is the executive director of the Academy for Integrated Arts, a prekindergarten through 6th-grade public school in Kansas City, Missouri. She has over 20 years of experience in urban schools as a teacher, teacher educator, and school leader. Tricia's research interests involve professional development processes for teachers that are meaningful, inquiry-based, authentic, and teacher-centered, leading to transformative learning for children and teachers.

ERIKA GRAY, B.S., director of education for Kohl Children's Museum, Chicago, Illinois, oversees Kohl's education department, which creates and facilitates all public programs, outreach, professional development grants, and workshops for children, caregivers, and teachers. Erika has been involved in Kohl's Early Childhood Connections Project Approach professional development program since its conception in 2001 and has been a coach-mentor to home-based and school district educators.

MAGGIE HOLLEY, Ph.D., was the director of Central Early Childhood Center, Kansas City, Missouri, for 22 years and was an early childhood instructor at the University of Missouri–Kansas City since 2008. She currently promotes the Project Approach through her coaching and research activities across a wide range of community programs and schools. Her passions involve supporting the full inclusion of diverse individuals in all settings.

NICK PETTIT, M.A., is a Kansas City, Missouri, based educator/principal who has worked with hundreds of students and teachers in Kansas City's urban core. Beginning his career in early childhood education, Nick has taught multiple grades and is now a building principal at Maplewood Elementary in the North Kansas City School District. Engaging students in student-centered learning experiences and creating impactful relationships drives his approach to leading.

LISA ROTI, B.S., is the executive director of Friends of Lakeside Lab. She received a bachelor's degree in business management from the University of Montana and a second bachelor's degree in elementary education from Buena Vista University. Lisa spent a decade teaching in kindergarten, 2nd, 3rd, and 4th grades. Since 2013, she has been involved with nature-based Project Approach training at Lakeside Lab in northwestern Iowa.

PAM SCRANTON, M.Ed., is the founder of UPC Discovery and adjunct professor at Bradley University in the teacher education department. Pam coaches teachers and undergraduate students in documentation and the Project Approach, and she provides leadership in the programs of UPC Discovery. She is co-author with Dr. Helm of *Teaching Your Child to Love Learning* and *Teaching Parents to Do Projects at Home*.

LIZ SMITH, B.S., Head Start director for the Mid-America Head Start program, is the administrator of a grant that serves 3,000 children in school district- and community-based programs. Liz is a strong advocate of the Project Approach and has worked to engage program and school district administrators and to ensure that funds are available for training, coaching, and the ongoing support of teachers in this important work.

PEGI STAMPS, M.A., has a diverse career in the field of early childhood education, with experiences in teaching, training, coaching, and leadership. She was a Head Start director of Education, Inclusion, and Mental Health; taught post-secondary education; and is currently the director of Early Learning for Constructive Playthings. Pegi is a Certified Young Investigator Trainer on the Project Approach.

REBECCA TEALL, B.A., has been working in early education for over 20 years and is currently a curriculum coach and prekindergarten teacher at St. George's Episcopal School in New Orleans, Louisiana. Rebecca has been an enthusiastic proponent for the Project Approach since joining the St. George's faculty in 2012.

NATALIE TYE, Ed.D., is a former early childhood educator and director. She is currently assistant professor of early childhood education at the University of Central Missouri, where she works collaboratively with cooperating teachers and teacher candidates in the university and public school settings. Natalie mentors teacher candidates through junior-level coursework, supporting their ability to create meaningful curriculum based on genuine student interest.

SUE VARTULI, Ph.D., received her master's and doctorate from The Ohio State University. Until her retirement, she was associate professor of early childhood education at the University of Missouri–Kansas City, where she was a teacher educator for 33 years. Her research is focused on teacher education, especially teacher beliefs, guidance, and curriculum. She currently volunteers with Head Start teachers as a coach for the Project Approach.

CATHERINE WILSON, Ph.D., retired from Park University as an associate professor in early childhood education, and afterward she became a consultant at Mid-America Head Start, learning together with coaches and teachers as they studied how to bring the Project Approach to the children and families in their programs.

REBECCA A. WILSON, M.S., current director and lead teacher of Van Meter Community Pre-Kindergarten in Van Meter, Iowa, has taught in a variety of programs using the Project Approach from preschool through 1st grade. These include dual language and bilingual Head Start programs. Rebecca is the author of several publications, including a chapter in *The Power of Projects* and co-author of *Teaching Parents to Do Projects at Home*.

CRYSTAL WOODIN, M.A., teaches kindergarten in Grain Valley, Missouri. She has taught in both rural and urban Missouri public schools for the past 9 years. She has utilized the Project Approach in her teaching for 8 years, and mentors other teachers in this style of teaching and learning through various professional development experiences. Crystal's project work with children has been published by edCircuit.